LAW AS INSTITUTIONAL NORMATIVE ORDER

The Edinburgh Centre for Law and Society
Series Editor: Professor Emilios A. Christodoulidis

Titles in the Series

Law and Agonistic Politics
Edited by Andrew Schaap

Public Law and Politics
The Scope and Limits of Constitutionalism
Edited by Emilios Christodoulidis and Stephen Tierney

Transformations of Policing
Edited by Alistair Henry and David J. Smith

The Universal and the Particular in Legal Reasoning
Edited by Zenon Bankowski and James MacLean

Law and the Politics of Reconciliation
Edited by Scott Veitch

Law as Institutional Normative Order

Edited by

MAKSYMILIAN DEL MAR
University of Edinburgh, UK and University of Lausanne, Switzerland

ZENON BANKOWSKI
University of Edinburgh, UK

Routledge
Taylor & Francis Group
LONDON AND NEW YORK

First published 2009 by Ashgate Publishing

Published 2016 by Routledge
2 Park Square, Milton Park, Abingdon, Oxfordshire OX14 4RN
711 Third Avenue, New York, NY 10017, USA

First issued in paperback 2016

Routledge is an imprint of the Taylor & Francis Group, an informa business

British Library Cataloguing in Publication Data
Law as institutional normative order. -- (The Edinburgh
Centre for Law and Society series)
1. Jurisprudence. 2. Law--Philosophy.
I. Series II. Del Mar, Maksymilian. III. Bankowski, Zenon.
340.1'12-dc22

Library of Congress Cataloging-in-Publication Data
Del Mar, Maksymilian, 1946-
Law as institutional normative order / by Maksymilian del Mar and Zenon Bankowski.
p. cm. -- (The Edinburgh centre for law and society)
Includes index.
ISBN 978-0-7546-7708-6 1. Law--Philosophy.
2. Legal positivism. 3. Jurisprudence. 4. MacCormick, Neil. 5. Law--Methodology. I. Bankowski, Zenon. II. Title.

K231.D45 2009
340'.1--dc22

2009008256

ISBN 13: 978-1-138-24912-7 (pbk)
ISBN 13: 978-0-7546-7708-6 (hbk)

Contents

List of Contributors

Zenon Bankowski is Professor of Legal Theory at the University of Edinburgh.

Maksymilian Del Mar is a doctoral candidate at the School of Law, University of Edinburgh and the Faculty of Social and Political Sciences, University of Lausanne.

Julie Dickson is Fellow and Tutor in Law at Somerville College, University of Oxford.

Jaap Hage is Professor of Jurisprudence at the University of Maastricht.

Andrew Halpin is Professor of Legal Theory at Swansea University.

Nils Jareborg is Professor Emeritus of Criminal Law at the University of Uppsala.

Massimo La Torre is Professor of Law at the University of Catanzaro and the University of Hull.

Neil MacCormick is Professor Emeritus of Public Law and the Law of Nature and Nations at the University of Edinburgh.

Frederick Schauer is David and Mary Harrison Distinguished Professor of Law, University of Virginia; George Eastman Visiting Professor and Fellow of Balliol College, University of Oxford; and Visiting Professor of Law, Harvard University.

Victor Tadros is Professor of Law at Warwick University.

William Twining is Quain Professor Emeritus of Jurisprudence at University College London and Visiting Professor at the University of Miami School of Law.

Magnus Ulväng is Reader in Criminal Law at the University of Uppsala.

Vittorio Villa is Professor of Legal Philosophy at the University of Palermo.

Chapter 1
Law as Institutional Normative Order: An Introduction

Maksymilian Del Mar

On 7 and 8 December 2007, a group of legal theorists got together to celebrate, but also critically discuss, Neil MacCormick's latest book, arguably his magnum opus, *Institutions of Law: An Essay in Legal Theory* (MacCormick 2007). This collection is a direct result of that meeting, which was generously sponsored by the Leverhulme Trust, and held at the School of Law, University of Edinburgh.[1] There had been a previous occasion, and also a previous collection (see Bankowski and MacLean 2006), where a chapter of MacCormick's earlier *Rhetoric and the Rule of Law* (MacCormick 2005) was discussed, but the publication of this book was clearly an event that merited its own careful attention.

Institutions of Law is the third book in a series of four books under the title *Law, State and Practical Reason*. The first book was *Questioning Sovereignty* (MacCormick 1999), and was followed by *Rhetoric and the Rule of Law* (MacCormick 2005). The series will be completed with *Practical Reason in Law and Morality* (MacCormick 2009). Whereas the first, second and fourth all contain important elements of MacCormick's legal theory (including his very significant revision, in the second of the above volumes, of his classic *Legal Reasoning and Legal Theory*, MacCormick 1978), they are also important contributions to political and moral philosophy, which leaves *Institutions of Law* as MacCormick's most consistent and most ambitious statement of his legal theory.

The date of the meeting that led to this collection was significant for two other reasons. The first of these was that 2007 marked the three hundredth anniversary of the School of Law at the University of Edinburgh. This anniversary, in turn, was tied to the establishment of the Regius Professorship in Public Law, and the Law of Nature and Nations, which was, for thirty-six years, the Chair held by Neil MacCormick. The second reason that 2007 was special was that early in the following year (2008) MacCormick was due to retire, becoming Emeritus Regius Professor, his chair to be taken up by Neil Walker. The meeting in 2007, then, was also an occasion to look back at a lifetime's contribution of a person who had given so much, not only to legal theory, and not only to political life (MacCormick was

---

1 The only contributor to this volume not present at the meeting was Julie Dickson, whose draft paper was nevertheless presented in abbreviated form by MacCormick and discussed by the group.

a Member of the European Parliament from 1999 to 2004), but also to academic life as an administrator, colleague and teacher.

However, as friendly as it is, and as much as it expresses the editors' and contributors' most sincere and heartfelt gratitude to MacCormick for the book's contribution to legal theory, this collection is not an exercise in hagiography. None of the contributors have refrained from criticism where they thought it was due. Each has taken his or her own considerable experience and expertise in legal theory to offer improvements or suggest new paths. That alone is a testament to MacCormick's dedication to the discipline of legal theory, and his relentless encouragement of alternative views. Indeed, MacCormick's intellectual leadership of the Edinburgh Law School has been characterised by exactly that unique mix of responsibility and openness. In all thirty-six years, he never once set out to impose his own vision on others; nor did he attempt to attract disciples. Rather, he set out to offer the best account he could of his own view, engaged with others in debate (often by way of anecdotes, and never without a great deal of humour), continued to read and comment generously on the work of others, and encouraged all of us to strive to meet ever-more demanding standards of scholarship.

The aims of this introduction are two-fold. First, a brief discussion is offered of some of the elements of the first four chapters of *Institutions of Law*. This is partly because these chapters comprise the philosophically most robust part of the book, and partly because many aspects of the other twelve chapters are covered in the contributions to this volume. Having provided such a discussion, the introduction then goes on to outline some of the themes pursued by the contributors to this volume and to summarise the basic features of their individual pieces.

1. Norms, norm-users and normative orders

In his earlier and justly famous work with Ota Weinberger (MacCormick and Weinberger 1986), MacCormick's legal theory rested on a distinction between brute and institutional facts. It will be useful to begin with this distinction because even though it is retained in *Institutions of Law*, and continues to play an important role, it is arguably surpassed in significance by another two sets of distinctions, i.e., between norm-users and norm-givers on the one hand, and normative orders and institutionalised normative orders on the other.

The distinction between brute and institutional facts is that brute facts are 'sheer physical facts' (MacCormick 2007, 11), while institutional facts are ones 'that depend on the interpretation of things, events, and pieces of behaviour by reference to some normative framework' (MacCormick 2007, 11). The key move from seeing something as an institutional fact, rather than a brute one – as in the move from seeing a piece of colourful plastic and recognising it is a credit card – is enabled, indeed presupposes, a 'body of legal or other rules' (MacCormick 2007, 11), e.g., in the above case, the rules concerning consumer credit. Without these rules, MacCormick says, 'the physical object would lack or lose its current meaning. Interpretation of the things and their use in the light of the relevant rules is what makes such physical objects have the meaning they have' (MacCormick 2007, 11–12). Recognising institutional facts, then, is a method for revealing the ontology of law, and thus also, though no doubt somewhat imperfectly, the 'omnipresent and inherent elements of social reality' (MacCormick 2007, 12).

In *Institutions of Law*, MacCormick does not wish to undermine the centrality of language or indeed the social reality it constructs, but, via the concepts of norm-users and normative orders, he does situate our picture of law on a different foundation. The opening chapter of the book contains a discussion of the practice of queuing, which MacCormick uses to illustrate these concepts. The practice of forming a queue, he says, 'occurs very frequently in the everyday experience of contemporary human beings' (MacCormick 2007, 14). This common experience is orderly, at least to the extent that people 'take their turn' (MacCormick 2007, 14). Of course, queuing need not work perfectly: either because 'there may always be somebody with brass neck enough to jump the queue' or because 'it is sometimes all right to go to the head of the line without waiting your turn' (e.g., in cases of medical emergency) (MacCormick 2007, 14). Nevertheless, even if it may not work perfectly, 'there is some minimum threshold of compliance below which the practice would be unsustainable' (MacCormick 2007, 14):

> It would be literally impossible to be the only person that 'takes her turn' because 'turns' require a mutually co-ordinated practice of two or more. When a substantial majority of potential competitors for a certain opportunity fails to acknowledge turn-taking, it amounts to pointless self-abnegation if one or a few act as though most others were ready to take their turn. (MacCormick 2007, 14)

From this it follows, says MacCormick, that 'turn-taking or queuing is … normative' (MacCormick 2007, 15):

> For where there is a queue for something you want, you ought to take your turn in it, and people who do take their turn do so because in their opinion that is what one ought to do – that is, ought to do in the given context. Such action-guiding 'ought' alerts us to the presence of some kind of norms, and to the normative character of the opinions that people hold in such a setting. (MacCormick 2007, 15)

The practice of queuing, then, is normative, but it is also a kind of normative *order*. 'People's positioning in a queue,' says MacCormick, 'is ordered, not random' (MacCormick 2007, 16). But this is not an order that can be studied '"externally" and reported statistically'; it is a '"normative order" because, or to the extent that, one can account for it by reference to the fact that actors are guiding what they do by reference to an opinion concerning what they and others ought to do' (MacCormick 2007, 16). The 'result', says MacCormick, 'is a kind of common action by mutually aware participants' (MacCormick 2007, 16).

Importantly, although MacCormick acknowledges that 'there can be normative order without explicitly formulated norms' (MacCormick 2007, 18), he continues to explain normative order as the functioning of implicit norms. 'People know how to queue', he says 'and can tell cases of queue-jumping, and protest about them, even if they have never articulated exactly what their governing norm is' (MacCormick 2007, 15). What explains this phenomenon is that 'implicit norms are in fact largely observed and respected, without any other element of supervision, direction or enforcement than that constituted by a pressure of common (not necessarily either universal or identically expressed) normative opinion among those who interact with each other' (MacCormick 2007, 18).

Interestingly, then, though he posits the possibility of a stratum of social behaviour that need not rely on pre-articulated norms, MacCormick nevertheless feels tempted to explain the order as one governed by mutual awareness of an implicit norm (or norms). Arguably, providing such an explanation allows for a smoother transition to the articulation of rules of conduct for the behaviour in question. It is a smoother transition because those rules can now be represented not as imposed from above, but as, in some sense, emerging from the practice of a normative order. In such a picture, those rules are an attempt, no doubt imperfect, and no doubt appearing in a formulation that not everyone might agree with, to make explicit the implicit norm or norms that norm-users had been following all along, though previously without the need for their articulation. The transition does not always occur – as MacCormick points out, 'normative order can exist in some cultural and social settings on the basis simply of mutual belief and inexplicit norms with overlapping mutual understanding and interpretation' (MacCormick 2007, 19). But sometimes it does become necessary to avoid 'problems of a kind apparently endemic in informal orders' (MacCormick 2007, 24) 'by resorting to the issuance of expressly articulated norms, making explicit what is to be done or decided in expressly foreseen circumstances' (MacCormick 2007, 14).

The difficulties MacCormick is grappling with here are at the heart of legal theory, as well as in many of the social sciences. On the one hand, we have this huge invisible ontology of institutional facts (i.e., the world of legal representations, managed, but not ruled over, by officials); on the other, we have people with their everyday activities, interactions, relations and practices. Providing an account of the relations between the two has been food for thought for a long time. Should we give explanatory priority to the representations themselves – i.e., is it they that constitute and regulate social life? Are our actions guided, more or less consciously, by these representations? Or, should we prioritise everyday activities, practices, interactions, relations and practices, which may at times rely on or manipulate representations, but which remain independent and autonomous, and which are subject to *post factum* praise or blame? Are these representations, then, only ever a significant reality for officials who are entrusted with them and under a duty to evaluate the behaviour of citizens only by reference to them?

One outstanding issue in MacCormick's suggestion that human beings are, at bottom, norm-users (and certainly before they are norm-givers), is how to account for the 'mutual understanding and interpretation' that is said to constitute the content of social normativity. Is the suggestion that we act with such implicit norms in mind – deliberating as to what is appropriate based on the expectation that everyone else will comply with these norms? Or is the suggestion that we somehow feel what is appropriate, and it is only when things go wrong, when something disrupts the usual run of expectations, that we begin to reflect on our practices, and perhaps, if necessary, attempt to articulate norms that are to be used in evaluating the behaviour that goes on in such practices in the future? In other words, can we describe our behaviour as a matter of rule-following, and our activities as rule-governed or as regulated by rules, even if there is no fact of the matter, at any one time, as to which rule we are following, or no fact of the matter about which rules we are being governed or regulated by?

This issue is not a matter, or at least not merely a matter, of articulating how much action is conducted under the conscious influence of institutional facts. The issue is deeper. The issue is whether or not our everyday social conduct can be described by reference to institutional facts, legal representations, implicit norms, or constitutive rules. More generally, the issue is the familiar one of the problem of the relationship between theory and practice.

The problem of the relationship between representations and reality, and between theory and practice, rears its head in another guise in *Institutions of Law*, namely in the gap between rules and habits. MacCormick tackles this problem in Chapter 4. His principal strategy is to incorporate the role of habits in his theory of law as institutional normative order by arguing that 'institutionalised legal orders depend on habits about rules, that is, on habitual references in some contexts to special sorts of text like those in the statute book and those in law reports' (MacCormick 2007, 69). MacCormick elaborates on this as follows:

> This involves the maintenance of a standing practical attitude towards institutionally established rule-texts … when these are cited and brought to attention as relevant to some context. … The habit or practical disposition of personnel engaged in legal work must include a disposition to give respect to and seek respect for any relevant provisions found in the texts of valid statutes and binding precedents, read in the light of the principles and values to which they give expression. (MacCormick 2007, 69)

Having acknowledged such a role for habits, MacCormick goes on to recognise that there are two kinds of gap between habits and law (the latter conceived of as institutionalised normative order). The first is that knowledge of the law on the books does not capture the knowledge and, equally, respect of the law in practice: thus, the success of lawyers in practice 'derives from a great deal more practical knowledge, know-how, and wisdom than could be gleaned from however voluminous a grasp of the whole body of statute law, whether or not supplemented with voracious reading of cases and precedents' (MacCormick 2007, 71). The second gap is the efficacy gap, namely, that:

> However legal professionals and legal officials negotiate their way around the law, it is very much an open question how much of the official law is any part of the working consciousness of laypersons. It is also questionable to what extent their sense of what is right and proper depends on, and how far it diverges from, what the official law enjoins either in the sense of abstract texts or in the mediated form filtered through professional and official practice. (MacCormick 2007, 71)

MacCormick addresses the difficulties arising from these gaps by pointing out that they are not always as large as we may think. 'There is,' he insists, 'a large conceptual framework [provided by law] which is available to people to appeal to, and to which they do frequently appeal' (MacCormick 2007, 71). People generally know they have rights, he says, and they know there are things that are crimes, and they can generally discern their own belongings from those of others. Further, states increasingly acknowledge 'international standards of acceptable conduct', and corporations 'acknowledge legal conditions for recognition of corporate activity wherever they engage in trade' (MacCormick 2007, 72). Finally, says MacCormick, there is such a thing as a 'civil society' – such that 'civility can obtain among persons who are relative [or complete] strangers to each other' (MacCormick 2007, 72). All these elements encourage us to 'consider whether [our] lived experience is not the best evidence [we] could have that law is at work to some reasonable extent in the state [we] live in' (MacCormick 2007, 74).

Again, the difficulties MacCormick is facing here are at the forefront of legal theory and the social sciences. H.L.A. Hart suggested that we recognise that at the foundation of all legal systems were social conventions. He left the task of characterising those social conventions to others, and legal theorists have since looked to philosophers, such as David Lewis, Michael Bratman and Robert Brandom, for aid in articulating the nature of social normativity. However, Lewis, Bratman and Brandom all tend to require the exercise of rationality, often deliberative and self-conscious, and sometimes in the name of liberation from traditional ways of life. Understanding ourselves, and requiring that laws and legal systems treat us, as capable of exercising practical reasonableness (including the capacity to criticise the status quo and lobby for change) is important: if anything, it helps thwart the imposition of laws that have no respect for the freedom and dignity of persons. However, what this approach makes difficult is understanding precisely that sense of traditionality, i.e., that which is taken for granted, tacit, and operating below the level of conscious deliberation. Worse, such an approach may define that sense of traditionally, which is probably more pervasive and tenacious than we realise, out of contention. To do so is dangerous, for it may make us think that we can, at any one time, be conscious of all that which influences our action. Although we need the confidence that comes with our belief in our capacity for rationality, we also need the modesty, and potential for alertness and sensitivity, that comes, or at least may come, with recognising we are always influenced more than we can, at any one time, be aware of or be critical about.

Providing an account of social normativity that takes that sense of traditionality seriously is clearly outside the scope of an introduction. However, what can be said about the prospects of such an account is that even if it were to successfully overcome the theoretician's prejudice to self-conscious deliberation by reference to representations, it would still leave open the question of the relationship between social normativity and representations, and theory and practice. We would still have to ask: at what point do we reach into ourselves, and look upon ourselves and our practices as objects of our own critical attention? What goes on when we do so? And how is such reflection linked to action, if at all?

Happily, it is these devilishly tricky questions, amongst others, that are dealt with in MacCormick's fourth and final volume in his magisterial series. Whatever we will think of the answers, there is no doubt that *Practical Reason in Law and Morality* (MacCormick 2009) will offer, just as *Institutions of Law* has, plenty of stimulus and ample room for discussion and debate. In the meantime, we can conclude these brief comments can be concluded by noting that we do not think that the answers to these questions need not affect the explanatory power of MacCormick's definition of law as institutional normative order, which is presented with such clarity and gusto in *Institutions of Law*. It is now time to highlight some of the themes and features of the individual responses, collected in this volume, to that definition and its exposition.

2. Themes and features of the contributions

This collection is divided into five parts. The first, containing contributions from William Twining, Frederick Schauer and Vittorio Villa, considers the importance, explanatory limitations and genealogy of MacCormick's concept of law as institutional normative order. The second, with pieces from Massimo La Torre, Victor Tadros, and Jaap Hage, turns more specifically to the nature of institutions and laws, as well as to the overlap between the treatment of these in legal and political theory. The third, with pieces by Nils Jareborg and Magnus Ulväng, is focused on criminal law. The fourth, which includes chapters from Andrew Halpin and Julie Dickson, focuses on the contribution MacCormick makes to the methodology of jurisprudence. Finally, the fifth part contains a reply to the chapters from MacCormick, which also includes a synopsis of the book and its place in the series. The four thematic divisions are not strict. There are, naturally, overlaps between the themes. Nevertheless, the chapters grouped under each of the four themes echo each other and can be productively read together.

One important issue at stake in the first part is whether legal theory can and should operate with one concept of law, or whether it needs several, each of which may have more explanatory value in different contexts and/or be better put to use for certain ends than others. Building on his previous work on the challenges of globalisation, non-state law and normative legal pluralism for legal theory, **William Twining** argues that although there are overlaps between his and MacCormick's concepts of law, there are also three significant differences. First, Twining argues that the standpoint MacCormick adopts, i.e., of an informed and engaged inside observer of a particular state legal system, does not fit other kinds of scholarly study, such as that of 'a jurist trying to construct an overview of legal phenomena from a global perspective or a legal theorist concerned with "laws in general".' The adoption of this participatory perspective by MacCormick is linked to the second difference in approach. Twining argues that the adoption of MacCormick's standpoint makes it difficult to make room for the 'relatively detached observer', which we need, says Twining, in order to see that we do not have to accept that law can '*only be understood* in terms of the orientation of those engaged in law-work towards peace, justice and related values' (MacCormick 2007, 297; emphasis added). There is just too much pluralism, according to Twining, of ideologies, religious beliefs and institutional forms, for us to assume, or assert without further investigation, that values such as peace and justice, which Twining characterises as 'a version of liberal democratic ideology', are universal enough to warrant making them necessary for an understanding of law in all times and in all places. The third difference, which is also connected to themes raised in the first part of this introduction, is that whereas MacCormick prefers to focus on normative orders, Twining argues for the use of the concept of social practice (and agglomerations of social practices), largely because of problems associated with the individuation of orders, including the difficulties with ascertaining under what conditions a normative order exists and to which system or agglomeration a particular norm belongs.

Disagreement over what kinds of concepts of law we need for which purposes is also at the forefront of **Frederick Schauer**'s contribution. Schauer tackles Ronald Dworkin's claim that conceiving of law as 'a kind of social institution', which Schauer takes to be the central part of MacCormick's enterprise, 'has neither much practical nor philosophical interest' (Dworkin 2006, 98). Schauer counters Dworkin's 'dismissive attitude towards institutional questions' by arguing that, to the contrary, such questions are of central importance to both legal philosophers and lawyers. The first part of Schauer's argument is designed to parry the idea that because the sociological concept of law is 'vague at the edges', so the concept itself is either 'unintelligible or worthless.' Even if we accept this, however, and thus step over the first hurdle towards recognising the intelligibility and possible worth of the sociological concept of law, we still need to show that law in a sociological sense 'is material to determining whether a proposition of law is true'. The sociological concept of law does this, Schauer says, because it enables us to identify the legal institutions from which legal propositions emerge. Given that this social validation thesis is a central plank of legal positivism, it turns out that, according to Schauer, Dworkin does not provide an argument against legal positivism, but rather presumes that the positivist account of a legal system is false.

Of course, this leaves open the question as to whether or not social validation is germane to legal enforceability, and here Schauer argues that although Dworkin is right that the doctrinal and sociological questions are conceptually distinct, he is wrong to deny or ignore that they are empirically and causally linked in most modern legal systems; that they are so linked, says Schauer, becomes evident when we acknowledge that 'the answer to the doctrinal question does, as a factual matter, often depend on the answer to the sociological question'.

One of the issues lurking in the background in Schauer's contribution is MacCormick's expression of and attitude to legal positivism. MacCormick's understanding of and stance with respect to the tradition of legal positivism has itself changed over time, and it is the task of **Vittorio Villa**'s chapter, the final in this trifecta of chapters in the first part, to provide us with an account of these shifts. Villa has not, however, confined himself to providing an accurate exegesis. Rather, he combines the historical reading with an evaluation of his own. Villa is critical of MacCormick's recent defence of 'post-positivism' – a term MacCormick himself uses in describing his own current position, which signals a retreat from his previously more clearly positivist perspective, and which consists in accepting certain tenets of the natural law tradition, especially those defended by Gustav Radbruch and Robert Alexy as to the claims of law to justice (which is a strategy that is also discussed in Julie Dickson's contribution). Villa's exegetical work and critical remarks rely on his longstanding interest in epistemological constructivism and the role of value judgements in the work of legal scholars and legal officials. Both of these themes play a crucial role in his argument that legal positivism and natural law are mutually exclusive conceptual oppositions. For Villa, legal positivism consists in two theses: first, that law 'historically represents the normative production of decisions and/or human actions that are historically contingent from the cultural point of view, and, therefore, more specifically, from the ethical-political point of view', which also means that 'there is no necessary legal content – and therefore a fortiori any necessary ethical content – that necessarily has to be part of positive law itself'; and second, which Villa calls 'methodological legal positivism', namely, that the taking into account of positive law by a legal scholar is a completely different activity and thus to be kept separate from 'what is concretised in a stance … towards law itself' (as acceptable or justifiable, or otherwise). According to Villa, if we accept this definition of legal positivism, we will see, contrary to MacCormick's most recent position, that there is a case to be made for a mutually exclusive conceptual opposition between legal positivism and natural law.

The first contribution of the second grouping of chapters also has a historical dimension, this time placing MacCormick's legal institutionalism into perspective, by comparing and contrasting it with contributions from Santi Romano, Maurice Hauriou, Carl Schmitt, Cornelius Costoriadis and others. Although these legal institutionalisms differ in many ways, they are also part of the push against 'formalism', i.e., they have in common, with many other traditions, the attempt to find a way out of a 'too narrow conception of law and legal science' and, primarily, the inability or unwillingness to place legal norms in a broader, social context. According to **Massimo La Torre**, however, legal institutionalism is the 'more epistemologically savvy' amongst all of these attempts. There are three basic features of legal institutionalist approaches: first, they emphasise sociality, which means understanding law as closely bound up with society; second, they support the idea of system, meaning that they understand law to form an order that is grounded on, and guarantees, orderliness; and, third, they embrace plurality, meaning that they understand the legal system to be plural in its makeup, with no 'single, coherent or self-contained system of law having effect over a single territory', but rather many systems integrated with one another. According to La Torre, what distinguishes MacCormick's contribution is that although he embraces these three features, he does not do so at the cost of leaving behind the notion of a norm and he does not descend into the anti-Enlightenment, irrationalist and anti-liberal perspective of Schmitt's decisionism. There are, continues La Torre, three characteristics of MacCormick's earlier work with Ota Weinberger: first, it is anti-reductionist, in that it does not understand social reality to be 'completely reducible to the material reality of space and time'; second, it is anti-prescriptivist, in that it says that 'norms cannot be explained as immediate imperatives, commands, or prescriptions'; and third, it is non-cognitivist in meta-ethical terms, meaning 'we can attain a knowledge of law, but not a knowledge of morality (understood as critical morality).' This already distinguishes it from other legal institutionalist approaches. *Institutions of Law*, however, according to La Torre, confirms this previous work, but also offers new insights. Arguably the most important, from La Torre's perspective, is that to previous uses of the concept of institution (e.g., on the back of John Searle's work), MacCormick adds the notion of an institution as 'a co-ordination scheme, a matter of reciprocal expectations and adjustments to conduct.' MacCormick's 'neo-institutionalism', then, offers 'an ontological foundation to the hermeneutical internal point of view', while also providing us with tools for seeing legal norms, phenomenologically, as not only constraining or simplifying conduct, but also 'opening up of a scope for action that would otherwise not be available'.

Although the chapter by **Victor Tadros**, the second in the second grouping of chapters, also focuses on the concept of institutions, it is quite different in key to La Torre's. Whereas La Torre is concerned with the conceptual issues at stake in the institutionalist picture of law, Tadros seeks out to investigate 'what institutions of law we ought to have, and what values they protect or promote'. Indeed, he is more explicit than that, asserting that the question as to whether law is institutional is both less interesting and also easier than the normative question. Although Tadros approves of MacCormick's attempt to investigate the values underpinning law's institutions, he is critical of MacCormick's method, i.e., rational reconstruction, because, according to Tadros, such a method 'will tend to suffer from conservatism', as it will 'tend to defend the values that the law in fact adopts'. Instead, Tadros sets out to 'outline some more foundational questions about justice, and to see how the institutions of law can best meet the demands justice makes of them.' In doing so,

Tadros first makes a distinction 'between the justification of having a state with some laws' in the first place, and 'the justification for the particular set of laws that we have'. Having provided such a distinction, he goes on to show how different institutions of law (such as public and private law, and subdivisions within these) each reflect aspects of a theory of justice, though none has a monopoly on attaining any one aim of justice (e.g., the proper aims of private law include elements of both corrective and distributive justice). Tadros also applies his approach to criminal law, and his criticism of MacCormick's reliance on civil peace as a justification for criminal law is profitably read together with Magnus Ulväng's contribution. Whatever one may think of the details of Tadros's arguments, one can surely agree with him that legal theorists ought to 'engage more closely with political theory than many of them have done to date'. Whether this means we ought to give up thinking about whether law is properly conceived of as institutional is, one might think, another matter; indeed, one might think that the two enterprises, descriptive and normative, not only intertwine but can also learn a great deal from each other's emphases (as indeed MacCormick's work exemplifies).

The final chapter in the second part focuses on the notion of a legal transaction. **Jaap Hage** defines legal transactions to be 'acts, performed with the intention to bring about changes in the world of law (legal consequences), to which legal rules attach the intended consequences because they were intended', which one can recognise everywhere in the law. The obvious example is that of contract law, from which, Hage says, the idea of a legal transaction may have emerged, but taken so abstractly the idea can apply to other areas of private law and some aspects of public law. Hage's treatment of the subject takes a good deal from MacCormick and Weinberger's analysis (1986) of rules (as institutive, terminative and consequential); indeed, Hage states explicitly that the starting point for his investigation is the institutional theory of law. Hage also relies on Searle's account of social reality, also endorsed by MacCormick, as well as Searle's account of speech acts. Building on these resources, and offering examples from both civil and common law, Hage argues that legal transactions can be understood to be a special species of constitutive facts. Hage's analysis of rules governing legal transactions also offers a welcome opportunity for a discussion of MacCormick's account of legal powers (in chapter 9 of *Institutions of Law*). Hage's careful analysis offers perhaps the clearest example in this collection of further applications of the explanatory framework of the institutional theory of law to complex legal phenomena across different legal systems and traditions.

The third part is dedicated to examining MacCormick's treatment of criminal law in *Institutions of Law*. The first of the contributions in this context is that of **Nils Jareborg**, who focuses on personality and corporate crime. Jareborg first discusses MacCormick's claim that corporations can be meaningfully considered morally or legally responsible for wrongful acts. Jareborg stresses, however, that this is but the first step in analysing, and justifying, corporate crime, for it must thereafter be established that a corporation can be blamed. Up to that point in his discussion, Jareborg is in agreement with MacCormick. He disagrees, however, with MacCormick's claim that 'in many systems ... the law has groped only slowly and uncertainly to a clear and principled resolution of this matter' (2007, 91). The remainder of Jareborg's contribution is dedicated to showing why we need to be careful about proceeding too quickly, and too ambitiously, with the criminalisation of corporate conduct. Apart from problems associated with agency, personal identity, and complicity, there are also, he says, difficulties concerning the sentencing of corporations, including the limited range of available sentences and the fact that 'dishonest corporations are suicide-prone', rendering it impossible to find anyone to punish or any assets to seize.

The second contribution in this part, by **Magnus Ulväng**, operates on a more a general level and tackles MacCormick's general definition of crime, in *Institutions of Law*, as 'behaviour violating the conditions of civil peace'. Ulväng argues that MacCormick's approach presupposes a universal right to punish, which, he further states, is not sufficient 'to offer a general justification for the existence of criminal law.' Rather than presupposing the universal right to punish, we ought, says Ulväng, to remain anxious and vigilant about any system that 'causes so much pain'. Further, in searching for a normative justification for criminalisation, including answers to vexed questions such as why we punish at all, what gives us the right to punish, and what are the functions of punishment, we cannot, argues Ulväng, rely solely on the concept of civil peace. In other words, the concept of civil peace will not have what it takes to help us draw the normative boundaries of criminal law. Ulväng reminds us that civil peace is not a matter exclusively for the criminal law, for civil peace can also be attained by 'promoting social welfare, economic stability, education, democracy, plurality, etc.'. He also notes that punishment, sanctified by criminal law, is 'not a particularly efficient way of solving conflicts or maintaining peace and stability'; indeed, he says, it is quite often to the contrary (i.e., punishment 'actually causes instabilities in societies'). Focusing on civil peace will also often have little to tell us as to why the deeds in question are blameworthy, especially those crimes classified as *mala prohibita.* Even where deeds violate civil peace, and are morally abhorrent, such as regulatory offences, there may be arguments against their criminalisation. Given the pain imposed by the criminal law, we should always be on the lookout, says Ulväng, for alternative measures and sanctions, such as those within administrative law, to maintain civil peace. For Ulväng, the starting point for our justifications of criminal cannot be 'the assumption that something is necessary in order to preserve civil peace, and then ask whether there are any moral constraints'. Rather, he asserts, 'we ought to begin with the normative element and ask why we think it is appropriate to intentionally inflict pain or suffering on someone'.

The final two chapters, both included in the fourth part of the collection, respond to MacCormick's methodological claims in Chapter 16 of *Institutions of Law*. The first of these, by **Andrew Halpin**, offers a wide-ranging discussion of the general enterprise of intellectual inquiry, the value of conceptual analysis and the role of theoretical methodology. Halpin proceeds from the assumption that the principal purpose of intellectual inquiry 'is to gain insight on a subject over which, prior to the inquiry, there existed a certain lack of understanding'. In considering the role of conceptual analysis within intellectual inquiry, Halpin argues against suggestions, particularly from those taken with the alleged priority of scientific inquiry, that conceptual analysis ought to play a stock-taking or domestic servant role. Halpin argues that if we acknowledge the contestable nature of scientific inquiry, we will also acknowledge the 'preliminary (if not prior) role for concepts'. For example, we will acknowledge that we first need a set of 'explanatory ideas/concepts' that allow us to embark on empirical testing; we will also see that we need concepts to offer 'further explanatory insight on matters for which empirical evidence is not yet available'. Further, we will recognise that concepts can be the drivers of the change and development of received scientific understanding. Halpin provides a detailed classification of different roles to be played by conceptual analysis, which are usefully accompanied by illustrations from legal and political theory. In applying his approach to MacCormick's discussion, Halpin finds much to agree with, though he is insistent in suggesting that a stronger link be drawn 'between sound theory and an experiential basis.' In the end, Halpin's point is that rather than seeking to establish a strong methodology or secure epistemology with which to defend a theory, the picture of intellectual inquiry we ought to adopt is that of the 'ability of the theory … to bump up against the world'. In this respect, he is also in agreement with MacCormick, whose modest approach to methodology is endorsed by Halpin.

The second contribution to the fourth part is by **Julie Dickson**. In a chapter rich with detailed exegesis and nuanced argument, including close readings of the work of both John Finnis and MacCormick, Dickson tackles the perpetually vexing issue of whether bad law is still and/or really law. Dickson ends up a defending a position at odds with Finnis, but akin (though not entirely) to MacCormick, wherein 'although it is necessary to understand law's aim, and the value which it ought to realise in order properly to understand its nature, the failure to achieve those aims or to realise those values does not thereby render something less than fully law'. Dickson's chapter offers a clear account of MacCormick's methodological claim in *Institutions of Law* and its position in the wider legal theoretical literature. For MacCormick, although law may fail to realise certain values less than successfully, and still be law, when it fails, radically and in an extreme fashion, to make good on law's implicit claim to justice, then it can no longer be called law. Dickson agrees with MacCormick when she argues that when we do not acknowledge that less than successful law is still law, we risk recognising the 'deep and pervasive effect on the lives of those living under law'; those being effects that 'persist when law fails to realise its moral point and fails to instantiate those values it ought to'. We ought not, says Dickson, forget about 'the social reality of law as it has actually been implemented in our societies', which we will do, she continues, if we neglect to grant the label of law to those instances of less than successful laws. However, Dickson does not endorse MacCormick's position that radically unjust law is not law; or, more accurately, she leaves the issue for another paper, while indicating her instinct is *contra* MacCormick.

The fifth and final part of the collection offers a response from **Neil MacCormick** to the chapters above, as well as outlining the major themes and occupations of the book and its place in the quartet of *Law, State and Practical Reason*. We shall not rehearse the arguments made in reply, save to reiterate our gratitude for such a characteristically careful and spirited reply.

Conclusion

As noted above, this collection does not aim – as it could not, given the magisterial scope of the book – to provide a comprehensive response to *Institutions of Law*.[2] The book speaks to many readers: advanced scholars and students alike, as well as legal, moral and political theorists. It also raises issues of general philosophical interest, including, as Halpin notes in his contribution, of how we might come to approach the construction of our theoretical pictures. In the spirit of MacCormick's scholarship and collegiality, we hope this collection opens doors for more discussion, debate and, no doubt, disagreement.

References

Bankowski, Z. and MacLean, J. (2006), *The Universal and the Particular in Legal Reasoning* (Aldershot: Ashgate).

Dworkin, R. (2006), 'Hart and the Concepts of Law', *Harvard Law Review Forum* 119, 95–104.

MacCormick, N. (1978), *Legal Reasoning and Legal Theory* (Oxford: Clarendon Press).

MacCormick, N. (1999), *Questioning Sovereignty* (Oxford: Oxford University Press).

MacCormick, N. (2005), *Rhetoric and the Rule of Law* (Oxford: Oxford University Press).

MacCormick, N. (2007), *Institutions of Law: An Essay in Legal Theory* (Oxford: Oxford University Press).

MacCormick, N. (2009), *Practical Reason in Law and Morality* (Oxford: Oxford University Press).

MacCormick, N. and Weinberg, O. (1986), *An Institutional Theory of Law: New Approaches to Legal Positivism* (Dordrecht: Kluwer Academic Publishers).

2 On that note, readers may be interested to know of a panel organised by the University of Oxford Jurisprudence Discussion Group on 20 November 2008, in which John Gardner, John Finnis, Jeremy Waldron and Nicos Stavropoulos discuss chapter 14 of *Institutions of Law*, 'Positive Law and Moral Autonomy'. The discussion was recorded and can be seen at http://www.law.ox.ac.uk/jurisprudence/jdg.

PART I
Concepts of Law

Chapter 2
Institutions of Law from a Global Perspective: Standpoint, Pluralism and Non-State Law

William Twining[1]

1. Introduction

Neil MacCormick has been a close friend and colleague for about forty years. I owe him many debts – personal, professional, and intellectual. So it is a special pleasure to be invited to comment on some aspects of *Institutions of Law*, the foundational volume of the four-volume series on *Law, State and Practical Reason*. The series provides a summation of MacCormick's positions on jurisprudence.

On most issues dealt with in this important book my views are very largely compatible with MacCormick's. How far this is due to affinity, influence or independent convergence is difficult to say. When we diverge, it is attributable more to difference than disagreement. We share similar values, similar conceptions of the scholarly enterprise, and a common concern to bridge the gap between analytical and empirical perspectives on academic law. Herbert Hart was an important starting-point for each of us and we both wish to go beyond *The Concept of Law* for related reasons.

In my view, we need to develop different conceptions of law for different purposes and contexts. MacCormick's idea of law as a species of institutionalised normative order is very close to my formulation for the purpose of viewing law in the world as a whole from a global perspective.[2] Our views on institutionalisation (influenced by Karl Llewellyn)[3] and on 'focal meaning' (influenced by Weber, Finnis and Dworkin)[4] are very close. To my surprise, we have independently concluded that, contrary to Hart's view, definition *per genus et differentiam* has a role to play in differentiating law from other social institutions (MacCormick

---

1 This comment focuses on MacCormick 2007. It draws heavily on three of my works that deal with most of the issues discussed here more generally: Twining 2000; Twining 2002; and Twining 2009.

2 Twining 2009, ch. 3. See below note 18.

3 Especially Llewellyn 1940. Acknowledged by MacCormick in, e.g., MacCormick 2008, 154–55.

4 MacCormick 2007, 295–96 and 304; Twining 2009, ch. 4.

2007, 1–2 and 281–85; Twining 2009, ch. 4). I find MacCormick's idea of 'explanatory definition' helpful in some contexts (MacCormick 2007, 1–2 and 281–85) and I am in general accord with his treatment of other connected concepts in his framework.

Of course, our paths have diverged in significant respects. Rather than pick over detailed points of difference, I shall focus here on three related topics that MacCormick acknowledges but does not develop: globalisation, non-state law, and normative and legal pluralism. MacCormick agrees that we should take 'globalisation' seriously and he emphasises throughout the book that 'law as an institutionalised normative order can be found in many contexts other than that of each single state' (MacCormick 2007, 288). Accepting the idea of non-state law, allied to the thesis that legal ordering has shifted 'beyond the sovereign state' (MacCormick 1999), supports the claim that MacCormick's theory, far from being anti-pluralist, 'seeks to contribute to the tide of contemporary opinion in favour of legal pluralism, not to subvert it' (MacCormick 2007, 288). However, *Institutions of Law* is explicitly limited to the municipal law of nation states. MacCormick justifies this on the ground that this is the law that matters most to ordinary citizens of such states, to legal professionals and law students. I shall argue that there are more fundamental reasons for this restriction: in brief, his commitment to a particular version of liberal democratic ideology, his insistence on a participatory standpoint, and his conceptualision of normative orders as systems or bodies of norms (rather than as norms *and* practices (MacCormick 2007, 6; see further below note 7), combine to constrain his perspective. I suggest that adopting a global perspective involves distancing oneself from each of these elements in *Institutions of Law*, without surrendering important personal commitments. This may lead on to a significantly different conception of what is involved in understanding law.[5]

MacCormick concentrates on state law because of its assumed practical importance and its relevance to a Western European or Northern audience. However, his institutional theory of law potentially has much broader implications. This suggests that there is room for a fifth volume, not necessarily by MacCormick himself, that examines these topics in detail as well as such matters as multiple levels of legal ordering and governance, interlegality, diffusion, and different kinds of supra-state, transnational and sub-state institutionalised normative orders and the connections between them.

5 MacCormick 2007 and Galligan 2007 are two important recent books that explicitly concentrate on modern municipal law, while accepting 'non-state law' and 'legal pluralism' as significant, if problematic concepts. This is a perfectly reasonable choice in books addressed to a Western legal scholars and law students. This comment is not a critique of such choices, but it points out some of the limitations.

2. Standpoint: external and global perspectives

What might such a fifth volume exploring the wider implications of MacCormick's institutional theory look like?[6] As a preliminary to answering this question, it is necessary to begin with the standpoint adopted in *Institutions of Law* and MacCormick's apparent defection from the legal positivist camp. In the Introduction and consistently throughout the book, MacCormick adopts the standpoint of an informed and engaged inside observer of a particular state legal system, her own:

> Law involves both front-line activities of law-making, judging, advocacy, counselling, drafting and doing, and second-line activities of observing these activities from within the practice taken as a whole. The actor of the second line, the student or scholar of law, concerned with jurisprudential or doctrinal exposition of it,[7] has a certain detachment by contrast with front-line actors. On the other hand, this second-line actor has a relatively high degree of engagement by contrast with purely external observers. These latter (for example) take the whole corpus of legal activity, including the output of legal scholars and legal theorists, as a subject matter for study from the standpoint of sociological or anthropological inquiry or of economics or political science. (MacCormick 2007, 5–6)

This 'observer from within' should seek for relative detachment guided by 'the ideal of objectively understanding the subject-matter of a branch of scholarly or scientific study' (MacCormick 2007, 291). The engaged inside observer differs from that of a 'purely external observer' in two respects: vantage point and role. First, someone observing a practice of which she is a part is equipped to understand the practice by virtue of such matters as intimate knowledge, socialisation, shared ways of thought, personal experience and easier access. Second, the engaged

---

6 This comment is concerned with the implications of MacCormick's ideas. My book, *General Jurisprudence* (Twining 2009), has quite strong affinities and overlaps with, but has a different starting-point and focus from this notional fifth volume.

7 MacCormick 2007 puts norms and exposition of norms (e.g., ch. 1 and 292) at the centre of his concept of law and what is involved in understanding law. By focusing on institutionalised social practices, interpreted as encompassing both norms and behaviour, I tend towards a view of understanding law that includes what is crudely designated as 'the law in action'. My starting-point, reflecting on my undergraduate study of the tort of negligence, was to ask the question: how could I be said to have understood the English law of negligence, if I knew nothing about insurance, settlement out-of-court, and the kinds of issues and phenomena dealt with in Atiyah's *Accidents, Compensation and the Law* (1970)? Of course, MacCormick deals with institutionalised enforcement etc., and is very sympathetic to socio-legal studies, but actual behaviour is not part of his conception of law as institutional fact.

scholar participates in and can contribute to the system by scholarly exposition of legal doctrine, commentary, critique, advice and suggestions for reform.[8]

The culture of academic law is strongly participant-oriented insofar as legal education caters for intending practitioners and many legal scholars consider themselves to be contributing to a particular legal order or system or preparing future participants.[9] MacCormick's shift away from positivism is directly associated with this second-order participant standpoint. For, if an academic lawyer is participating in such ways, in one view she ought to be committed to the basic values of that system.[10] If that system belongs to a modern liberal democratic state, these values can be broadly summed up in terms of peace, justice and civility (MacCormick 2007, 297 and 299). According to MacCormick, an internal critic can point to divergences between underlying values and what happens in fact as gaps between aspiration and reality (MacCormick 2007, 299–300; see Twining 2009, ch. 10, 'Surface Law'). She can no doubt clarify and refine these basic values; but she cannot be a genuine participant if she is seeking to overthrow, subvert or revolutionise the system.

MacCormick's perspective may or may not be appropriate if one is studying one's own legal system or is involved in promoting the aspirations of a particular kind of normative order, such as a liberal democratic constitutional state. But it does not fit some other kinds of scholarly study: for example, an account of a foreign legal system to guide potential foreign investors; a teacher of comparative law or a medieval legal historian (in non-Whiggish mode); a member of Amnesty International or Human Rights Watch reporting on or assessing the human rights record of a foreign country (its legal provisions as well as specific 'violations') or a jurist trying to construct an overview of legal phenomena from a global perspective or a legal theorist concerned with 'laws in general'. All of these are concerned with legal orders in which they are not first or second order participants and to which they owe no allegiance. Their standpoints are by no means all the same, but the objects of their studies are generally the products of other people's

---

8 On the roles of academics in the legal system, see Cane and Tushnet 2003, ch. 41.

9 On law as a participant-oriented discipline, see Twining 1994, 128–30; cf. MacCormick's somewhat different treatment of the relative heteronomy of law (MacCormick 2007, 248–58).

10 'But the character of the whole enterprise determines that its intrinsic ends, or 'final causes', are the realisation of justice and the common good, according to some reasonable conception of these. Hence you cannot sincerely participate in this enterprise without serious orientation to these values, and you cannot intelligibly participate in it without at least pretending to have such an orientation' (MacCormick 2007, 264). This is, in my view, too simple: for example, it does not allow for revolutionaries who use existing structures for their own ends or the dilemmas of legal masochists (on legal masochism see Twining 1994, 78). See also the debate on the suggestion that critical legal scholars should move from law schools to other parts of the academy: see Carrington 1984.

power (Twining 2000, ch. 5).[11] All involve a switch of standpoint from an engaged internal observer of a particular example or type of a modern legal system to that of a relatively detached observer, scholarly or otherwise. The vantage point can be much the same in that the scholar can, indeed largely must, draw on the concepts, insights and accumulated insights of her own intellectual tradition. Similarly, the audience may not be significantly different. But the role inevitably shifts from an engaged insider to a relatively detached outsider – not necessarily 'purely external' (whatever that is) nor social scientific, but *an external juristic observer*.[12]

This point brings us back to positivism. Hart's project to develop a descriptive theory of law involved the standpoint of an external juristic observer, taking into account the internal point of view of actors, but not claiming to be engaged in any particular legal system. Leaving aside difficulties associated with his use of 'description', Hart's standpoint seems more appropriate than MacCormick's for many such external perspectives, including the study of all state systems of ordering, whether or not they are more or less admirable or wicked, weak, corrupt, inefficient, incoherent or unjust.[13] Hart's focus was on the 'Westphalian Duo' of municipal law of states and public international law conceived as governing relations between sovereign states. He was not much interested in non-state institutionalised normative orders.[14]

MacCormick only partly distances himself from Hart. He preserves versions of the idea of 'the internal aspect' of rules and rule-governed conduct (MacCormick 2007, 61), and both the separation thesis and the social sources thesis of modern analytical positivism. However, he modifies the separation thesis by introducing the idea of the engaged observer, who is committed to the basic values of a particular

11 MacCormick's interesting treatment of the relative heteronomy of law is more concerned with the perspective of the juristic insider than with that of the bad man or foreign observers.

12 On problems relating to the internal/external distinction see Twining 2000, ch. 5, especially 129–33.

13 A thorough external juristic observer assessing the human rights record of a foreign regime, typically considers how far the regime's 'official law' conforms with a given set of human rights norms on the surface; how these norms are interpreted and applied locally; how far they are effectively enforced in practice; and the extent to which the regime's officials or agents observe both the 'official law' and international human rights norms. Such an assessor typically postulates that the regime has law *before* evaluating the system according to external standards. If the situation turns out on investigation to be so bad that a non-positivist assessor concludes after that this is not a 'legal system', the judgement does not seem especially significant for her given task: she needs a further vocabulary for giving an accurate account of 'official law' as it is and the operative rules and practices.

14 Galligan 2007, 217, defends Hart's distinction between pre-legal orders and mature legal orders on the ground 'that the contrast is conceptual not anthropological'. That may be so, but Hart nevertheless can be criticised for not paying sufficient attention to the literature of legal anthropology, which by 1960 had begun to construct a much richer picture of so-called 'primitive law'.

kind of legal system as an institutionalised normative order. The engaged observer can be relatively detached and critical insofar as 'the-law-in-books' or 'the-law-in-action' falls short of the aspirations of that system as she interprets them.

MacCormick also acknowledges that a student of foreign or comparative law has a somewhat different standpoint. In criticising Dworkin's over-extensive claims for 'constructive interpretation', he acknowledges that:

> I do not have to be thinking how to make French law to be seen in the best possible light when I am seeing that French law really has law that is interesting and perhaps fruitfully comparable with Scots, or American, or English law … [T]here can and should be no assumption for this purpose that our duty is to depict any particular legal order in the best light possible, showing how it can best realize justice with least adverse side-effects. (MacCormick 2007, 297)

However, he goes on to say:

> Used comparatively and as a tool for understanding common elements among different states, law can indeed only be understood in terms of the orientation of those engaged in law-work towards peace, justice, and related values, albeit often ineptly and sometimes with deeply undesirable side-effects. (MacCormick 2007, 297)

Here MacCormick and I part company. Even if one is comparing modern Western legal systems allegedly based on broadly similar liberal democratic ideologies, this statement seems to be inappropriate for a comparative lawyer. To be sure, exploring the underlying ideology of a given foreign system or part of it may be illuminating and one may enquire (as functionalist comparatists do) whether similar 'solutions' to 'shared problems' are reached by different routes (Örücü and Nelken 2007). But to claim that law can 'only be understood' in such terms is an overstatement. For the purpose of studying other legal orders in the world, including non-state legal orders, adopting such a view would be ethnocentric. For we live in a world of pluralism of ideologies, religious beliefs, and institutional forms, and one cannot just impute liberal democratic ideology or giving priority to 'peace, justice, and related values' to all other legal traditions, systems and orders. There may or may not be some shared 'universal' basic values, but that is a matter for external juristic inquiry and interpretation, not bare assertion. Moreover, one cannot assume the good faith of those in power or of professional actors within a system.

MacCormick acknowledges the significance of globalisation (e.g., MacCormick 2007, 2, 5, 288–89 and 304), but does not pursue its implications. It is not necessary here to enter debates about the meaning, history, nature, and likely consequences of 'globalisation'. A broad conception refers to those processes that intensify world-wide social relations not only in respect of economy, but also of communications, health, ecology, culture, and so on (adapted from Giddens 1990;

see Twining 2000, ch. 1). For present purposes, it will suffice to switch standpoint from that of an engaged internal observer of a particular kind of modern Western legal system to that of a relatively detached external observer adopting a global perspective on law in the world as a whole.

Institutions of Law is clearly rooted in the Anglo-American (including Scottish) tradition of legal theory, and is informed by developments and ideas from Western Europe. Like much of this kind of legal theorising, it is vague about its geographical reach.[15] The focus is on modern Western legal systems in liberal democratic states broadly conceived, and it clearly has implications for other states that broadly conform to this model. *Institutions* is not concerned with religious law (but see MacCormick 2007, 267–70) and the index contains no reference to non-Western traditions, or Islam, China or Africa. So the book makes no strong geographical claims, but clearly the institutional theory of law has wider implications. My argument is that with some modification it has a broader potential than it claims.

The focus of *Institutions of Law* is largely on constitutional law-states (*Rechtstaat*), 'especially what they have in common despite manifold differences' (MacCormick 2007, 296 note 36). MacCormick grounds his conception of constitutional states and liberal democracy in an argument about the moral autonomy of individual agents (MacCormick 2007, 249–52). In this view, the ends of the enterprise of governance under law are realisation of peace, justice and the common good (MacCormick 2007, 304; cf. 'peace and civility'; MacCormick 2007, 297 and 299). Anticipating criticism, he emphasises:

> The fundamental premises of the argument from moral autonomy come first, as far as I am concerned. Human societies are societies of persons with a capacity to realize moral autonomy in their lives. (MacCormick 2007, 303)

I broadly share MacCormick's political views, his vision of scholarship, and, more cautiously, his moral commitments. I can understand how an engaged internal jurist may make these moral views and political commitments an integral part of her

---

15 It is not necessary here to enter into the question whether *Institutions of Law* is a contribution to Anglo-American, Western, general, universal or global jurisprudence (see Twining 2000, ch. 2). It seems to be broader than the retreat into the idea that a political or interpretive legal theory generally addresses the society from which it emanates (e.g., '[I]nterpretive theories are by their nature addressed to a particular legal culture, generally the culture to which their authors belong' (Dworkin 1986, 102; cf. Rawls 1987, 421)). Dworkin explicitly distinguishes interpretive theories from abstract philosophical theories, (and justifications of legal systems based on different ideologies), which are not confined in this way (discussed in Twining 2000, 33–47, and 72 note 1). How far can a jurist properly claim to be an engaged insider beyond her own society or region? MacCormick is qualified to claim to be a citizen of Europe in addition to Scotland and the United Kingdom. An engaged 'citizen of the world' might claim an engaged standpoint in relation to a putative 'global law', but in my view that is at best aspirational and typically dubious, if one accepts pluralism of beliefs as a significant social fact (see further Twining 2009).

work – although I am more sceptical. But the standpoint of the scholarly external juristic inquirer needs to be more detached than that. I believe that pluralism of beliefs and ideologies is a fact and that legal phenomena are immensely varied and complicated. I also share Herbert Hart's view that '[T]he identification of the central meaning of law with what is morally legitimate, because orientated towards the common good, seems to me in view of the hideous record of the evil use of law for oppression to be an unbalanced perspective, and as great a distortion as the opposite Marxist identification of the central case of law with the pursuit of the interests of a dominant economic class' (Hart 1983, 12).

So, for the purposes of the scholarly understanding of law from a global perspective, but within our shared intellectual tradition, I prefer Hart's strong version of the separation thesis to MacCormick's weaker one.[16]

Can the institutional theory of law be adapted for this purpose? MacCormick seemingly thinks not;[17] I think it can. That depends on one's interpretation of detachment. If the detached observer can be detached from all moral and political commitments except to honest scholarship – an admittedly controversial matter – one can make the shift by substituting for 'the point of law' some functions that are less closely associated with a particular moral theory or political ideology. One formulation is: 'law is a form of institutionalised normative order oriented towards ordering (i.e., patterning) relations between persons (i.e., legal subjects)' (see Twining 2009, ch. 3).[18]

16 MacCormick has recently acknowledged Hart's assessment that he was a 'harder' positivist than MacCormick suggested in the first edition of *H.L.A. Hart* (1981) (MacCormick 2008, 15–16).

17 In addition to giving priority to his political commitments, MacCormick acknowledges 'that the institutional theory of law *in its present form* though originally developed within the strand of thought known as 'legal positivism', is not now a 'positivist' theory … it is certainly post-positivistic' (MacCormick 2007, 5; emphasis added). My argument is that the institutional theory of law still has a wider application without any major change of form. *Institutions of Law* can be interpreted as MacCormick's attempt to work through the implications of his liberal democratic ideology for a systematic account of constitutional states (one kind of state), but from a more detached positivist standpoint, the basic ideas also have real value.

18 This explanatory definition (formulated for the project of constructing a total picture of law in the world as a whole) differs from MacCormick's in two main respects: first, 'ordering relations' is substituted for 'the intrinsic ends of governance under law' (realisation of justice and the common good) as the orientation ('point') of law as an institution. This is more abstract and less tied to a particular ideology. Second, social practice (and agglomerations of social practices) are preferred to 'normative order' because there are difficult conceptual problems concerning the individuation of 'orders' and related concepts such as system, code, bundle, body or muddle. It is, of course, the case that almost all rules belong to some larger unit, such as a legal system or a code of behaviour, but these analytic constructs are problematic not only in regard to questions such as 'under what conditions is it true to say that a normative order exists?' (e.g., is this a queue?), but also

3. Non-state law

MacCormick acknowledges that the idea of 'non-state law' is important and can be given a sufficiently precise meaning to be used as an analytic concept. He is emphatic that there are institutionalised normative orders which are appropriately categorised as legal, but which are more or less detached from states (e.g., MacCormick 2007, 288). He focuses on municipal/state law largely because it is the most important form of law for his audience and for engaged legal scholars.

Throughout, MacCormick suggests that he is 'presenting a theory in which the comparative practical importance of state law can be seen for what is' (MacCormick 2007, 289). Judgements about the relative importance of state law in relation to other forms involve difficult conceptual, empirical, and interpretive questions that cannot be pursued here. Suffice to say that if one adopts a global perspective, it is not self-evident that state law is always or even generally the most important, especially from the point of view of users.[19] That depends on one's standpoint, criteria of importance and access to a great deal of data that is not at present easily accessible or does not exist.

Elsewhere, I have made the case for taking non-state law seriously. From a global perspective, a map or picture of law in the world that omits non-state religious, or customary law, ideas and practices considered as law by other juristic traditions, emerging supra-national institutionalised normative orders and various forms of 'soft law', just leaves out too much for many scholarly and practical purposes. I have sought to allay fears that adopting a broad conception of law dilutes mainstream legal education and scholarship, threatens democratic values, or obscures the distinctiveness of state law as a form of normative order (Twining 2007; Twining 2009, ch. 12). Of course, there is the problem of the definitional stop: if one's conception of law includes even a few examples of non-state law, how is one to draw a line or differentiate between legal and non-legal social phenomena? My position is that what counts as an appropriate conception of law depends largely on context (Twining 2009, ch. 4).[20]

---

with regard to which system or agglomeration a particular norm belongs (e.g., what kind of norms does a particular instance of 'queue-barging' violate? – see below).

19 Obvious candidates include areas where 'custom' or 'religion' are strong and the authority of the state is weak, 'no-go' areas in many cities, and some spheres of ordering of transnational relations. It is wrong to assume that non-state law is mainly important in poorer countries, especially in rural areas. There is a growing literature on the importance of social practices among ethnic and religious minorities in Europe (e.g., Ballard 1994; Yilmaz 2005; and Pearl and Menski 1998 on *angrezi shar'iat*). MacCormick's institutional theory of law, with its emphasis on norm-users (e.g., MacCormick 2007, 286), is clearly hospitable to such studies. From a global perspective, I suspect that both MacCormick and Galligan are over-confident about the dominance of state law (Galligan 2007, 175–78; and MacCormick 2007, 2–3; 69–70 and 287–89), but that raises complex issues of interpretation.

20 For the purpose of viewing law from a global perspective, for instance in constructing a map or overview of law in the whole world or generalising about legal phenomena across

MacCormick's conception of law fits modern Western states that are underpinned by values that fall within a broad conception of liberal democracy. It can be extended to other states that broadly fit this ideal type and perhaps even to what Rawls patronisingly calls 'decent non-liberal peoples' (Rawls 1996). It is less clear whether other states – wicked, undemocratic, or bureaucratic states that merely pay lip service to formal versions of the rule of law[21] – fit MacCormick's conception of law, but it is not necessary to pursue this much-debated taxonomic issue here. And what of wicked, etc., non-state institutionalised normative orders?

In the present context, not many examples of non-state institutionalised normative orders fit MacCormick's post-positivist conception of law. Indeed, there is a school of thought that maintains that the form of the modern liberal democratic state is the best, perhaps the only, form of governance that offers a stable prospect of realising values embodied in the rule of law, justice, human rights, and democracy (e.g., Abraham 2007). That, rather than the factual dominance of state forms, may be the most important reason for treating the law of constitutional states as of primary importance. Even strong versions of that view (which I do not share) do not mandate that legal scholars should confine their conceptions of law to state or law-state legal orders. On the contrary, to develop this view requires taking non-state institutionalised normative orders seriously in order to bring out by contrast the special virtues of the state form. In this context, whether such phenomena are labelled non-state law, unofficial law or institutionalised non-state normative orders is normally of secondary importance.

Santos rightly warns us that it is a dangerous error to romanticise the ideas of pluralism and non-state law:

> [T]o my mind there is nothing inherently good or progressive or emancipatory about legal pluralism. Indeed, there are instances of legal pluralism that are quite reactionary. (Santos 1995, 114–15, c4. 58)

If the subordination of women or torture or the treatment of certain classes as sub-human, or certain embedded customs are reactionary, one does not have to

---

legal traditions or cultures, my 'thin functionalist' solution is very close to MacCormick's: law can usefully be viewed as a form of institutionalised normative practice oriented towards ordering relations between subjects at various levels of relations and of ordering. As suggested above, note 18, this differs from MacCormick's formulation in substituting (institutionalised) social practice for normative order and the broader and more inclusive concept of ordering (in the sense of patterning) for specific liberal democratic values, which interpret justice, peace and civility in a particular way.

21 For example, a regime that observes formal of law requirements by subjecting governance to publicised rules, but where the main orientation of the rulers is towards maintenance and expansion of their power, furthering the interests of only some citizens, or naked self-interest.

look very far for examples of both state and non-state normative orders. However, it is important not to fall into trap of some top-down commentators who assert or assume that custom and tradition are necessarily inimical to Western liberal values and economic development.[22]

Thus, non-state law is of great practical importance to many people in many different contexts and it is a mistake to assume that it is generally incompatible with liberal values in relation to gender and other issues. It is also theoretically and practically significant wherever state law interacts substantially with other normative orders. To give just one example: social scientists have characterised one of the most common errors in diffusion studies as 'the empty vessel' (or 'blank slate') fallacy (Rogers 1995, 240–42). The error is repeated in the literature and practices of 'transplantation' of laws. It is wholly exceptional for foreign state law to be imported into a total normative vacuum, even in respect of 'modern', e.g., commercial laws, such as banking or bankruptcy or intellectual property. To introduce reforms without awareness of pre-existing norms and practices (such as Islamic prohibitions on *riba*) because they were 'customary', or 'unofficial', or 'not really law', is to ignore the main sites of potential conflict, resistance to or incomprehension about what is intended.[23]

4. Legal and normative pluralism

> ... it seems to me that the great mass of confusion and distress must arise from these less evident divergencies – the moral law, the civil, military, common laws, the code of honour, custom, the rules of practical life, of amorous conversation, gallantry, to say nothing of Christianity, for those that practise it. All sometimes, indeed generally, at variance; none ever in an entirely harmonious relation to the rest; and a man is perpetually required to choose one rather than another, perhaps (in his particular case) its contrary. It is as though our strings were each tuned according to a completely separate system – it is as though the poor ass were surrounded by four and twenty mangers.
> 'You are an anti-nomian', said Jack.
> 'I am a pragmatist', said Stephen.
>
> (O'Brian 1971, 319)

MacCormick explicitly accepts the idea of legal pluralism, but does not say much about it. He implicitly acknowledges that acceptance of the idea of non-

22 Such views are criticised in Twining 2009, ch. 11. A prime example of egregious wholesale condemnation of 'customary law' is by the Secretary-General to the Commonwealth, Don McKinnon (2006) in a speech on 'The Rule of Law in Africa'. A useful counterbalance is Örebach et al. (2005), a central theme of which is: '[E]ach customary law system needs to be evaluated on its merits' (Bosselman in Örebach et al 2005, 441).

23 A classic account is Pistor and Wellons 1999.

state law mandates acceptance of the existence and importance of legal pluralism as a social fact. My suggestion is that his institutional theory of law provides a potentially fruitful juristic framework for studying this complex phenomenon.

One definition of legal pluralism is: 'A state of affairs in which two or more legal orders co-exist in the same time-space context.' The term is sometimes treated as a perspective, either one that treats legal pluralism as a very important phenomenon (sometimes in contrast to state-centrism) (e.g., Griffiths 1986) or else which is linked to some version of post-modernism or epistemological relativism (see below). This seems to me to be unnecessarily confusing. One can accept the idea of legal pluralism as a social fact without being committed to any form of epistemological relativism nor to a denial of the proposition that in many contexts state law is the most important form of law or the most relevant to present or intending legal practitioners. Nor indeed, as noted above, is there any need to romanticise legal pluralism. But 'legal pluralists' are sometimes referred to as an exotic sect, rather like 'flat earthers'.[24]

Discussions of legal pluralism have been bedevilled by a series of debilitating and, in my view, largely unnecessary controversies. One way out of the confusion is to distinguish between puzzles and concerns about legal pluralism as such and broader conceptual and normative issues. For this purpose it is helpful to treat legal pluralism as a species of normative pluralism. Normative pluralism exists when two or more bodies of norms co-exist in the same time–space context.

First, we encounter and navigate this phenomenon every day of our lives, as the quotation from Patrick O'Brian illustrates (see Twining 2000, 83).[25] So lawyers should not be surprised by the idea of co-existing normative orders.[26] Most of the time we are not puzzled by it, but if we pause to think about it, a whole host of

24 Von Benda-Beckmann 2002, 37, criticises the emergence of a bogeyman called 'the legal pluralists', 'the legal pluralist movement' or a 'legal pluralist project': 'The creation of two camps, one of so-called pluralists and one of state law adherents therefore does not make much sense and only detracts attention from the really interesting methodological questions' (Von Benda-Beckmann 2002, 74). He attributes this hostility to Tamanaha 1993 and Roberts 1998. I agree with the thrust of his argument, but consider the treatment of 'legal pluralism' as a distinct perspective rather than as a form of phenomenon to be more widespread than he suggests. Galligan 2007, ch. 10, acknowledges the existence of parallel legal orders, and gives a quite balanced critique of 'extended legal pluralism' and its concerns. However, he refers to 'legal pluralists' and criticises them for adopting too broad or too vague conceptions of law.

25 O'Brian in this passage emphasises conflict, competition and tension between sets of norms, but relations are more varied than that and can include supplementation, reinforcement, co-optation, or peaceful co-existence, for example. The cryptic exchange at the end of the quotation could be interpreted as representing two views of pluralism: as a challenge to centralised authority ('anti-nomian') and a pragmatic acceptance of normative pluralism as a social fact.

26 Of course, judges and other legal actors within a particular system may have to decide how far to recognise, take account of, or tolerate claims to attention based on other

issues arise. I suggest that some of the most profound philosophical and conceptual problems about legal pluralism are best treated as issues about normative pluralism: the nature of norms, institutionalisation, the idea of a normative 'order' or 'system' and the individuation of units such as rules, codes, systems for the purposes of study are issues that concern normative orders in general, not just legal orders. The problem of individuation – what can be treated as one legal order? What counts as one rule? What counts as one law?[27] – has concerned jurists from Bentham to Raz to Galligan, without much specific reference to pluralism (Bentham 1782/1970; Raz 1970; and Galligan 2007, 100). Problems of individuation are often more acute with some kinds of non-state phenomena than with state legal systems. For example, with tacit social norms, when a norm is invoked, it is sometimes unclear to what body or system of norms it belongs: if one complains about queue-barging by saying 'There is a line', is one invoking a specific queuing norm or an intermediate set of norms about turn-taking or some broader regime such as good manners, fair procedures or equal treatment? These and many related questions are in need of further development within the general theory of norms.[28]

Second, treating legal pluralism as a species of normative pluralism raises the question: how to differentiate between legal and non-legal phenomena in this context. This problem of 'the definitional stop' has re-surfaced in the context of debates about legal pluralism.[29] But this is not a specific puzzle about legal pluralism as such, but is part of the perennial topic of how best to conceptualise law.

Thirdly, pluralism is sometimes linked with some version of post-modernism or epistemological relativism. Gunther Teubner has elegantly suggested that legal pluralism fits the post-modern mood:

> Postmodern jurists love legal pluralism ... The crucial question of how to reconstruct the postmodern architecture, the connections between the social and legal fields finds a highly vague answer: interpenetrating, intertwined, integral, superposed, mutually constitutive, dialectical ... we are left with ambiguity and confusion. After all, this is the very charm of postmodernism. (Teubner 1992, 1443–44)[30]

---

normative orders and, in some cases, this may turn on whether they can treat them as 'law'. For some interesting examples of such issues, see Judicial Studies Board 1999.

27 It is often misleading to talk of rules as discrete units but it is sometimes necessary to talk *as if* they can be individuated (e.g., the Rule in *Rylands v Fletcher*). (Twining and Miers 1999, 143–46.)

28 Twining 2009, ch. 15 deals briefly with the concepts of order and system; whether every rule or norm belongs to some larger unit, such as a system or code; and the problem of individuating legal and normative orders. But there is a great deal of work still to be done on such questions.

29 This is a particular concern of Tamanaha 1993 and 2001, discussed in Twining 2007, 42–46.

30 Discussed in Twining 2000, 87–88.

However, one can accept the idea of legal pluralism as a social fact without being committed to any form of epistemological relativism. It is clear from MacCormick's writings that he does not accept strong versions of epistemological relativism or post-modernism, although he is sensitive to the complexities of social phenomena and the value of multiple perspectives in understanding such phenomena.[31]

Fourthly, under the rubric of 'state centralism', some complex ideological issues have been raised concerning the role of the state, its claims to a monopoly of legitimate force, and claims to independence or autonomy by or on behalf of non-state legal orders.[32] Again these are general issues of political theory, which have been debated in the context of legal pluralism rather than questions about legal pluralism as such.

If one pares away broader issues that belong to the general theory of norms, or problems of conceptualising law, or epistemological issues about post-modernism and relativism, or ideological issues about 'the state', it is relatively straightforward to conceive of legal pluralism as a social fact. Its scope depends in large part on one's conception of law. Discussions of the subject have been plagued by broader epistemological concerns and by the re-surfacing of puzzles about defining law. In particular, where to draw the line between legal and non-legal orders has permeated the debates. However, this should not pose special problems to the institutional theory of law. A 'focal point' perspective indicates in broad terms where the line between legal and non-legal phenomena can appropriately be drawn, and where the rest can be left to a specific context. Very often not much turns on the distinction anyway. The interesting phenomenon is the co-existence in the same time–space context of two or more institutionalised normative orders, whether or not one or more are characterised as 'legal'.

There are, however, specific theoretical issues concerning legal pluralism that deserve attention within jurisprudence as well socio-legal studies. How should one conceptualise 'pluralism', 'co-existence' and different forms of 'interlegality' (Von Benda-Beckmann 2002; Santos 1995; and Twining 2007)? Can one construct a useful typology of forms of pluralism or of relations between legal orders? What kinds of task are best done by informal legal orders rather than by state law or a combination of these (Galligan 2007, 179)? To what extent, if at all, are the values embodied in one or other conception of human rights and the rule of law furthered or undermined by a given example of legal pluralism? As Von Benda-Beckmann argues, once the broader conceptual, epistemological and ideological issues are clarified, most of the interesting questions about legal pluralism are empirical and

31 On the distinction between imaginative post-modernism (exemplified by Italo Calvino) and irrationalist or sceptical post-modernism (exemplified by Richard Rorty) see Twining 2000, ch. 8 (reprinted in Twining 2002, ch. 9).

32 Galligan 2007, ch. 10, forcefully criticises claims to strong autonomy by non-state orders, but allows much weaker claims for semi-autonomy or semi-independence. These complex issues cannot be pursued here.

need to be set in some broader intellectual framework, including that of orthodox jurisprudence (Von Benda-Beckmann 2002, 74).

As conceptualised in *Institutions of Law*, the category of non-state law and the phenomena of legal pluralism will be quite constricted, as they are limited to institutionalised orders oriented to a particular set of values. But this is not a necessary implication of the institutional theory of law, as long as it allows for different conceptions of law appropriate to different standpoints – a post-positivist conception for the scholar engaged in their own legal system or some broader ideological enterprise, but a positivist conception, such as Hart's, for the external juristic observer concerned to understand the many forms of institutionalised normative ordering oriented to many kinds of function and interacting in many complex ways. As soon as 'non-state law' is placed on the jurists' agenda, a whole range of conceptual, normative and empirical issues come to the surface. There has been much interesting theorising about some of these issues, for instance in relation to 'customary law'[33] and 'religion' (e.g., Huxley 2002). But much of this work has taken place in specialised contexts or marginalised fields. The extension of the institutional theory of law to encompass non-state law and legal pluralism, subjects hitherto generally neglected in mainstream jurisprudence, would provide one route to theorising these important subjects within a coherent framework and re-establishing close contact with mainstream legal theory.

5. Conclusion

Most Western legal theory, legal scholarship and legal education are and will continue to be participant-oriented, focusing mainly on the municipal law of a particular legal system or tradition. MacCormick's *Institutions of Law* is a masterly exposition and analysis of an intellectual structure that by and large fits this orthodox enterprise. However, insofar as he hints that his institutional theory of law can accommodate the ideas of non-state law and legal pluralism, these ideas are in need of development. A putative fifth volume might lead to a reconsideration of the standpoints that are most appropriate for conceptualising not only a broad and realistic vision of law in the world as a whole, but also less ethnocentric and unempirical orientations towards comparative law, international law and forms of local law than our mainstream academic legal tradition caters for.

I am not advocating that Neil MacCormick himself should sit down and write the imagined fifth volume. That may not fit his engaged agenda. Rather, I am suggesting that anyone addressing such questions would do well to consider the

33 There has been a striking revival of theoretical interest in custom and customary law recently, for example Örebach et al. 2005; Polanski 2007 (internet law); Tasioulas 2007 (international law); and Perreau-Saussine and Murphy 2007, but this has been largely separate from mainstream jurisprudence.

implications of MacCormick's institutional theory, freed from the limitations that he has set on his own version of it.

References

Abraham, D. (2007), 'The Boundaries and Bonds of Citizenship: Recognition and Redistribution in the United States, Germany and Israel' in M.S. Rodriguez and A. Grafton (2007), 201–49.

Atiyah, P. (1970), *Accidents, Compensation and the Law* (London: Weidenfeld & Nicolson).

Ballard, R. (ed.) (1994), *Desh Pardesh: The South Asian Presence in Britain* (London: Hurst).

Bentham, J. (1782/1970), *Of Laws in General*, Hart, H.L.A. (ed.) (London: Athlone Press).

Cane, P. and Tushnet, M. (eds) (2003), *The Oxford Handbook of Legal Studies* (Oxford: Oxford University Press).

Carrington, P. (1984), 'On Law and the River', *Journal of Legal Education* 34, 222–28.

Dworkin, R. (1986), *Law's Empire* (London: Fontana).

Galligan, D.J. (2007), *Law in Modern Society* (Oxford: Oxford University Press).

Giddens, A. (1990), *The Consequences of Modernity* (Stanford: Stanford University Press).

Griffiths, J. (1986), 'What is Legal Pluralism?', *Journal of Legal Pluralism* 24, 1–55.

Hart, H.L.A. (1983), *Essays in Jurisprudence and Philosophy* (Oxford: Oxford University Press).

Huxley, A. (ed.) (2002), *Religion, Law and Tradition* (London: Routledge Curzon).

Judicial Studies Board. (1999–), *Handbook on Ethnic Minority Issues*, available online http://www.jsboard.co.uk.

Llewellyn, K.N. (1940), 'The Normative, the Legal, and the Law-Jobs: The Problem of Juristic Method', *Yale Law Journal* 49, 1355–1400.

MacCormick, N. (2008), *H.L.A. Hart* (Stanford: Stanford University Press).

MacCormick, N. (2007), *Institutions of Law: An Essay in Legal Theory* (Oxford: Oxford University Press).

MacCormick, N. (1999), *Questioning Sovereignty* (Oxford: Oxford University Press).

MacCormick, N. (1981), *H.L.A. Hart* (London: Edward Arnold).

McKinnon, D. (2006), 'The Rule of Law in Today's Africa', *Commonwealth Law Bulletin* 32:4, 649–55.

O'Brian, P. (1971), *Master and Commander* (London: Fontana).

Örebech, P., Bosselman, F., Bjarup, J., Callies, D., Chanock, M., and Peterson, H. (2005), *The Role of Customary Law in Sustainable Development* (Cambridge: Cambridge University Press).
Örücü, E. and Nelken, D. (eds) (2007), *Comparative Law: A Handbook* (Oxford: Hart Publishing).
Pearl, D and Menski, W. (1998), *Muslim Family Law* (London: Sweet & Maxwell).
Perreau-Saussine, A. and Murphy, J. (eds) (2007), *The Nature of Customary Law: Legal, Historical and Philosophical Perspectives* (Cambridge: Cambridge University Press).
Pistor, K. and Wellons, P.A. (1999), *The Role of Law and Legal Institutions in Asian Economic Development 1960–1995* (Oxford: Oxford University Press).
Polanski, P.P. (2007), *Customary Law of the Internet* (The Hague: T.M.C. Asser Press).
Rawls, J. (1987), 'The Idea of an Overlapping Consensus', reprinted in Rawls 1999a, ch. 20.
Rawls, J. (1999a), *Collected Papers*, Freeman, S. (ed.) (Cambridge, Mass.: Harvard University Press).
Rawls, J. (1999b), *The Law of Peoples* (Cambridge, Mass.: Harvard University Press).
Raz, J. (1970), *The Concept of a Legal System* (Oxford: Clarendon Press).
Roberts, S. (1998), 'Against Legal Pluralism: Some Reflections on the Contemporary Enlargement of the Legal Domain', *Journal of Legal Pluralism* 42, 95–106.
Rodriguez, M.S. and Grafton, A. (eds) (2007), *Migration in History: Human Migration in Comparative Perspective* (New York: University of Rochester Press).
Rogers, E.M. (1995), *Diffusion of Innovations* (New York: The Free Press).
Santos, B.S. (1995), *Toward a New Common Sense* (London: Routledge).
Tamanaha, B. (1993), 'The Folly of the "Social-Scientific" Concept of Legal Pluralism', *Journal of Law and Society* 20, 192–217.
Tamanaha, B. (2001), *A General Jurisprudence of Law and Society* (Oxford: Oxford University Press.)
Tasioulas, J. (2007), 'Customary International Law and the Quest for Justice' in Perreau-Saussine and Murphy (2007), 307–335.
Teubner, G. (1992), 'The Two Faces of Janus: Rethinking Legal Pluralism', *Cardozo Law Review* 13, 1443–62.
Twining, W. (1994), *Blackstone's Tower: The English Law School* (London: Sweet and Maxwell).
Twining, W. (2000), *Globalisation and Legal Theory* (London: Butterworth and Evanston: Northwestern University Press).
Twining, W. (2002), *The Great Juristic Bazaar: Jurists' Texts and Lawyers' Stories* (Aldershot: Ashgate).

Twining, W. (2006), 'Schauer on Hart', *Harvard Law Review Forum* 119, 105–12.
Twining, W. (2007), 'General Jurisprudence', *University of Miami International and Comparative Law Review* 15, 1–59.
Twining, W. (2009), *General Jurisprudence* (Cambridge: Cambridge University Press).
Twining, W. and Miers, D. (1999), *How to Do Things With Rules* (London: Butterworth).
Von Benda-Beckmann, F. (2002), 'Who's Afraid of Legal Pluralism?', *Journal of Legal Pluralism* 47, 37–82.
Yilmaz, I. (2005), *Muslim Laws, Politics and Society in Modern Nation States* (Aldershot: Ashgate).

Chapter 3
Institutions and the Concept of Law: A Reply to Ronald Dworkin (with some help from Neil MacCormick)

Frederick Schauer[1]

In *Justice In Robes* (Dworkin 2006a, ch. 8), and in an earlier commentary on one of my own articles (Dworkin 2006b, replying to Schauer 2006), Ronald Dworkin makes the arresting claim that thinking about law 'as a kind of social institution' 'has neither much practical nor philosophical interest' (Dworkin 2006b, 98). The institutional question of distinguishing a legal system from the normative systems of morality or religion, or from the behavior-altering institutions of force or terror, Dworkin insists, might be of some interest to sociologists and others of that ilk, but has scant relevance to lawyers, to judges, or to legal philosophers.

If Dworkin is correct, then thinking about law in institutional terms, as Neil MacCormick has championed for decades,[2] and as others of us have, perhaps belatedly, come to recognise (see Schauer 2004), is a misdirected enterprise. If we legal theorists wish to decamp to sociology departments and become obsessed with labelling normative systems as law or not, Dworkin suggests, then he would have little objection. But as long as we persist in claiming to do legal theory, and in particular legal philosophy, and as long as we purport to speak to the concerns of lawyers and philosophers of law, then perhaps we are best checking our sociology and our talk of institutions at the door.

In this chapter, I seek to reply to Dworkin's dismissive attitude towards the institutional questions. Such questions, I argue, are important both to the philosophy

1 This chapter was originally presented as a paper at the Symposium on Neil MacCormick's *Institutions of Law*, held at the University of Edinburgh on 7 December 2007, and has benefited greatly from the audience comments on that occasion. Earlier versions of the central argument are contained in an essay entitled 'Is There a Concept of Law?', presented as a plenary lecture at the Congress of the International Association for the Philosophy of Law in Krakow, Poland, in August, 2007; at Ronald Dworkin's Colloquium on Legal, Political, and Moral Philosophy at University College, London, in February, 2007; and at Seana Shiffrin's Jurisprudence Colloquium at the University of California, Los Angeles, in January 2007. For all of its remaining errors, the current version is better for the opportunity of having discussed with such helpful audiences.

2 Much of this work is crystallised in MacCormick 2007. The most important precursor is MacCormick and Weinberger 1986.

of law and to the real concerns of real lawyers and real judges. To hold otherwise, as Dworkin so plainly does, is to assume (and not to prove) the correctness of Dworkin's own anti-positivist and 'seamless' account of law and adjudication, an account that is at the very least controversial and more likely empirically and institutionally mistaken. In rejecting the philosophical and practical importance of looking at law through the lens of legal institutions, Dworkin exposes just how much his own account of law depends on a view of the irrelevance of law-identifying institutions, a view that poorly captures the way in which the legal systems with which we are most familiar actually operate. Or so I argue here.

1. Dworkin's argument

In large part because it is a direct reply to me, I will use the version of Dworkin's claim that appears in the *Harvard Law Review Forum* (2006a), and not the substantially similar, but not identical, version in *Justice in Robes*. In the version on which I focus, Dworkin distinguishes two 'questions about the nature of law.' One he describes as 'sociological', and he sees the sociological question as one about 'what makes a particular structure of governance a legal system rather than some other form of social control, such as morality, religion, force, or terror' (Dworkin 2006b, 97–98). This is the question that Dworkin takes to have 'neither much practical nor much philosophical interest' (Dworkin 2006b, 97–98).

By contrast, what is of 'enormous practical and considerable philosophical significance' is that which Dworkin calls the 'doctrinal question' (Dworkin 2006b, 97–98). This, he says, is the question of 'what makes a statement of what the law of some jurisdiction requires or permits true' (Dworkin 2006b, 99). What makes this question so important, Dworkin argues, is that '[j]udges and other political officials justify decisions of great consequence by citing propositions of law …'. Thus, '[i]t obviously matters very much whether any such proposition is true, and therefore what test should be used in determining its truth.' And as a result, [t]he philosophical depth and interest of the question are also apparent ...' (Dworkin 2006b, 99).

Dworkin contrasts the importance to lawyers, judges and political officials of the doctrinal question with what he describes as the sociological question's dependence on 'the sociological question of law: it refers to law as a kind of social institution'. But that is the concept that has little practical or philosophical importance because it 'is vague: it has no precise or settled boundaries in ordinary language' (Dworkin 2006b, 98). Thus,

> We agree that Massachusetts has a legal system but we disagree about whether to call customary commercial practices enforced only by commercial sanctions a form of legal regulation or whether to call a frozen set of rules with no legislative or enforcement mechanisms a legal system. (Dworkin 2006b, 98)

But these issues, Dworkin claims, 'are verbal not substantive disagreements. Social scientists, of course, need more precise definitions of law for their research', but 'it would be a mistake ... to treat these definitions as attempts to excavate the very concept of law in the sociological sense or to capture the essence of legal systems and structures' (Dworkin 2006b, 98).

Thus, Dworkin sees the attempt to designate a system as legal or not as essentially a definitional enterprise, on which '[n]othing turns' 'so long as we make plain what further point we wish to make in speaking that way. So the issue as traditionally posed has neither practical importance nor philosophical interest'. In this respect, Dworkin plainly sees many modern disputes about the nature, character, phenomenon or concept of law in ways that parallel classical disputes about whether unjust law is 'really' law. Dworkin's view thus might be seen as reminiscent of the position of Glanville Williams, who in 1945 lamented that we could transcend the debates about what is or is not law (especially in the context of international law) simply by making it clear what it is that we were talking about (Williams 1945).

2. Avoiding the vagueness fallacy

Dworkin says that the 'sociological concept of law' is 'vague: it has no precise or settled boundaries in ordinary language.' That is of course true, but it hardly distinguishes law from much else. And in order to see Dworkin's argument in its best light, we ought not to saddle him with the burden of the fallacious rhetorical move from vagueness to incomprehensibility. Ever since Wittgenstein purportedly asked whether it was still 'chess' if the game were played without the queen (see Wisdom 1952, 259), we have recognised that most of our words and most of our concepts have fringes as well as cores.[3] Hart distinguished the core from the penumbra as a way of talking about legal language and the difference between clear and not-so-clear applications of the language contained in a rule (Hart 1994; see Schauer 2008), but the point is every bit as applicable not only to the words we use to describe clusters of social phenomena, but to the clusters themselves. Insofar as law (and not just the word 'law') is a sociologically differentiated institution,[4] there will be phenomena that clearly are part of the institution (national courts, for example), phenomena that clearly are not part of the institution (cookbooks, for example), and phenomena whose inclusion within the institution is partial and debatable, such as, for example, the systems of informal dispute resolution, and the functions of *notaries* in French-speaking countries. So although it is true that neither law nor the word 'law' in the sociological sense has precise or settled boundaries, neither does chess, baseball, education, medicine, or, for that matter,

3 Indeed, the point well precedes Wittgenstein. See Russell 1923.

4 And this is one of the running themes in MacCormick 2007. See also Luhmann 2004; and 'The Unity of the Legal System' in Luhmann 1988.

sociology. That there are or can be disagreements around the edges says no more about the (sociological) concept of law than it says about the concept of baldness, to use Russell's famous example (Russell 1923), or games, to use Wittgenstein's (Wittgenstein 1958), or night, to use Burke's.[5] That we might disagree about whether commercial practices enforced only by commercial sanctions, to use Dworkin's example, should be counted as law says little about whether a decision by the Court of Appeal interpreting an Act of Parliament counted as law, and although we might disagree about whether a professor of law was exceeding her remit if she taught and wrote about the informal dispute resolution mechanisms of medieval Iceland, there would be far less disagreement about the permissibility of the same person teaching and writing about the law of tort, and about the impermissibility of her teaching and writing about plasma physics or the future prospects of Manchester United Football Club.

If we thus rescue the sociological concept of law from the *sorites* fallacy, we can see that its undeniable vagueness at the edges hardly makes it unintelligible. Universities distinguish their faculties of law from their faculties of medicine with little difficulty, just as we have a pretty good sense of what holds together most of the books published by Butterworth's and Sweet and Maxwell (or, for Americans, the West Publishing Company), just as we do not think it nonsensical for a bar examination to test legal knowledge for purpose of granting a licence to practice, and just as we immediately know the difference when someone at a cocktail party identifies herself as a lawyer and someone else identifies herself as a rocket scientist. Moreover, and perhaps more importantly, we recognise the family resemblance among lawyers, judges, bar examiners, legal publishers, and law professors, just as we recognise the non-crisp distinction between this family of individuals and institutions from the family consisting of surgeons, medical schools, pharmaceutical companies and hospitals. The sociological concept of law, and thus the very idea of law not only as a collection of institutions but as an institution itself, may be vague, but that it is vague at the edges hardly makes it either unintelligible or worthless.

3. The sociological foundations of the doctrinal question

That there *is* a sociological concept of law, however, does not necessarily make it valuable for what Dworkin calls the 'doctrinal question', i.e., what it is that makes a proposition of law true, and what test or tests should be employed to determine whether a proposition of law is true. Dworkin is correct that this is indeed a question of great practical and philosophical importance, and he is correct that its importance lies substantially with the way in which lawyers and judges use the

5 'Though no man can draw a stroke between the confines of night and day, still light and darkness are on the whole tolerably distinguishable.' Edmund Burke, 'Thoughts on the Case of Present Discontents' (1770; see Burke 1881, 258).

truth of propositions of law to *justify* 'decisions of great consequence.' But then the issue is whether the sociological concept of law can provide any assistance in answering the undeniably important doctrinal question.

To pose the issue most squarely, we thus need to ask whether 'law' in a sociological sense is material to determining whether a proposition of law is true. This is the question to which Dworkin gives a negative answer, both in the work under discussion and in previous work (Dworkin 1977 and 1986). For Dworkin, the existence of a norm within (or the promulgation of a norm by) the social system commonly called the legal system is neither a necessary nor a sufficient condition for it being legally true. That it is so is a defining characteristic of legal positivism, and it is precisely this claim of legal positivism – the claim that the truth of a legal proposition is a function of its institutional pedigree – that Dworkin has devoted much of his career to refuting. But is Dworkin's refutation sound, and what is the relationship between that refutation and his newer distinction between the sociological and the doctrinal concepts of law?

Consider first the question whether the institution of Parliament (or Congress) is relevant to determining whether a proposition of law is true. Suppose the question is whether, to take a recent and controversial example at the time of this writing, it is legal for the government of the United Kingdom to detain without formal charges someone suspected of terrorism for a period of 56 days. Or, to put it in propositional form, is the proposition that it is lawful to detain, without trial or formal charges, a person suspected of terrorism for 56 days true?

The answer to this question is plainly 'no,' and one important reason that the answer is 'no' is that after extensive and public discussion of the possibility of a 56 day limit, such a possibility was taken off the table and the eventual enactment passed by Parliament limited the period of such detention without charge or trial to 42 days. And we know that the limit is 42 and not 56 days because we know that Parliament is an institution understood by the relevant rule of recognition to have at least presumptive law-creating authority.[6] I say 'at least presumptive' because it may be, as various versions of the natural law tradition would have it, and as Dworkin has often insisted certainly in the common law context and at times suggested even in the statutory context (Dworkin 1987), the fact of emanation from a law-making body such as Parliament may, even if on occasion a necessary condition for the creation of law, not be a sufficient condition. That is, Parliamentary enactment may produce only defeasible law, defeasible in the service of morality, most obviously, but possibly also in the service of various other goals and values.

But even if enactment by Parliament is not a sufficient condition for a proposition of law being true, and, moreover, even if such enactment is not a necessary condition, it would be foolish to suggest that enactment by Parliament was not even relevant to the question of whether some normative proposition was a proposition of law. Consequently, it appears simply implausible to assert that

6 Technically, the Queen in Parliament.

the social fact of behaviour by a certain institution is not highly relevant, i.e., it is of great practical importance, in the determination of what is or is not law. And thus the behaviour of an institution turns out to be highly relevant to the doctrinal question, the question that Dworkin describes as being both deep and important. Moreover, it is the determination that the institution is a *legal* one that makes it relevant, or more relevant to the doctrinal question. It may be that acceptance by the society of some norm would also make it, especially for Dworkin, relevant to the doctrinal question, but it would be hard to claim with a straight face that Parliamentary enactment of the 42 day rather than the 56 day limit was of no doctrinal importance in the face of a social determination or moral fact that 56 days was preferable to 42 days. And thus not only is the promulgation by an institution of great importance to the doctrinal question, but the determination that that institution was a legal one – the sociological question – is also of great importance to the doctrinal question.

If the social fact of production by the institution that we call Parliament is relevant to the determination of whether a proposition of law is true, and if the social fact of that institution being a legal one is also relevant to the determination of whether a proposition of law is true, then it would hardly be startling if the social fact of norm production by some other institution would, or at least could, have the same effect. Suppose, for example, that one of the criteria for the truth of a legal proposition in some society were to be the existence of the social fact of announcement, endorsement or promulgation of that proposition by a court, or by the society's highest court, or by the collective opinion of authoritative commentators. What if it were a necessary condition for a proposition being a legal one that it had been promulgated *either* by Parliament or by a court? Or what if it were a sufficient condition for a proposition being a legal one that it had been promulgated by a *legal* institution? If that were the case, then the sociological question of which institutions were legal institutions would have huge practical importance, because the identification of those institutions as legal ones would enable judges to determine which propositions to draw on in determining the rights of those who came before them; would instruct law enforcement officials about which propositions to enforce; and would enable citizens to ascertain which propositions they should permit to limit what would otherwise be their all-things-considered decisions about what to do or what to decide. Moreover, under such circumstances the sociological question would have great philosophical significance as well, because the sociological question would raise the question of when, if at all, the emanations of some institution or cluster of institutions should be permitted to override an individual's or an official's best moral judgment about what to do.

4. Legal positivism and the doctrinal question

As will be obvious by now, what I have just described is a central case of legal positivism. The point of the exercise was to demonstrate that *if* legal positivism, as a descriptive matter, were true, then what Dworkin calls the doctrinal question would depend on the answer to what he calls the sociological question, and not only would the two questions no longer be distinct, but the latter question would have a practical and philosophical importance that would be hard to deny. So Dworkin's argument cannot be taken as an argument against positivism. On the contrary, it presupposes the descriptive falsity of a positivist account of the legal system under discussion. If positivism poorly describes such a system, and thus if the distinction between legal and non-legal institutions has no relevance to determining whether a proposition of law is true, then the sociological question – the distinction between legal and non-legal institutions – indeed has little practical or philosophical importance. But if a positivist account of some legal system is true, then the identification of an institution as a legal one becomes crucial, because it's legal-ness, as it were, is precisely what gives the institution its capacity to render a proposition a legal one, and thus gives the institution its capacity to render a proposition of law true.

Thus, if Dworkin's argument is intended as an argument against positivism, it fails, because it assumes the very conclusion its sets out to prove. Moreover, even the weakest of positivist claims survives Dworkin's attack. If, for example, as McCormick himself now appears to argue in the concluding portions of *Institutions of Law* (see, e.g., 252–61 and 277–79), the institutional status of some norm or directive is a necessary, but not a sufficient, condition for its legality, it would still be the case that the sociological question of whether the institution promulgating the norm was or was not a legal one would have enormous practical importance, for the answer to the sociological question would determine whether a judge or police officer or other official with the power to bring the state's use of force to bear would in fact do so.

Moreover, the very fact that this could be so is of equally great philosophical interest. How is it, we might ask, that the truth of a proposition of law depends, even in part, on its source and not on its content? And if that is a possibility, is this a morally undesirable state of affairs, as generations of skeptics about source-based authority have argued (e.g., Simmons 1979)?

5. The limited domain of the law

Implicit in the foregoing is an understanding of legal positivism that will strike contemporary legal philosophers as non-standard, but it is one that Dworkin and I appear to share. That is, rather than (or, charitably, in addition to) being a claim about the concept of law, which would be the contemporary understanding, positivism could also be a description of particular legal systems, or perhaps of families of legal systems. Under this view, a view that has its roots in Bentham and Austin, even if not in Coleman and Raz, and arguably (but controversially) not in Hart, a legal system is a positivist one to the extent that the norms that are enforced within the system are enforceable just insofar as a social fact – the pedigree, in

Dworkin's terminology – says they are. For Dworkin, therefore, the sociological differentiation between law and non-law – between legal and other sorts of institutions – is uninteresting and unimportant precisely because for him nothing about legal decisions turns on the distinction. Thus, if Dworkin's characterisation of modern legal systems as non-positivist turns out to be descriptively accurate – if the social fact of production by a legal institution was neither necessary, nor sufficient, nor even just probabilistically causal of the legal enforceability of a norm – then it is true that the sociological concept of law would be of no legal importance. But if Dworkin's description of modern legal systems is inaccurate – if positivism is instead the accurate description of a system in which social validation was germane to legal enforceability – then the sociological concept of law would take on enormous significance.

Thus, everything turns on the descriptive claim. I have argued elsewhere that if this conception of positivism is understood as presumptive and not absolute, then Dworkin's claim about modern common law legal systems is largely false (Schauer 2004; see also Schauer 1991).[7] Even if the kinds of norms that generated the outcomes in cases like *Riggs v. Palmer*[8] and *Henningsen v. Bloomfield Motors*[9] were not subject to a pedigree-based test, these cases are nevertheless epiphenomenal. Far more typical, even with respect to the very issues that these cases raised, is that the existence of a distinctly *legal* norm generates the outcome, even where the outcome is inconsistent with the best interpretation of a society's full collection of legal, political, and moral norms, or even where the outcome is simply unjust. Unconscionable contracts are enforced because they are contracts according to pedigreed legal norms, and beneficiaries no less unworthy than Elmer Palmer inherit precisely because of the literal words of the legal institutions we call legislatures.

---

7 In *Legal Reasoning and Legal Theory* (1978), MacCormick argues with much force that many of the supposedly non-pedigreed principles that provide the linchpin for Dworkin's claims had in fact been recognisable and recognised by a rule of recognition. This strikes me as correct, but my empirical argument is different. It is the theoretically thinner claim that some of Dworkin's examples of principles (in his sense) trumping rules (in his sense) are exceptional, and that in the normal operation of the English and American legal systems rules often prevail in the face of loftier principles that would have produced more desirable outcomes in particular cases. I do not claim that such principled-based departures from rules are lawless, but only that an accurate description of Anglo-American adjudication (and, a fortiori, norm application outside of the courts) must recognise the way in which rule-of-recognition recognised legal rules often prevail even in the face of legal, political, and moral principles that would produce superior outcomes in the pertinent case. That law operates this way may or may not be morally desirable, but any description of law that ignores its positivity and consequent occasional sub-optimality cannot provide a satisfactory explanation of the phenomenon of law as it actually operates.

8 22 N.E. 188 (N.Y. 1889).

9 161 A.2d 69 (N.J. 1960).

It thus turns out that in actual legal systems lawyers often argue on the basis of legal rules whose decision-determining capacity (whether that makes them legally 'true' may not be the best way of putting the issue) is a function of their promulgation or endorsement by some institution, and that judges often justify (and make) decisions according to those same institutionally legitimated rules. As a result, the difficulty with Dworkin's argument for the practical and philosophical unimportance of the sociological question is not only that it assumes the conclusion, and not only that it presupposes the falsity of an account of law in which a common answer to the doctrinal question (albeit not the only answer, and not the answer in all cases) is dependent on the answer to the sociological question. It is also that in the actual operation of actual legal systems the answer to the doctrinal question genuinely does, as a factual matter, often depend on the answer to the sociological question. The keystone of Dworkin's argument turns out, as a result, to be as empirically mistaken as it is argumentatively elusive. The doctrinal and sociological concepts of law may indeed be conceptually distinct, and Dworkin has performed a valuable service in illuminating this useful distinction. But although the two are conceptually distinct, they are empirically and causally linked in most modern legal systems. As a contingent and not a necessary truth, therefore, to treat the sociological concept of law as being of no practical or philosophical importance is to neglect something of great significance, both practically and philosophically, about the legal systems that pervade our individual and institutional lives.

6. Conclusion: The institutional dimension of norm-generation

In *Institutions of Law*, Neil MacCormick analyses at great length and depth the central feature of modern legality – its institutional status. Much of his focus is on institutions as norm-users, but a great deal of what he has to say is relevant to institutions as norm-issuers as well. If we neglect the way in which institutions can issue norms, we will have missed much of importance about the centrality of institutions in modern society. And if we neglect the way in which the norms that are issued by institutions can become important just because of their institutional issuance, we will have missed much of importance about law. It is precisely because the norms that institutions generate have much to do with adjudication that we need to attend to them, and to believe that the sociology of institutions 'has little to do with adjudication', as Dworkin insists, is in the final analysis to ignore, as MacCormick decidedly has not, what may be law's most salient characteristic.

References

Burke, E. (1881), *Works of Edmund Burke* (Oxford: Clarendon Press).

Dworkin, R. (1977), *Taking Rights Seriously* (Cambridge, Mass.: Harvard University Press).

Dworkin, R. (1986), *Law's Empire* (Cambridge, Mass.: Harvard University Press).
Dworkin, R. (1987), *A Matter of Principle* (Cambridge, Mass.: Harvard University Press).
Dworkin, R. (2006a), *Justice in Robes* (Cambridge, Mass.: Harvard University Press).
Dworkin, R. (2006b), 'Hart and the Concepts of Law', *Harvard Law Review Forum* 119, 95–104.
Hart, H.L.A., (1994), *The Concept of Law* (Oxford: Clarendon Press).
Luhmann, N. (1988), *Autopoietic Law: A New Approach to Law and Society* (Berlin: Walter de Gruyter).
Luhmann, N. (2004), *Law as a Social System* (Oxford: Oxford University Press).
MacCormick, N. (2007), *Institutions of Law: An Essay in Legal Theory* (Oxford: Oxford University Press).
MacCormick, N. (1978), *Legal Reasoning and Legal Theory* (Oxford: Clarendon Press).
MacCormick, N. and Weinberger, O. (1986), *An Institutional Theory of Law* (Dordrecht: D. Reidel).
Russell, B. (1923), 'Vagueness', *Australasian Journal of Psychology and Philosophy* 1, 84–92.
Schauer, F. (1991), *Playing By the Rules; A Philosophical Examination of Rule-Based Decision-Making in Law and in Life* (Oxford: Clarendon Press).
Schauer, F. (2004), 'The Limited Domain of the Law', *Virginia Law Review* 90, 1909–56.
Schauer, F. (2006), '(Re)Taking Hart', *Harvard Law Review* 119, 852–83.
Schauer, F. (2008), 'A Critical Guide to Vehicles in the Park', *New York University Law Review* 82, 1109–34.
Simmons, J. (1979), *Moral Principles and Political Obligations* (Princeton: Princeton University Press).
Williams, G. (1945), 'International Law and the Controversy Concerning the Word 'Law'', *British Yearbook of International Law* 22, 146–63.
Wisdom, J. (1952), 'Ludwig Wittgenstein, 1934–1937', *Mind* 61, 258–60.
Wittgenstein, L. (1958), *Philosophical Investigations* (New York: Macmillan).

Chapter 4
Neil MacCormick's Legal Positivism

Vittorio Villa

1. Introduction

In the last few decades Neil MacCormick has been one of the most important figures in contemporary analytical legal positivism. His thought has roamed over many important areas of legal philosophy and theory, producing important contributions on many different occasions. I am particularly interested in highlighting two of these contributions.

The first concerns his thesis on the importance of recognising, under certain conditions, a *cognitive value* in a whole series of 'discourses on norms' developed by legal theorists and jurists (from now referred to cumulatively as 'legal scholars'), also for the purpose of clearly separating cognitive discourses from ones with an ideological function, whether upholding positive law or rebelling against it. It is a thesis that I too have striven to develop, ever since the beginning of my research (in this connection, I can mention a period of research spent in Edinburgh way back in 1983), convinced as I was that this thesis, among other things, could furnish further support to the *principle of the separation of powers*, which is fundamental for the contemporary rule of law. The fact is that if we affirm that it is possible to produce 'genuine' knowledge of positive law, then this strengthens the thesis that law (as a product of legislative power) *exists*, in some sense, *as an object of knowledge*, before being applied (by judicial power).

The second contribution is the one relating to the fact that, in its formulation, the theory of legal reasoning becomes the central point of the theory of law. It is an important shift that many other authors (Dworkin and Alexy, for instance) have enacted today, thus helping to determine a crucial turn in contemporary legal theory: the passage from *objectual* conceptions (which see law as an *object* that exists in a prior and independent way in relation to the activities of interpretation, application and social use that make reference to it) to *practice-oriented conceptions* (which see law as a normative social practice).

In this chapter I will dwell on one of the most important points in MacCormick's thought – one in connection with which his reflection has perhaps proved more difficult and tortuous, accentuated with some major changes of opinion: his conception of *legal positivism.* The treatment of this profile will allow me not only to illuminate a very significant aspect of MacCormick's thought, but also to face, in a direct and complete way, two themes that have always been discussed by us, but unfortunately never fully and exhaustively: the theme of epistemological constructivism as a 'background' perspective for legal theory, and that of value judgments as a central (and necessary?) element of discourses of a cognitive character produced by legal scholars and legal operators (judges and public officials).

Speaking of legal positivism, I will say frankly what my opinion is, thus anticipating the conclusions of my chapter and immediately indicating a point on which I disagree with MacCormick. Unlike what he maintains today, I believe that the opposition between legal positivism and legal naturalism still has a central role in contemporary legal thought, provided one is careful to define the two notions adequately. In my opinion, the definition of legal positivism that I will furnish in the next section determines a *mutually exclusive conceptual opposition* between the two traditions of thought on the subject (Villa 1999, 25–26). In this definition of mine, moreover, both the adoption of an epistemological constructivist perspective and the thesis of the presence (necessary, on certain conditions) of value judgments in the cognitive discourses of jurists and operators play an important role.

The chapter will develop in the following way. In the next section I will present my *conceptual definition* of legal positivism, deriving from it, by negation, that of legal naturalism. In the third section, in the light of the proposed definition, I will try to reconstruct, in its various phases, the conception of legal positivism advanced by MacCormick. In the final part of the chapter I will develop some critical observations on MacCormick's thought. The observations will be organised in the following way. In the fourth section I will make some comments of a general character on the way in which MacCormick sees the notion of 'legal knowledge', and on the type of relationship that he establishes between legal knowledge and value judgments. In the last section I will endeavour to examine critically the various theses advanced by MacCormick on positivism and on his opposition – if any – to natural law.

2. A conceptual definition of legal positivism

In proposing a conceptual definition of legal positivism, I follow the 'concept/conceptions' scheme (used, for instance, by Dworkin 1986, 70–71), in a very peculiar version. This scheme is particularly appropriate in cases in which we are dealing with *essentially contested* notions (Gallie 1955–56, 167–98), that is to say, with notions structurally open to divergent interpretations, i.e., conflicting attributions of meaning. The word 'concept' is used here with reference to the most consolidated part, to the so-called *solid area* (Jori 1985, 277) of a determined notion of common or scientific language. In this sense, this concept is formed by all those assumptions that express the content of beliefs of a *substantial* character (connected, that is, to the common presuppositions of several theories), or of a *semantic* character (connected, that is, to the common core of meaning of a notion susceptible to several interpretations), on which there is the unproblematic consensus – which may also be absolutely implicit – of the members of a given community. It could be said, from this point of view, that the members of the community in question (be it social or scientific) rely on such beliefs, or 'deem them certain' (Wittgenstein 1979, §94, §115, §125, §163, §337 and §341).

Naturally no theory, be it scientific or philosophical, can stop at the threshold of the concept, which only represents the shared starting point, the assumptions that are commonly relied on. *Conceptions*, precisely, represent the first stage that knowledge goes through as soon as it breaks away from the solid ground of what is 'deemed certain' (which precisely for this reason is not strictly part of knowledge, but of its presuppositions), to move to the much more slippery terrain of what can be the object of falsifiable conjectures that always run the risk of being confuted. From this point of view, *conceptions* are those assumptions in a given field of experience that furnish a preliminary interpretation of a concept, as the first stage of the endeavour to produce a theory in a given field of experience.

Giving a conceptual definition of 'legal positivism', precisely one fixing the *concept* of it, is an operation making it possible to achieve some important results. It is first of all able to give a contextual account, in a more adequate way than other types of definition, both of the unitary elements (precisely at the level of the *concept*), and of the no less important elements of differentiation (at the level of *conceptions*) that are present in legal positivist conceptions. For instance, in the absence of a unitary conceptual definition, I believe it is more difficult to adequately explain the contextual confluence, in legal positivist theories, of elements of continuity and elements of differentiation; the risk that one runs, in short, is ending up sacrificing one or the other of the two aspects, confusing the level of the concept with that of conceptions, and vice versa. In my opinion, MacCormick makes this mistake (most recently in *Institutions of Law*), insofar as he expresses the belief, in his latest works, that the opposition between legal positivism and natural positivism (an opposition said to derive from a 'two-way-divided universe of jurisprudence'; MacCormick 2007a, 278) is no longer fruitful (MacCormick 1992, 131). He fails to take into account the strong conceptual distinction that instead exists between the two notions, privileging analysis of conceptions and thus making the thesis of the opposition or of the substantial homogeneity between the two traditions of scholarship depend on the search for possible differences or similarities at the level of conceptions.

The conceptual definition of 'legal positivism' (Villa 1999, 25–33) that I propose consists of two theses that, though they are not logically connected, nevertheless *jointly* express the conceptual nucleus of legal positivism in its *full sense*, its *minimal conceptual content* shared by all the conceptions that can entirely be qualified as such in a full sense. The first will be labelled a *thesis on law* (and, therefore, in a sense, an *ontological* thesis), and the second a *thesis on the knowledge of law* (and, therefore, a *methodological* thesis).

According to the first thesis, all the phenomena (firstly the norms) to which the appellative 'law' is appropriate invariably constitute instances of *positive law*, and, therefore, of law that historically represents the *normative product* of decisions and/or of human actions that are historically *contingent* from the cultural point of view, and, therefore, more specifically, from the ethical-political point of view.

In agreement with the second thesis, (so-called *methodological legal positivism*) the legal scholar 'taking into account' positive law is a completely different activity, and clearly one to be kept separate from what is concretised in a stance (of acceptance or otherwise, of justification or otherwise, etc.) towards law itself.

As I have said before, the concept of legal naturalism can be constructed beginning from the negation of the concept of legal positivism. One can thus obtain the concept of legal naturalism by applying the 'negation sign' to both of the previous theses.

As regards the first conceptual thesis, this would mean that the legal naturalist denies that all law is entirely contingent; which means, in a positive sense, maintaining that there are legal contents that are in a sense *necessary* – taken away from the domain of contingency – which can be qualified as such for reasons independent of the contingent decisions of historically determined political communities.

As regards the second conceptual thesis, what springs from its negation is that the legal naturalist does not admit that it is possible to separate the 'description of positive law' from a 'stance towards it'. This means, developing the contrary thesis, that, according to the legal naturalist, 'describing positive law' necessarily implies an attitude of an evaluative type taking a stand regarding the correspondence or otherwise of a determined positive law to ethical-political criteria. In other terms, according to the legal naturalist, describing positive law requires us prejudicially – or at least contextually – to consider the problem of *correct law*, i.e., of the conformity of the contents of a certain positive law to a particular ideal of justice.

What has just been said suggests a reflection of a general character on the true meaning of the opposition from the ontological point of view. It is not on the basis of the level of the theory of positive law that the two traditions of scholarship can be clearly differentiated. Within this level there can well be agreement between legal naturalist theories and legal positivist theories of positive law. Furthermore, I believe that for many scholars this agreement exists today, regarding the approach that looks at law as a *social practice*. The problem, instead, is the recognition or otherwise of a further (legal?) level. For this purpose, according to what was said before, it seems to me that the deep sense of the opposition between legal naturalism and legal positivism has a fundamentally meta-ethical nature. By this I mean that the problem is not so much whether to recognise (or not) the existence of a *law* or a *natural right* (one can be a legal naturalist even without this recognition), but rather whether to accept (or not) the thesis of the possibility of an absolute and objective foundation of values (in this case *legal* ones), or at least of some of them, in a transcultural and non-contingent key. In other words, at a meta-ethical level, the opposition is between absolutism (legal naturalism) and relativism (legal positivism). In this connection, it would be interesting to understand clearly which of these two approaches corresponds to the position of the most recent MacCormick. I will return to this point later.

For the moment, having come to the end of the section, it seems appropriate to make some observations on both the levels of the definition of legal positivism, the ontological one and the methodological one.

As regards the *ontological* level, it comprises, in a sense that I will clarify, the *separability thesis*, i.e., the thesis – which for many is the fundamental element of the opposition between legal naturalism and legal positivism – that it is not conceptually necessary in any sense that positive law mirror particular contents or demands of a moral character (for a very clear exposition of this thesis, see Füsser 1996, 119–62). From the point of view of the conceptual definition adopted here, the *separability thesis* is not a postulation or a fundamental axiom of legal positivism, but, more correctly, a *corollary* deriving from the first conceptual thesis mentioned above. In this connection, if the thesis that all positive law derives from contingent decisions is accepted, then one also has to accept, as a necessary implication, the thesis that there cannot be any *necessary* legal content – and therefore a fortiori any necessary ethical content – that necessarily has to be part of positive law itself.

At the *methodological* level, it is extremely important to realise that this thesis is by no means identical to the one that obliges legal scholars to assume a *non-evaluative attitude* in the sphere of their activity, traditionally called – though improperly – *descriptive*. In the penultimate section, I will return to the latter thesis, which most legal positivist scholars (see, for instance, Bobbio 1972, 125–26) consider, in my opinion erroneously, as an essential characteristic of legal positivism. Here, I will simply say that it is one thing to maintain that the positive law scholar must clearly separate the activity of 'description of positive law' from what is concretised in a 'commitment' towards it; while it is another thing, a completely different one, to maintain that the aforesaid jurist, within his 'descriptive' activity, must take up a non-evaluative attitude. These two theses are not logically connected in any way. In other words, maintaining that the description of a given positive law requires taking a non-evaluative attitude means making a further move, namely interpreting a conceptual assumption, developing a conception starting from an element of a conceptual character. The operation that is performed is the following: the activity of description of the positive law is interpreted as an activity of a non-evaluative character, through a move that is not at all obvious or logically determined, but which, on the contrary, could also produce completely different results. I believe that in given situations (to be specified later), the cognitive discourses of jurists are marked by the presence – a necessary one – of evaluative appreciations. I am not at all sure of what MacCormick's position is on the issue today. But I will also return to this later.

3. A reconstruction of Neil MacCormick's legal positivism

It is not simple to reconstruct MacCormick's conception of legal positivism, because it has developed, not without uncertainties and tensions, through different phases, down to a position that at least in his opinion is not clearly identifiable either as legal positivist or as legal naturalist.

However, starting from the many occasions on which MacCormick has grappled in his works with legal positivism, schematising to the utmost, it is possible to isolate three big phases representing three important 'conceptual interchange points' at which MacCormick has expressed three different positions on legal positivism.

The first phase expresses a convinced defence of the 'legal naturalism/legal positivism opposition'; the second phase constitutes a moment of critical revision, at which the opposition is questioned, but not entirely abandoned; the third phase is marked by abandonment of this opposition and the working out of a conception that rejects this distinction, deeming it not to be significant and fertile from the explanatory point of view. But let us proceed in order, starting from the first phase.

For reasons of expository economy, I will condense the first phase in exclusive reference to the first edition of *Legal Reasoning and Legal Theory* (MacCormick 1978). Here, MacCormick expresses a very clear-cut position, presenting an almost exclusively methodological version of legal positivism that he substantially limits to some theses on the way in which the legal scholar should approach legal positivism. However, the premise to what he says is a real 'constant' in MacCormick's thought, and it is the affirmation that 'there is nothing antipositivistic about saying that law is not value free' (MacCormick 1978, 233). With this affirmation MacCormick means not only that the law of our contemporary legal organisations incorporates values that are contained in legal statements incorporating principles, but also that the acceptance of the content of such principles, expressed by the members of those organisations – or at least by some of them – has a clear *ethical value*, in the sense that these people express adhesion to these contents because they aim to realise states of affairs that they deem 'correct' and/or 'good'.

In my view this is a point that it is absolutely possible to share. MacCormick develops it by extending the notion of acceptance of the legal system that Hart (introducing the *internal point of view* of the participants) certainly considered in too neutral and thin a way. MacCormick continues by saying that 'the point of being a positivist is not to deny obvious truths of that sort. The point is rather in the assertion that one does not have in any sense to share in or endorse these values in order to know that law exists, or what law exists' (MacCormick 1978, 233). In short, one can perfectly well – and perhaps has to – take into account the principles in force in a certain historical-institutional context without for this reason having to accept them; and MacCormick concludes by offering a minimal definition of legal positivism, which characterises this tradition of scholarship 'minimally as insisting on the genuine distinction between description of a legal system as it is and normative evaluation of the law which is thus described' (MacCormick 1978, 239–40).

Two further observations are required in order to pave the way for the critical observations that will follow in the next two sections. The first is that MacCormick, in this first phase of his thought, on one side identifies the cognitive discourse of the legal scholar as a 'merely descriptive' discourse, and on the other side, does not distinguish between commitment to legal positivism and evaluative appreciations. In this way it is rightfully inscribed in that conception that in some of my papers I have called *descriptivist* (Villa 1999, 90–95), a conception that is an alternative to the constructivist one, which MacCormick embraces in quite a clear-cut way in his latest works.

The second observation is that in the background to this definition there lies, very correctly in my opinion, a meta-ethical option of a markedly non-cognitivist character, which I considered in the preceding section (in a relativistic version) as the most plausible justification of a legal positivist conception. According to the 'early MacCormick', on the basis of ultimate values (of whatever type they are, and, therefore, also of those contained in legal principles) there are dispositions of the will and affective attitudes not further justifiable through reasons. It does not seem to me at all by chance, I will add, that this first definition of legal positivism – which in MacCormick's thought expresses the greatest distance between legal positivism and legal naturalism – is accompanied by a meta-ethical option of a non-cognitivist character, precisely signalling the close connection that exists between the two options.

In the second phase I include the works published by MacCormick in the 1980s and in particular *H.L.A. Hart* (MacCormick 1981) and *An Institutional Theory of Law* (MacCormick and Weinberger 1986).

In the work on Hart, alongside the methodological definition of legal positivism (which he had already given previously and which he here reaffirms), MacCormick places the ontological one too, which bases law exclusively on social practices. In this connection, he gives a definition that includes both the thesis of law as a human product and that of the absence of a necessary connection between law and morality (but the two theses are not clearly connected to one another). In this sense, according to MacCormick, legal positivism expresses the thesis that 'all laws owe their origin and existence to human practice and decision concerned with the government of a society, and … they have no necessary correlation with the precepts of an ideal morality' (MacCormick 1981, 6 ff).

In *An Institutional Theory of Law* MacCormick further specifies the thesis about legal positivism that I have called *ontological*. He presents, as the 'first tenet of positivism', the thesis that 'the existence of laws is not dependent on their satisfying any particular moral values of universal application to all legal systems' (MacCormick and Weinberger 1986, 128), which, according to him, can be derived from Austin's well-known affirmation that 'the existence of a law is one thing, its merits or demerits another'. Here, one can notice the presence of that confusion between ontological level and methodological level that I pointed out in the previous section. The fact is that Austin's thesis would be all right as a *methodological thesis.*

Secondly, MacCormick derives from the 'first tenet' a 'second tenet of positivism', which is substantially the *social thesis,* according to which 'the existence of laws depends upon their being established through the decisions of human beings in society' (MacCormick and Weinberger 1986, 129). Actually, as I will observe in the final section, the 'second tenet' logically has priority over the first one. It is precisely from the thesis that law depends on contingent social practices that it is possible to derive the thesis that the existence of law does not depend on the satisfaction of universal moral values, and not vice versa.

In this second phase, however, taking a critical attitude to Hart, MacCormick further reaffirms the thesis that moral values enter into our legal systems, precisely because inside them there are principles serving to realise moral values. The recognition of this presence now begins to worry MacCormick, because it throws serious doubts (in my opinion unjustified, as I will say afterwards) on the 'first tenet' of legal positivism, according to which the existence of law would not depend on moral reasons. MacCormick resolves them once again, provisionally, jumping from the ontological level to the methodological one: the fact that the members of the legal community express moral preferences does not imply that the scholar too has to do it in his 'descriptive' activity. Incidentally, looking carefully at the matter, one can observe that these are two different issues: one thing is the issue of the connection (necessary or otherwise) between law and ethics; another thing is the issue of what the methodological attitude of the legal scholar has to be.

In general, in this second phase it is the whole thesis of the opposition between legal naturalism and legal positivism that starts to lose weight and importance in MacCormick's thought. In *An Institutional Theory of Law*, as an argument against this opposition, he uses the fact that in Great Britain today something can only become compulsory by law if it can be justified through reasonable value judgments. According to MacCormick, recognising this brings legal positivism very close to contemporary legal naturalism, for instance in Finnis's version, even though an important point of dissent remains: namely, the issue of the absoluteness and objectivity of values, on which however MacCormick does not dwell (and this in itself can be interpreted as a sign of another element of doubt regarding his previous positivistic formulation).

As regards the third and last phase, which covers the period from the 1990s to the present, I will primarily use the works *Natural Law and the Separation of Law and Morals* (MacCormick 1992), *The Ideal and the Actual of Law and Society* (MacCormick 1997b) and, of course, *Institutions of Law* (2007a).

In this third phase MacCormick's thought becomes much more complex and hence requires more marked summarisation: I will necessarily have to make some simplifications. I will therefore simply highlight some fundamental profiles of the conception of legal positivism recently expressed by MacCormick.

A first profile is characterised by the fact that in the most recent years in MacCormick there is much more marked attention to the issue of legal knowledge, and therefore of the possible cognitive value of the activity of legal scholars. I will dwell on this where I make critical comments. Here, I will simply observe that recognition of the importance of such qualification blends with adhesion to a constructivist model of knowledge. MacCormick associates the conception of epistemological constructivism, applied to the study of law, with that of an investigation that *rationally reconstructs* what would otherwise be the 'multiform chaos' of legal experience, imposing an order on it (MacCormick 2005, 134–35). The general idea that he communicates through these affirmations is that scholars 'reinterpret phenomena as parts of a coherent and well-ordered whole' (MacCormick 2005, 134). What we would see, if we observed without a 'background theory', would be a 'chaotic flux of activity and process'. I will postpone to the next section my comments on this position of MacCormick's, which will allow me to argue that he does not consistently develop his constructivist project.

A second profile, connected to the first one (because it concerns a further profile of cognitive activity, interpreted in a constructivist key) is that of the role of values and value judgments within legal knowledge. Here it is important to distinguish three different issues, which MacCormick tends to confuse but which are not logically connected.

A first issue is that of the moral value possibly attributable to positive law, in relation to the fact that law, in MacCormick's opinion, has a moral meaning for officials and for at least a part (those that express full acceptance) of the members of the given legal community. MacCormick reaffirms this rather clearly in *Institutions of Law*, when he radically contests the idea that 'law or its doctrinal exposition can be in any interesting sense 'value free' (MacCormick 2007a, 304). The fact that he does not, however, appropriately distinguish, in that context, between 'law' and its 'doctrinal exposure' introduces an element of conceptual confusion that is destined to be of weight in the continuation of his analysis.

In any case, in these affirmations one perceives the influence of the thought of Finnis and Dworkin, but it is above all Finnis and his thesis of *focal meaning* of law (Finnis 1980, 12–18) that influences MacCormick's positions. What happens is that MacCormick's previous theses are further corroborated by the appeal to some theses by Finnis on *focal meaning*, a thesis that supplants, in MacCormick's theory Hart's *central case*.[1] According to Finnis (and MacCormick), some examples of human activities are 'more central' examples than others, because they better exemplify the values towards which the enterprise is oriented, and therefore only the theory that produces the most attractive account of what has value for human beings, within that given practice, can give true knowledge of that field of experience. In more specific terms, for Finnis (and MacCormick), the explanation of what counts as law depends on the adoption of a point of view on what count as good examples, central ones, from the point of view of value, of the

1 MacCormick 2007b says that 'the focal meaning of any conceptual term dealing with matters of human interest identifies something that is really good … or well-working example of object of study.'

kind considered; and this implies having a vision of those goods towards which the practice in question is directed. On this subject MacCormick says that 'laws, like other social institutions, are fully intelligible only by reference to the ends or values they ought to realise, and thus by reference to the intentions that those who participate in making or implementing them must at least purport to have. This does not entail any acceptance of substantive moral criteria as criteria of legal validity, but it does involve acknowledging the moral quality of the relevant ends and values, namely justice and the public good' (MacCormick 1992, 113). One of the most important values (an absolute value?) of law is that of *legality* (which can be considered as a part of moral good), destined to remain stable in time, while other legal values can be the object of clashes and disputes. This presupposes that the participants have a 'sense of good', and, therefore, the ability to formulate judgments on what is good for them. In other words, the activities of the various subjects that operate within the legal system can only be justified on condition that some reasonable conception of justice is implied by their own activities. One cannot sincerely participate in the legal enterprise without having an orientation towards these values. In MacCormick's words, 'a certain pretension to justice, that is, a purported aspiration to achieve justice … is necessarily evinced in the very act of law-making in the context of a law-state' (MacCormick 2007a, 276).

A second and different issue is the strictly methodological one linked to what, in this situation of 'evaluative contamination', the jurist's attitude towards his object should be. Here the question is: must this attitude in turn be evaluative or not?

Unfortunately, we are forced to observe that the later MacCormick's answer to this question is not at all clear. He oscillates within a spectrum of positions which has, at one extreme, the thesis of the persistent non-evaluative dimension of the discourses of legal scholars (even in a situation in which among legal materials there are values and value judgments), and, at the other extreme, the thesis that evaluative contamination of the object would seem to require further evaluative commitments for them. But let us proceed in order.

First of all, the common presupposition of this analysis by the 'later MacCormick' is that the activity of scholars represents a sort of *second line* in relation to the activity of professional participants (MacCormick 2007a, 5–6); an activity that, however, is 'inside the system' (we are talking about *observers from within*), and that therefore requires a certain degree of *engagement*. What MacCormick suggests here, in short, is a sort of *mixture* between *detached description* and *value oriented activity*.

Setting out from this common starting point, in his latest works MacCormick has made a certain number of affirmations that are not entirely consistent with one another. I spoke, above, of two extremes of a spectrum of positions. On one side, there are some affirmations that maintain that nothing changes in the attitude of neutrality with which the law scholar should present himself, even if he is forced 'to have dealings with values'. From this point of view he says (in MacCormick 1997b) that the values discussed are always 'imputed to law' as its values, and not appreciated by the scientist as his own (MacCormick 1997b, 15 ff). The scholar, it is true, should opt for the 'best set of values' that can be imputed to law, but should not commit himself to these values himself. Undoubtedly, in this way the scholar, precisely because he is engaged in his activity, would also show an orientation towards a value; but it would be a 'truth value' and not a practical value.

Subsequently, however, MacCormick seems markedly to attenuate the force of these affirmations, above all because he comes up against the problem of the richness and possible incoherence and contestability of the materials evaluated that the scholar deals with. The presence of these elements would require of the scholar a critical account, selection and rectification of the material investigated. In MacCormick's words:

> It is undoubtedly controversial what function should be ascribed to law in general or to particular laws … Failure to confront and account openly for value involved, and to defend one's own proposals as to what the relevant values are, may confer on work about law an apparently greater objectivity than if a proper openness were practised. But it is this concealment of value-orientation, not its open avowal, that it is ideological in a sinister sense. (MacCormick 2007a, 305)

I will return to this important point when I make some critical comments.

A third issue is that of the way in which, at the meta-ethical level, we should look on the question of the justification of these values and these value judgments. For me, this is a crucial point, seeing that I have characterised legal positivism, from the meta-ethical point of view, as a relativistic conception. In this case too, MacCormick's thought is rather changeable and not very perspicuous. Indeed, he frankly says at one point (MacCormick 2005), that this is an 'open problem.' He clearly affirms, it is true (I would almost say 'unfortunately'), that he has renounced non-Humean cognitivism, but admits at this point that he has the onus of providing an alternative explanation (MacCormick 2005, 30).

Actually, precisely on this point an explanation by MacCormick himself would be useful, because I do not understand clearly what type of position he wants to maintain regarding this issue. I will simply endeavour to put order in some affirmations of his. He clearly denies that for some fundamental value judgments we can speak of 'self-evident values' (MacCormick 1992, 125–29); a situation of this kind would create serious obstacles to the principle of tolerance. However, on various occasions, he does not rule out the possibility that in some ethical and legal controversies there can be 'correct answers', even if we fail to find them (MacCormick 1996, 166–67).

A third and last profile concerns MacCormick's (definitive?) position on legal positivism and on the 'legal positivism/legal naturalism' opposition. What remains of the original opposition in the later MacCormick?

Examining his affirmations in *Institutions of Law*, we would say that almost nothing is left. In this context, MacCormick challenges a pillar of legal positivism, affirming that 'provisions which are unjustifiable by reference to any reasonable moral argument should not be considered valid as laws'. What he substantially means here is that if the normative content of a given disposition cannot be justified by one of the possible conceptions of justice (for instance from the point of view of human rights) which can be advanced by reasonable people, then this content could not be considered as *legal* (MacCormick 2007a, 242).

Besides, MacCormick himself affirms that nowadays he moves in the orbit of a non-positivist or at all events post-positivist position (MacCormick 2007a, 278). I believe it can be said that in his position today there are aspects related to legal positivism and aspects related to legal naturalism, but there is no longer a clear and recognisable opposition between the two traditions of scholarship. The dichotomy between legal positivism and legal naturalism does not reveal any important truth for him, an expression, as it is, of a thesis that prefigures a 'two-way-divided universe of jurisprudence' (MacCormick 2007a, 278), something which in his opinion it is no longer possible to share.

4. Some critical observations on legal knowledge and values

There would be a great deal to say, in the sphere of critical comments, on MacCormick's positions regarding all the issues raised, but unfortunately there is insufficient space for going into greater depth and detail. Hence, I will limit myself to some schematic observations, possibly referring the reader to some papers of mine for a more organic treatment of some crucial points. My comments will concern three themes, which I will deal with in the following order: the theme of legal knowledge and that of legal value judgments, which will be dealt with in this section; the theme of the conception of legal positivism and of the possible opposition between it and legal naturalism, which will be dealt with in the last section.

As regards the theme of legal knowledge, there is a point on which, as I clarified in the introduction, I wish to express full and strong agreement with MacCormick's position. The thesis of the cognitive value of the activity of legal scholars has always exerted great fascination on legal philosophers, but in the past it primarily – but certainly not exclusively – interested scholars in continental countries, who had in front of their eyes legal dogmatics and legal theory in a context of codified law. Some of them (for instance, Bobbio, Scarpelli and Ross), a few decades ago (more exactly in the 1950s and 1960s), worked out the theme, under the thrust of neo-positivistic epistemological conceptions, in the terms of an investigation of the *scientific value* of positive legal disciplines (for an analysis of these positions, see Villa 1984). Probably it was not possible to do otherwise, in a context dominated by the thesis of the equation between 'knowledge' and 'science'. Besides, investigation of the method promoted by these legal philosophers started, on the basis of these presuppositions, from the premise constituted by *methodological monism* (for a definition of 'methodological monism' see Villa 2003, 63): in other words, jurists were asked to ape the empirical method of natural scientists (Ross), seen as the only possible way of 'doing science'.

Today, in a profoundly different cultural climate, in which post-positivistic epistemological conceptions dominate the field, the thesis of the equation between 'knowledge' and 'empirical science' is now rejected and the *imperialistic* formulation of methodological monism is challenged, in favour of methodologies inspired by *methodological pluralism* (Villa 2003, 142).

In this context, many scholars, including myself (Villa 1999), have chosen the alternative pathway consisting in sounding out the cognitive value of the activity of legal scholars and legal operators, regardless of conformity to the over-rigid model afforded by the empirical sciences. MacCormick, too, has moved in this direction, certainly a more fertile one, with the objective of clearly distinguishing cognitive activities in our field (though with different modalities and objectives), from activities that are concretised, with reference to positive law, in ideological operations, in political discourses, in normative stands and in critical discourses. This strategic choice reveals, it seems to me, that there still lingers in him an irrepressible and genuine positivistic inspiration, related to that *methodological positivism* that for me constitutes, as I have already said, one of its two fundamental aspects.

As I have already observed in the previous section, the pathway chosen by MacCormick, within post-positivistic conceptions, is that of *epistemological constructivism*. My impression, nevertheless, is that this project has not been consistently developed by MacCormick to its extreme conclusions: what emerges is much too weak a version of constructivism. On this subject two points need highlighting.

The first point is that MacCormick limits the constructive role of knowledge, on a more general plane, to the profile of the rational reconstruction of a field of experience; to the establishment of an order within it (MacCormick 2005, 134–35). But the constructivist conception, interpreted correctly,[2] goes further, as far as the operation aiming to cut out, within a field of phenomena, those that inside a given conceptual scheme represent the 'base objects', and to select those of their properties that are deemed most significant that are part of a given field of experience. It does not seem to me that MacCormick moves consistently in this direction. That this is the case is also shown by the reference that he makes, again in a constructivist key, to Popper's thesis of 'World 3' (MacCormick 2007a, 292), relating to the modality of existence of cultural and institutional facts, in this case of norms and other 'legal objects' (Popper 1972, 103–22, 153–65). This is a thesis strongly marked by *objectual* premises, which it is not possible to place within a constructivist conception. Popper's position amounts, in fact, to a very sophisticated version of neo-positivism.

2 Good examples of constructivist epistemological conceptions are Goodman 1978 and Putnam 1981.

The second point concerns the issue of the value-freedom of knowledge (in general and as regards legal knowledge), on which, as I said before, MacCormick expresses ambiguous and wavering positions; yet criticism of the principle of value-freedom, in its strong version, is an integral part of a constructivist conception of knowledge.[3] But this point is already part of the second theme, which I will deal with presently.

As regards the second theme, that of the relationship between value judgments and legal knowledge, I can only reaffirm what I said in the preceding section. MacCormick seems uncertain about the type of strategy to be undertaken in order to face this delicate problem, torn as he is between the desire to satisfy two opposite demands: recognising, in the legal field too, the characteristic of objectivity that should characterise all cognitive discourses; objectivity that by and large he continues to link to the paradigm of 'non-evaluative description'; and that of the presence in law of evaluative materials that are certainly not secondary (for instance, the principles that introduce fundamental rights), which would require of the observer a certain degree of evaluative commitment. It is a tension that remains unresolved, at least in my opinion.

For my part, I think that MacCormick could have been more daring, seeking precisely in constructivism the epistemological resources[4] in order to recognise how it is possible today to challenge the principle of value-freedom of knowledge from a general point of view, and also to put into question, but in a different and stronger sense, the principle of value-freedom of legal knowledge. In my opinion, this recognition implies two different theses. It first of all implies, from a general point of view, the removal of a methodological prohibition, the one issued by the value-freedom principle. The first result could be dubbed the 'minimal thesis on value-judgments.' What this thesis amounts to so far is, *negatively*, only that there are no persuasive epistemological reasons which could support the presence of this prohibition. But the possible *positive* presence of value judgments, in one or the other domain of knowledge, is something that must be ascertained or argued afresh, with the intervention of different arguments. In other words, in order to get a further, and more important, result (and this represents my second thesis), i.e., that of arguing in favour of *the necessary presence of value judgments in legal knowledge*, we must build a much more complex and articulated argument.

It is not possible here to present this argument in detail (for a more detailed analysis, see Villa 1997, 447–77). I can only briefly sum it up. In the field of legal experience, as in that of all human sciences, the subject already contains values and value judgments. Even values, as far as they are objects of knowledge, have to be approached in a constructivist fashion; this means that they have to be selectively reconstructed and interpreted, in the light of a given conceptual framework. In other words, even values have to be carved up by the active intervention of legal

3 A good example of a constructivist-oriented criticism of value-freedom principle can be found in Hesse 1980, 133 ff; 188 ff; and 193 ff.

4 I tried to steer this way in Villa 1997, 447–77.

knowledge: and this may require jurists choosing a privileged interpretation of their semantic content, establishing hierarchical priorities between them, highlighting some features of them, leaving other features in the darkness, etc. Think, for instance, of the complex situation in which jurists find themselves when the objects of their investigation are the evaluative content of the constitutional principles of a charter society. In these cases, their difficult task could be that of settling conflicts between different principles, or of deciding which of them is more relevant from an ethical point of view, or of balancing their different weight; and this could be done either for knowledge's sake, or also for justifying or supporting some concrete decision by the courts. In any case, it should be clear that legal values (like values in general) are not equipped with self-identifying labels.

On this basis, we can in the end draw the final conclusion of the argument, i.e., that this interpretive and selective work, which, under the constructivist epistemological image, is needed by jurists in order to get adequate knowledge of these values, cannot suitably be done without requiring them to formulate *second order value judgments* (that is, value judgments referring to values), aiming to express the best possible appreciation of those values which are already present inside the legal system. Putting it very schematically, here the methodological slogan to be coined should be this: 'you need values for dealing with values'.

Returning, now, to MacCormick's theses, I find it impossible to accept his argument serving to save the neutrality of the cognitive discourses of jurists, according to which there would be a difference between value judgments of a scientific character (for instance directed towards the value of truth) and value judgments of an ethical character. As a matter of fact, some legal philosophers (see, for instance, Dickson 2001, 32–33) advance this type of argument. It amounts to saying that we should distinguish between *committed value judgments*, coming from inside a given legal system, and *neutral evaluations*, coming from the outside, which are close to traditional scientific values (truth, simplicity, etc.). To sum up, the latter express judgments of the relevance and importance of the phenomena to be investigated, but do not imply, after all, any kind of ethical appreciation.

It seems to me that here again we end up peeping into the old demarcationist position of traditional positivism, according to which ethical evaluations always imply adopting an internal position and taking a stand in favour of – or against – the given legal system. From this point of view, evaluating ethically is always a step in the practical process of justifying or of 'accepting/refuting' something. The external location, on the contrary, is that which is at the disposal of the scientist (or 'para-scientist') who neutrally describes phenomena (even normative phenomena).

To this position, I respond with two kinds of criticism. With the first one, I point out that there is no logical or conceptual connection between adopting an internal or committed position and expressing ethical value judgments. It is perfectly possible, that is, to stand outside the legal system, and, therefore, to adopt an uncommitted point of view, and to be almost forced to express ethical value judgments in order to reach a better understanding of the value-laden material contained in that legal system.

With the second criticism, I raise many doubts on the distinction between 'ethical' and 'merely evaluative', which seems to me quite *ad hoc*, that is, drawn only for the reason of saving legal knowledge from the intrusion of strong value judgments. I do not think that it is possible to draw a clear line, of a qualitative character, between different value judgments with specific regard to their content; I believe, on the contrary, as I will show in a moment, that a viable distinction should only regard the function of value judgments. To strengthen this point, it can be useful to make reference once again to Putnam's thinking. According to Putnam, all values are *in the same boat*; he says very forcefully that 'if values seem a bit suspect from a narrowly scientific point of view, they have, at the very least, a lot of "companions in guilt": justification, coherence, simplicity, reference, truth, and so on, all exhibit the same problems that goodness and kindness do, from an epistemological point of view'; and he concludes that 'we should recognise that all values, including cognitive ones, derive their authority from our idea of human flourishing and our idea of reason' (Putnam 1981, 140–41).

Of course, taking up this position in the legal field, a position which is openly critical of the principle of value-freedom, requires a series of specification and distinctions that it is not possible to make here. One, however, seems particularly important to me, and I want to mention it. I am talking about the distinction between *value judgments exhibiting a cognitive function*, whose task is that of contributing to a better understanding of a given legal system; and *value judgments exhibiting a strong creative function*, whose task is to import values from the outside, in order to change the legal system in the direction of the protection of ethical values or of the pursuit of political ends, values and ends which should not be considered at the moment as part of the system. But, of course, these 'membership judgments' have always a constructive character, in the sense that they do not neutrally describe values or ends as something autonomously existing in reality, like pieces of the 'furniture of the universe'.

On the contrary, value judgments having a cognitive function (as long as they are introduced with the goal of getting a better knowledge of a given legal system) cannot come freely from the outside as the result of a completely discretional intervention of the jurist, perhaps coloured by strong political or ideological motivations.

I would like to add, lastly, that, according to what I have just said, the position that I have tried to defend on this point cannot at all be qualified as that of a paleo-positivist or a disguised legal naturalist. My approach remains firmly, I believe, in the legal positivist camp, because, among other reasons, it appreciates and protects, to the highest possible degree, one of the most important features that legal positivism has ever attributed to the operations performed by jurists (something which MacCormick too has openly recognised and that remains the residual component of his legal positivism), namely, that one of the most important tasks of jurists is that of giving an objective knowledge of positive law, a knowledge that is independent both of its moral acceptance or refusal, and of its ideological manipulation. I would like to stress again, at the end of this section, that the difference between a positivist and a naturalist no longer lies in the fact that the former thinks that positive law can be described without expressing value judgments, and the latter thinks that positive can only be so described. The difference lies, on the contrary, in the kind of justification that legal positivism and legal naturalism think, respectively, can be offered of these kinds of judgments. Here, the alternative is between *objective* (legal naturalism) and *relative* (legal positivism) justifications, i.e., between a justification which founds itself on objective values and a justification which rests on values that are only contingently valid, i.e., valid relatively to a given context.

5. Last words on MacCormick's legal positivism

I would like now to conclude my chapter returning to the theme of the various conceptions of legal positivism expressed by MacCormick. My personal impression is that the most solid and consistent position among those expressed by him is by and large the original one, though in a context dominated by epistemological and theoretical premises of a traditional kind. This being the case, my personal preference would be for affirmation of a clear conceptual opposition between legal positivism and legal naturalism, accompanied by epistemological and theoretical premises that are more up-to-date than those expressed by MacCormick in *Legal Reasoning and Legal Theory* (1978).

In any case, I want briefly to recapitulate the criticisms I have already made of the positions expressed by MacCormick in his works. This series of criticisms concerns, as a matter of fact, the phase in which he accepts, more or less fully, the opposition between legal positivism and legal naturalism, because on the subsequent phases I have already fully expressed my criticisms in the previous section.

From this point of view, the first criticism is that he fails at all events to make a clear distinction between the levels of concept and conceptions, and therefore does not show precise awareness of what remains stable in legal positivism and what is subject to change.

The second criticism, connected to the first one, is that in MacCormick's thought there is no distinction between the two different ontological and methodological levels of the definition of legal positivism. This gap produces those logical jumps that I have already identified in the previous sections and to which I will not return. But even remaining on the ontological level, it is not clearly specified that the thesis that logically has priority, of the two that he brings into play, is the *social thesis*, and, hence, that from it there derives, as an implication, the thesis of the separability between law and morality. A further proof of this misunderstanding is given by the fact that, fearing (without reason) that the thesis that certain moral values penetrate into law can challenge the positive law thesis of separability, he tries to resolve the difficulty by jumping from the ontological level to the methodological level: thus, he maintains that the fact that the members of the legal community express moral preferences does not imply that the scholar has to do this too. As I have said, however, these are two different issues: one thing is the issue of the connection (necessary or otherwise) between law and morality, while another thing is the issue of what the methodological attitude of the legal scholar has to be. It seems to me that on the first issue the *inclusive* versions[5] of legal positivism have many arrows in their sheaths, and are able to show that the reference of a given legal organisation to certain values as an integral part of positive law is, by and large, a contingent element, which depends on the criteria of recognition accepted inside that legal system.

The third criticism is linked to the fact that MacCormick fails to stress that the true crucial element on which to found the opposition, at the ontological level, between legal positivism and legal naturalism is set at the meta-ethical level and concerns the distinction between absolutism and relativism. Besides, the proof of the importance for MacCormick himself of this type of meta-ethical justification is given by the fact that the phase in which he abandons the non-cognitivist meta-ethical premises coincides with the phase in which he seriously starts to challenge the significance and importance of the opposition between these two traditions of scholarship.

The last criticism, already mentioned several times, concerns the methodological level of the definition. MacCormick fails to distinguish the *conceptual thesis*, crucial for each legal positivist, which consists of the distinction between 'describing positive law' and 'taking a stand on it', from the *thesis concerning the level of conceptions*, a thesis that some – but certainly not all – positivist scholars stress, according to which cognitive discourse has to be rigorously non-evaluative in any case. Failure to recognise this distinction causes further problems for his theory; and in this case too, not by chance, as soon as his trust in the non-evaluative character of the cognitive discourses of legal scholars starts to waver, his taking side with legal positivism starts to waver too.

By way of conclusion, over and above these specific critical comments, I can only reaffirm that MacCormick's conception remains a fundamental turning point in contemporary analytical legal theory, or, perhaps, as one might also say, in contemporary analytical legal positivism, considering that MacCormick's position, at least from the methodological point of view, can still be placed in the field of legal positivism.

References

Bobbio, N. (1972), *Giusnaturalismo e positivismo giuridico* (Milano: Edizioni di Comunità).

Dickson, J. (2001), *Evaluation and Legal Theory* (Oxford: Hart Publishing).

5 A particularly persuasive version of inclusive legal positivism is that given by Waluchow 1994.

Dworkin, R. (1986), *Law's Empire* (London: Fontana Press).
Finnis, J. (1980), *Natural Law and Natural Rights* (Oxford: Clarendon Press).
Füsser, K. (1996), *Farewell to 'Legal Positivism': The Separation Thesis Unravelling*, in George 1996.
Gallie, W.B. (1955–56), 'Essentially Contested Concepts', *Proceedings of the Aristotelian Society* LVI, 167–98.
George, R.P. (ed.) (1992), *Natural Law Theory: Contemporary Essays* (Oxford: Clarendon Press).
George, R.P. (ed.) (1996), *The Autonomy of Law: Essays on Legal Positivism* (Oxford: Clarendon Press).
Goodman, N. (1978), *Ways of Worldmaking* (Indianapolis and Cambridge: Hackett).
Hesse, M. (1980), *Revolutions and Reconstructions in the Philosophy of Science* (Brighton: Harvester Press).
Jori, M. (1985), *Saggi di metagiurisprudenza* (Milano: Giuffrè).
MacCormick, N. (1978), *Legal Reasoning and Legal Theory* (Oxford: Clarendon Press).
MacCormick, N. (1981), *H.L.A. Hart* (London: Edward Arnold).
MacCormick, N. (1992), 'Natural Law and the Separation of Law and Morals', in George 1992.
MacCormick, N. (1996), 'The Concept of Law and *The Concept of Law*', in George 1996.
MacCormick, N. (ed.) (1997a), *Constructing Legal Systems* (Dordrecht: Kluwer).
MacCormick, N. (1997b), 'The Ideal and the Actual of Law and Society', in Tasioulas 1997.
MacCormick, N. (2005), *Rhetoric and the Rule of Law: A Theory of Legal Reasoning* (Oxford: Oxford University Press).
MacCormick, N. (2007a), *Institutions of Law: An Essay in Legal Theory* (Oxford: Oxford University Press).
MacCormick, N. (2007b), 'Legal Positivism: Hart's Last Word', paper presented at the *The Legacy of H.L.A. Hart Conference*, University of Cambridge, 27–28 July 2007, unpublished.
MacCormick, N. and Weinberger, O. (1986), *An Institutional Theory of Law* (Dordrecht: Reidel).
Popper, K.R. (1972), *Objective Knowledge: An Evolutionary Approach* (Oxford: Clarendon Press).
Putnam, H. (1981), *Reason, Truth and History* (Cambridge: Cambridge University Press).
Tasioulas, J. (ed.) (1997), *Law, Values and Social Practices* (Aldershot: Dartmouth).
Villa, V. (1984), *Teorie della scienza giuridica e teorie delle scienze naturali: modelli e analogie* (Milano: Giuffrè).
Villa, V. (1997), 'Legal Theory and Value Judgments', in MacCormick 1997a.
Villa,V. (1999), *Costruttivismo e teorie del diritto* (Torino: Giappichelli).

Villa, V. (2003), *Storia della filosofia del diritto analitica* (Bologna: Il Mulino).
Villa, V. (2004), *Il positivismo giuridico: metodi, teorie e giudizi di valore. Lezioni di filosofia del diritto* (Torino: Giappichelli).
Waluchow, W. (1994), *Inclusive Legal Positivism* (Oxford: Clarendon Press).
Wittgenstein, L. (1979), *On Certainty* (Blackwell: Oxford).

PART II
Institutions and Justice

Chapter 5
Institutional Theories and Institutions of Law: On Neil MacCormick's Savoury Blend of Legal Institutionalism

Massimo La Torre[1]

1. Preliminary remarks

The current of thought known as legal institutionalism finds its place within a wider jurisprudential research programme somewhat hostile to formalism. This is true of the 'classic' institutionalism associated with Santi Romano and Maurice Hauriou, but it might be true as well of the more recent neo-institutionalism put forward by Neil MacCormick. As an anti-formalist stance, institutionalism is one of several attempts at finding a way out of a host of problems caused by a too narrow conception of law and of legal science, the one essentially equated with the command of the 'political superior,' or state sovereignty; the other understood as a purely descriptive, or 'external', and systematic analysis of norms and normative orders.

This narrow conception has a name: it is legal positivism, which forestalls any recourse to strong normative (moral, political) argument, and usually also dismisses as pointless any taking into account of the broader, social context in which legal norms are set. Opposition to this view comes from various scholarly traditions, the common theme being a concern with asserting the relevance of practices against mere forms or rules and stressing the normative, and hence the legal value of social facts against a purely semantic approach. One of these traditions, and also the more epistemologically savvy among them, is legal institutionalism.

1 This chapter was first presented as a paper at the 2007 Symposium on Institutions of Law, held in Edinburgh. I was first in Edinburgh twenty years ago, in the summer of 1987, to work on my translation of Neil MacCormick's and Ota Weinberger's *An Institutional Theory of Law* (1986), a book which collected, among other papers, MacCormick's inaugural lecture, 'Law as Institutional Fact.' I had at that time the privilege to discuss my translation (MacCormick and Weinberger 1990) with MacCormick. Presenting this paper again gave me the opportunity to discuss with him. For this renewed privilege, I declare my gratitude to the University of Edinburgh and the Leverhulme Trust.

2. 'Classical' institutional theories

In Santi Romano's work, we have the first, specific theory of institutionalism as a legal doctrine (his full account can be found in his 1917 book, *L'ordinamento giuridico* ('The Legal Order'; see Romano 1977). Two basic tenets come together in his work: the legal order is an institution, and institutions are organised social forms. This amounts to breaking with one of the two main dogmas of legal positivism, namely, the oneness of all forms of law – all of them state-sourced, or finding their single, defining form in the statute. Romano's institutionalism, therefore, presents itself as a doctrine making a case for the plurality of legal orders and for their openness to society and their movements. But this much it achieves at the expense of sacrificing, to a large extent, the concept of norm, which finds itself set rather starkly against that of institution.

Romano takes an anti-voluntarist stance on the question of the sources of law – and he might even be said to be 'anti-creationist' in this respect. For him, law takes shape by spontaneous production and is always already in effect wherever there are social relations that support it. Law, he argues, is never the commencement of law: it is rather an accretion that builds on top of pre-existent law or else a modification of that law. The legislator, then, does not properly *create* law.

Another important version of institutionalism comes to us by way of the French constitutionalist, Maurice Hauriou. But he only saddles Romano's construction with three devices. First, he introduces a questionable ontology of legal objects by drawing the distinction between person-institutions and object-institutions. Second, he politicises the notion of a person-institution by making it in essence equivalent to that of a representative state. Lastly, he puts forward a questionable conception of representation and develops it in a non-rationalistic sense – but this he does by introducing the interesting notion of a 'guiding idea.' This is a force-idea making up the foundation of each institution, and the representation afforded by the institution thereby becomes essentially an existential notion, the bearer of that idea. The upshot of a theory so framed is what will sometimes be a bluntly anti-liberal outlook.

Indeed, Hauriou's conception of representation connects up with Eric Voegelin's theory of an 'authoritative state.' The same goes for the spurious German institutionalism of the 1930s, whose most prominent exponent was Schmitt: again, Schmitt sets norms against institutions, but this time dramatising the contraposition because, among other reasons, he sees a principle of equality inherent in the idea of a norm, and equality cannot be tolerated in a radically anti-democratic line of thought such as his.

We have, therefore, three versions of 'classic' institutionalism, two of them legitimate, so to speak, and a third one more or less 'illegitimate,' meaning that its specific use of 'institution' as a basic concept is idiosyncratic and contested. The first two versions, the 'legitimate' ones, are the French and the Italian, as exemplified in the work of Maurice Hauriou and Santi Romano, respectively. The third, and 'illegitimate', version is the Germanic one, its earliest examples being found in conservative political thinkers like Rudolf Smend and Eric Voegelin, but most notably in the constitutionalist theory of Carl Schmitt, especially in the period spanning from the early 1930s to the mid-1940s, a theory that also goes by the name of *konkretes Ordnungsdenken* (doctrine of the concrete order).

It may be a telling factor that all the authors mentioned above study public and constitutional law. What this suggests is that institutionalism comes as an answer to questions that are of greatest concern to public law, such as the need to integrate people under collective structures and ensure stable social relations, and the need to secure the legitimacy and efficacy of political authority.

Even with the above-mentioned differences among the three 'classic' versions of institutionalism, we can make out some shared features. In all three versions, law is found to have a few basic characteristics: call them sociality, system and plurality. *Sociality* means that law is closely bound up with society, or a social group, so much so that there are institutionalists that understand the two terms as synonymous. *System* means that the legal system is precisely that, a system or an order, or that it is grounded on, and guarantees, what MacCormick now defines as 'orderliness' (MacCormick 2007, 11; for a similar statement, see Romano 1977, 26). *Plurality* means that the system is plural in its makeup, in that there is not any single, coherent, self-contained system of law having effect over a single territory as its 'law of the land'; rather, there are believed to be, for each such territory, plural legal systems integrated with one another. In this sense, an institutional legal order would always tend to be an institution of institutions, and sort of a 'mixed constitution'.

The two 'legitimate' theories of institutions, as was observed only a moment ago, are those of Hauriou and Romano. But still, there are important differences between them. A statement of these differences will help us have an overall picture of 'classical' legal institutionalism.

Hauriou understands institutions as somehow prior to law. An institution, he says, is 'a project-idea behind an undertaking' that gets carried out through the law over time in a social environment. Romano, in contrast, understands law and institutions as coinciding. 'Every legal system', he says, 'is an institution and, vice versa, every institution is a legal system: the equation between the two concepts is necessary and absolute.' In Hauriou, furthermore, institutions properly so called are constitutional and representative in form, meaning that they must effect a sort of rule of law, on however small a scale. This idea meets with zestful criticism from Romano, who sees it as mistaking description (the 'scientific' task of the theoretical jurist) for prescription, that is, the task befitting the moralist or the politician and foreign to 'the science of law'.

The elements constitutive of an institution, on Hauriou's conception, are: its giving course to an idea of social action; its using to this end an organised power; and the fact of that idea finding widespread acceptance in society. Romano, instead, sees these elements as encapsulated in a plurality of subjects; in the organisation that binds them together; and in a power to regulate by which the organisation expresses itself.

Hauriou operates under the influence of Bergson's vitalism, and his theory is, therefore, sometimes cast as a political philosophy. Romano is deeply entrenched in the legal-positivist tradition, and his influence, if we have to pin it down, is that of Otto von Gierke's *Genossenschaftstheorie*: he spills over into sociology. Thus, Hauriou makes the ideal moment the decisive moment and, further, he cannot welcome just any 'project-idea' as the institution's normative core, but only that idea which expresses the principles underlying the rule of law and political representation. Romano is more realistic – more cynical, by another name – and so counts even the mafia as an institution. What matters, for something to qualify as an institution, is how organised it is, how developed, and how effective in doing what it does.

Let us look now at the 'illegitimate' version of institutionalism, whose essential traits are sketched out paradigmatically in *Über die drei Arten des rechtswissenschaftlichen Denkens* ('Three Types of Juristic Thinking'), an essay that Schmitt wrote in 1934 for a specific occasion. Here we find institutions set in stark opposition to norms and made to agree, instead, with the notion of 'decision'. The institution fleshed out in the *konkretes Ordnungsdenken* is an organic community not founded on any convention, with different people finding themselves set within a single whole that they cannot transcend, a community whose regulation is inherent: the organism regulates itself and so does not necessitate norms (in the sense of abstract and general norms); rather, it comes through in the concrete vital manifestations that transpire among its members, and it comes through as well, or rather in the first instance, in the decisions of individuals who enjoy a privileged connection with the community.

An institutionalism so framed rejects normativism: it is wary of conventional rules, understood as provisions that can be universalised (albeit only within the scope of single legal categories), and it is also wary of explicit reasons for action, insofar as these can become an object of reflection on the part of individuals. Schmitt, then, uses institutionalism as an ideology with which to justify decisionism – the final outcome and practical import of his *konkretes Ordnungsdenken*. Of course, neither Hauriou nor Romano are decisionists; and further, Romano defends the normativist perspective, and does not set against it the institutionalist approach, as Schmitt does. 'Legitimate' institutionalism remains harnessed to a rationalistic conception of the world, and one that in Hauriou is still in certain respects an Enlightenment conception. Not so in Schmitt, whose unifying theme is anti-Enlightenment, irrationalist and anti-liberal.

3. Institutionalism revisited

The neo-institutionalism developed by MacCormick, which proceeds not so much from anti-formalism, as rather from ordinary-language philosophy and from the idea of 'institutional facts' is quite different. The basic difference, with respect to the first kind of institutionalism, is that now we see the notion of a norm fully recovered. Nor do we find here any trace of the former's anti-liberal mood.

Legal neo-institutionalism results from the merging of two traditions of thought: analytical jurisprudence, as renewed in the work of H.L.A. Hart (of whom MacCormick is, I would say, the most faithful disciple), and the pure theory of law, in the critical, heterodox and somewhat 'materialised' version of it developed by the Czech-born Ota Weinberger. Indeed, Weinberger's work could hardly be labelled as 'pure theory' in Kelsenian terms, though Kelsenian motives are permanent and central in all his views.

Despite some differences, some of them significant, in the way MacCormick and Weinberger approach neo-institutionalism, there are features common to both. There is, in the first place, an anti-reductionist attitude that both of them take. This attitude is manifest in the ontology the two authors put forward: neither understands social reality to be completely reducible to the material reality of space and time (as the Scandinavian realists did before them, following the lead of Axel Hägerström), and a distinction is drawn between 'brute facts' on the one hand and 'institutional facts' on the other (taking up a suggestion of the philosopher John Searle). So, too, law does not find itself reduced to the norms that make it up, however much in the manner of a system; rather, it is thought that in working out a concept of law we need to take additional elements into account, such as the practices made possible and meaningful by norms, or the spheres of action enabled by norms and the principles of action expressed in a given social context: these are the elements from which legal norms draw inspiration and which guide their application. Further, in neither author are norms viewed in an obsessively prescriptive manner, as acting only to restrict spheres of action: norms, on this view, not only restrict but also, on occasion, expand spheres of action. As MacCormick puts it, institutions – contract, property, matrimony, and the like – enable us to increase the number of facts existing in the world without necessarily increasing the number of objects physically present among us.

But neo-institutionalism is also and especially a methodological anti-reductionism, in that legal concepts cannot, on this view, be reduced to the structures designed to represent norms and prescriptions: they cannot be reduced to instruments placed in the hands of the dogmatist, as the realists à la Ross would have it.

There are other features of neo-institutionalism common to MacCormick and Weinberger. One of them is its anti-prescriptivism, which says that norms cannot be explained as immediate imperatives, commands, or prescriptions. Another one is its moderate legal-positivist stance, whereby law, though conceived as the product of human will, rather than as an entity unsusceptible of any design or purposive intervention, will admit of the possibility of norms not expressly laid down by the legislator. Still another feature, despite some reservations expressed by MacCormick in this regard, seems to be a meta-ethical non-cognitivism: we can attain a knowledge of law (once its constituent norms have been set forth), but not a knowledge of morality (understood as critical morality), and the two spheres, law and morality, will accordingly have to be kept in clear distinction.

If we draw a comparison with 'classic' institutionalism, neo-institutionalism will prove much more methodologically refined. Even so, noteworthy affinities do exist between the two versions. Thus, Romano would resist ontological reductionism as much as he would resist methodological reductionism; he would welcome without too much hesitation a non-prescriptivist view of law; and he would not shrink from upholding the separation of law and morality. So he, too, can easily be described as a moderate legal positivist. But then, again, there are also important differences, at least two of them.

MacCormick and Weinberger both understand 'institution' as mainly equivalent or related to 'institutional fact.' Romano, instead, understands it as equivalent to, or overlapping with, 'society.' (Of course, not every institutional fact constitutes a society: witness the example of a contract). So, too, Romano, at one point in the course of his theoretical exploration, attempts to reduce the 'ought' (the validity of norms) to the 'is' (to their efficacy) – not so neo-institutionalism, which maintains an unequivocal distinction between the two categories, even if at the expense of incurring obscurities and ambiguities, a few too many in fact. How, for instance, can one accept the idea of institutional fact without at the same time taking on board the idea of constitutive rules, as explained by Weinberger (see, for instance, MacCormick and Weinberger 1986, 23–24)?

4. Institutions and social facts

The notion of an institution is in certain respects a 'compromised' notion, in that it carries implicit and concrete normative assumptions. Also 'compromised' is its history, a history none too simple or merely conceptual.

In one sense of institution – a non-theoretical sense – the notion is assumed to be equivalent to that of an organisation, authority, or power. On this assumption, the expression *public institution* may well be taken to mean 'public power.' In another sense, a specific sense framed within legal theory, an institution is understood as an *Anstalt*, this being a fundamental concept in the legal-philosophical thought of Friedrich Julius Stahl (his magnum opus is Stahl 1830, 1833, 1837). The concept was developed as an alternative to that of free association, expressive of the will of the people in a community or body politic, and it idealises the medieval guild, understood as the authentic, immediate and non-reflexive expression of the social fabric. *Anstalt* is language, spontaneous construction, the product of human activity, but not of human design: language is indeed the paradigmatic model for this concept.

The institution of which *Anstalt* might be the German translation is, therefore, conceived from the outset in contraposition to the sphere of voluntary relations and to deliberation, and also to the notion of norms as the manifestation of a will, i.e., an intentional and reflexive purpose. But it is only with Santi Romano and Maurice Hauriou that the notion of an institution becomes explicitly and specifically relevant in legal theory, so much so that they use it to bring out the very concept of law. An institution, says Romano, is 'any entity or body having a stable and permanent framework and forming a body in itself, with a life of its own' (Romano 1983, 82).

On this definition, an institution looks very much like a community, and therefore finds its theoretical antithesis in the notion of an individual. It carries an anti-individualistic normative conception by implying the ontological primacy of the community over the individual, and in Romano's formulation it also implies a separation of law and morality, with law pertaining to the sphere of community, and morality to the subordinate sphere of individuals and subjectivity. The same theoretical scheme frames the notion of institution in the definition of it offered by Maurice Hauriou: an institution is 'the idea that stands behind an effort or undertaking and is carried through and lasts under the law in a social environment' (Hauriou 1933, 96). For Hauriou, who distinguishes between 'people-institutions' and 'object-institutions,' even norms are institutions (they are 'object-institutions'). This institutionalist reductionism is driven by a communitarian engine that grows ever more powerful, beginning with the Thomistic radicalisation of Hauriou's doctrine that we find in the French scholar George Renard (see Renard 1933), all the way to the raving aggrandisement the notion of institution goes through in German legal philosophy at the hands of scholars like Carl Schmitt, Karl Larenz, and Arnold Gehlen. For Schmitt and Larenz, law is an institution understood as *Selbstgestaltung:* as the community's self-formation. For Gehlen, even the individual is an institution!

Worthy of mention is also the ambitious theory developed by Cornelius Castoriadis (he died in Paris in 1997) (see Castoriadis 1974). For him, an institution designates in the first instance human social reality at large, and the law can be said to be only a 'second institution'. Castoriadis understands institutions to be the point of intersection of two constant movements proper to human sociality – its 'instituting' moment and its 'instituted' one – in a continuing dialectic by which meanings and forms of life fuse and crystallise. Reality, or 'being', is not only ruled by a deterministic movement. The unexpected or the 'new' are intrinsic to 'being'. Now, this ontological creativity within a social or human context finds its most powerful expression in the growing of institutions – novel reality formations which enrich and increase human scopes of action. Castoriadis's theory thus is underpinned by an articulate and refined metaphysics and could serve to impart philosophical direction to the research project carried on by legal institutionalism, a project that has so far proved rather ambiguous in its attempt to free itself of the dogmas of neo-empiricism and positivism.

It is a different series of reflections that leads to the notion of institution, as it takes shape in *political*, not legal, neo-institutionalism. In fact, even in political science there has been, in the more recent past, a renewed interest in the notion of institution, no longer studied from the merely behaviourist, or utilitarian, perspective informed by the myth of an idealised *homo oeconomicus*. From *legal* neo-institutionalism we get a notion of institution based on a notion of 'institutional fact' understood as pertaining to the sphere of rules and as resulting from such rules. From the neo-institutionalism of political science, which finds two effective defenders in James G. March and Johan P. Olsen (see March and Olsen 1989), we instead have a reaction against the reductionism proper to decision theory and to the methodological individualism of empiricist origin. Institutions, organisations, states especially – they tell us – are not transparent to individual, utilitarian or prudential calculations.

In the several versions we have of institutional theories, anyway, the notion of an institution seems to to be driven to face an alternative. On the one side, it is seen as restraining chances of behaviour, reduction of complexity. Gustavo Zagrebelsky, a former judge of the Italian Constitutional Court and a distinguished constitutional lawyer, believes that 'institutions were born out of a fear for freedom's possibility' (Zagrebelsky 2006, 30). They nevertheless – he says – play an emancipating role, in so far as they take from human beings' shoulders the heavy burden of too many choices and of too frequent decisions. The map of social action is thus simplified through institutions. They give us that other freedom which is the outcome of reducing uncertainty and keeping under control insecurity, *Entlastung* – to use Arnold Gehlen's expression (see Gehlen 1997).

Now, this is the prevailing sense of the notion in much legal theory and in political science and sociology. Some philosophy about the concept supports this view: Arnold Gehlen or Carl Schmitt's elaborations go in this direction. However, one may wonder whether this is the sense we can extract from MacCormick's insights about institutional practice. Indeed, I wonder whether this is the better way to give the notion of an institution an independent and fruitful purport. In fact, I tend to believe that it would be much less 'compromised', so to speak, or less ambigous, and certainly more promising, to look in the opposite direction. It is so, especially, if we do not want to blur the experience and intuitions we have of a normative domain which, as MacCormick often points out, seems to be more enabling than disabling, that is, enlarging rather than narrowing our grip over the world.

5. Institutions and the law

Now, MacCormick's latest book, *Institutions of Law* (2007), and indeed the whole of his institutional theory, is a step forward in the 'compromised' and complex story of institutionalism. I have elsewhere argued that among H.L.A. Hart's disciples, the Scottish scholar can be considered the closest to the old master's views, and the one who has attempted to keep the two fundamental promises made by the English jurisprudent. These are: (i) a hermeneutical methodology in the study of law centred around an internal point of view; and (ii) a notion of law rescued from its traditional dependence upon an authoritarian view of social relationships and a more or less acute reference to command and to coercion. MacCormick makes the two promises the core of his own research programme. Thus, MacCormick's neo-institutionalism seems to represent a radical turn in the story of institutionalist doctrines towards an open acknowledgment of democratic political arrangements and a discursive concept of law.

All this is confirmed in MacCormick's latest book, though here we find some important new insights. Throughout the Scottish scholar's theoretical work, and already clearly outlined in his jurisprudential manifesto, his inaugural lecture held in Edinburgh in 1973, we find four main declinations of the notion of 'institution': two more philosophical, the other one more sociological. MacCormick's first use of the notion overlaps with John Searle's 'institutional fact'. Actually, this is the opening move of neo-institutionalism, which, as matter of fact, can claim to be a special theory of law only in so far as 'institution' assumes a strong theoretical purport and is not just equated with formalities, procedures, agencies, i.e., with 'institutions' in the non-philosophical sense. Indeed, there is hardly a theory of law that does not reconnect this to some form of agency, or procedure, or in this sense 'institution'. An 'institution' is first of all assumed to be a special kind of fact, indeed an 'institutional fact'.

> There are more things in heaven and earth than were known in Horatio's philosophy, and many more things exist than can be accounted for in terms of physics, physiology, and behavioural psychology. (MacCormick 1973, 2)

But, MacCormick says, there is a second 'philosophical' sense, or better, the first is reinterpreted in terms of a second sense, that is more or less equivalent with the basis or the essence of a (legal) concept. Institutions are reshaped into 'institutes', which is an English translation of the German 'Rechtsinstitut' or of the Italian 'istituto giuridico', a notion for a legal concept viewed through essentialist eyes as something endowed with a thick ontological dimension. 'Institutional terms, as used by lawyers, can only be understood as the organising and connecting terms between complex sets of institutive, consequential and terminative rules' (MacCormick 1973, 13).

However, these two senses are considered to be too abstract. Philosophy should cede the way to sociology. Institutions are better understood as 'organisations'.

> There are certain types of social system or subsystem, such as universities, schools, hospitals, orphanages, libraries, sporting organizations, and the like, to which we often refer as 'institutions'. These are organizations of people which retain their organizational identity through time even though their personnel may change, because they are getting on with some job, and getting on with it in an organized way. (MacCormick 1973, 9)

Such sociological reading can, however, be offered by pointing out that institutions, as organisations, grow from a differentiation process whereby some conduct is addressed not only through primary rules of obligations, but also, and more specifically, through secondary rules which confer powers. This is made visible and effective by the operations of special actors such as arbiters, umpires or judges. Here, an 'institution' would overlap with what H.L.A. Hart defines as a 'developed' normative order where systemic rules are certified through a meta-rule offering membership criteria.

Institutions in this sense are the outcome of 'institutionalisation', which, in MacCormick's reconstruction, takes place through the existence of a 'second tier of practice' which is given by the performances of 'supervisors' impinging upon a first tier of conducts that could originally subsist only following some informal pattern.

In his latest and rich book *Institutions of Law*, we find, however, a fifth use: here, an institution is basically seen as a co-ordination scheme, a matter of reciprocal expectations and adjustments to conduct, though it should soon reach the stage of 'institutionalisation' and of being related to a 'second tier' of supervision practices. Queuing up in a line now emerges as the paradigmatic case for an institution. (This, by the way, was also the view held by two Italian legal philosophers, both adopting institutionalism as their conception of law, Widar Cesarini Sforza and Guido Fassò.) We can, then, safely affirm that MacCormick's use of the notion ('institution') is pluralistic, and that it has evolved in time, including now in more clear terms the issue of co-ordination.

Nonetheless, the question remains whether this pluralistic use is not a trifle too plural and loose and whether it might be reconceptualised in terms of a unitary view of what an institution is. The question, also, is whether, after the turn given to that notion as primarily related to co-ordination of conduct, we could maintain that there is a basic continuity in MacCormick's institutionalist approach. It might well be that by aligning an institution mainly with co-ordination problems, the very idea of a special 'institutional fact' dimension evaporates. However, we have seen that in MacCormick's inaugural lecture his conclusions were quite sceptical about the epistemological purport of 'institutional facts'. MacCormick's conclusion there was:

> Many important elements of law can be profitably contemplated as institutional facts in the philosophical sense, but we cannot squeeze the whole of the law into that category; in other aspects, it can only be comprehended as an institutional phenomenon in the sociological sense. (MacCormick 1973, 30)

In the end, then, we might find that there is indeed a continuity in MacCormick's approach, and that this is what I would call a sceptical institutionalism, which, on the one hand, raises the claim of a special ontological layer for the law ('institutional facts'), but, on the other, plays down he implications of such a claim by pointing to an empirical, 'external' reading of the facts of law in sociological terms.

However, an 'institution' as a novel and far-reaching notion for the concept of law cannot but have an ontological turn. This was, as a matter of fact, MacCormick's original view, in spite of all his Humean scepticism: law is an 'institutional fact'

– this is the central thesis of his inaugural lecture and of much work that was to follow. Institutionalism is thus meant to offer an ontological foundation to the hermeneutical, internal point of view. In this way, furthermore, we would close the way to imperativism, prescriptivism and decisionism. To have and practice law is not just commanding and obeying, sanctioning and being sanctioned, but we need particular normative rules that institute a new dimension for action by qualifying a situation and/or an object in a non-empirical way. Here, rules are not only prescribing conduct, or ascribing values; they produce or express sense, Wittgenstein's 'Witz', where there is yet none. Phenomenologically, law is here not so much a constraint or a reduction of chance in human conduct; it is rather the opening up of a scope for action that would otherwise not be available. It is not really the reduction of complexity, but rather, the production of a plurality of existence modes. Without the rules and the institution of chess we could not have the opportunity of playing chess. Without the institutive rules and the institution of trust, we could not have trusts and all the actions which follow from the fact there is a legally valid trust.

The logical structure which lays the ground for the institution is a rule of the form 'x stays for y', or in other terms 'x means y'. We take an object or a fact, and by a rule of that kind, and the application of the rule itself, we transform different objects or facts. A piece of metal is taken for a coin, some words are equivalent to a promise or a contract or a baptizing; a gathering of people is a parliament, a piece of land a Fatherland. Naturally, this transformation of x into y, of a group of people into a parliament or into an army regiment, makes possible and easier a particular co-ordination of conduct, and people often have to be trained to fit into a parliament or into an army. But logically, that co-ordination is only possible once we have the institutive rules being applied and the normative transformation herein implied taking place. Such transformation is not, of course, an empirical one: a piece of metal which is now taken and used as a coin has not changed its physical status or properties. Money cannot be reported through external statements focusing on states of fact in the physical world. Internal statements, statements which take as reference the relevant institutive rule and its subsequent application, will not, however, have too much trouble in offering an understanding and giving an account of the new 'reality' which they are here concerned with.

It is very doubtful that an institution as an institutional fact could be conceived as just a matter of co-ordination. An institutional fact is a state of affairs whose 'status' and 'function' are additional to the 'brute' or non-institutional fact which supports it. This is even more evident as far as institutional 'objects' are concerned. A screwdriver is not an institutional object because its function is already given through its material or physical shape. There is no added value in it. The same, for instance, holds for a chair. Something is a chair if one can sit on it thanks to its physical or material structure and shape. There is no y added to the x here given by the 'brute' object. Now, if we consider co-ordination as a situation where some actions, which are fully meaningful as an individual piece of conduct, can be more easily and effectively carried out if taken in conjunction with other actions of the same type, we do not have an additional value added to the single action in question.

Queuing up might be a situation of this kind. One queues up because one waits for something. It is collective waiting for a performance or a service. Queuing up is better and more effective (and fairer) than just rushing all together to reach for what we are waiting for and wish to have: a theatre ticket, a bus, some good to purchase, a passport to show and so to be allowed into a foreign country. We could perhaps be happier if we should not have to queue up, and our happiness would increase with the number of people giving up queuing. The sense of a collective enterprise is indeed very low in a 'line', so that it is doubtful that we face here an institution as a space for collective action additional to the sum or bundle of individual actions considered. In any case, if we consider co-ordination as a matter of instrumental rationality we would not yet be in the domain of an 'institutional' practice.

6. Institutional facts and normativity

An institution, as a special and non-trivial dimension of social reality, is something 'new' with respect to the empirical world and to instrumental rationality. It is 'new' with respect to the empirical world, since it cannot be reported from the external point of view and a mere causalist perspective. Its relations are given through a normative backlash of the form 'x stays for y'; 'y' is not caused by 'x'; it is a matter of ascription or, if you like, of stipulation in some sense. This special feature of institutional facts make it impossible to reconstruct them in terms of instrumental rationality. Instrumental rationality lays upon a bedrock of causalist moves, that is, it centres around the empirical property of x to bring about y. This is no longer central within an institutional space that is mainly governed by normative arrangements, through constitutive rules.

Constitutive rules, and with them in some context law, produce a 'new' scope for actions. They do not just regulate actions possible on principle without the rules. They are not restraining provisions. They do not lessen social complexity. Quite the opposite, they heighten it by creating additional chances and reasons for actions. For, as Hannah Arendt has stressed, speaking of the rules of a state, 'the point of these rules is not that I submit to them voluntarily or recognise theoretically their validity, but that in practice I cannot enter the game unless I conform' (Arendt 1978, 157). Without those rules I could not play the game of citizenship and co-operation which is so fundamental for who I am.

But, one could object, there are several institutions and constitutive rules outside the law and the space of citizenship – a fact that could point out that institutions and constitutive rules are not so intimately related to legal and political practice. The reply to this could be as follows. True, there are institutions and constitutive rules that do not have anything to do with law. To have the institution of law we need more than constitutive rules and institutional facts. We need *special* constitutive rules and *special* institutional facts.

But when, under which conditions, is such specificity to be found? I believe that it is the 'point', the 'Witz', the general sense of rules and institutions, to convey the difference. MacCormick shares this view. 'We may say', he writes in *Institutions of Law*, 'that an explanation of any institution requires an account of the relevant rules set out in the light of its point' (MacCormick 2007, 36). Now, it is uncontroversial, I would say, that law's 'point' has to do somehow with *justice*. Consider the following statement by Karl Llewellyn – otherwise a 'realist' – that we find in the introduction to his book, *The Bramble Bush*:

> No man sees law whole who ever forgets that one inherent drive which is a living part of even the most wrongheaded and arbitrary legal system is a drive – patent or latent, throbbing or faint-pulsed, impatient or sluggish, but always present – to make the system, its detail and its officials more closely realize an ideal of justice. (Llewellyn 1991, x)

There is in law a claim to justice that makes of it a very special institution, that is, a scope for action where an orientation to moral values is of central significance.

All this is very well understood by MacCormick, according to whom a legal order has indeed a necessary pragmatic connection to morality, not in the sense that law has to satisfy requirements of a single, substantive morality, but rather in so far as a legal order cannot but raise some claim to be just. 'That legal reasoning', MacCormick says, 'is a sub-species of practical reasoning, and hence either strongly analogous to, or even a specialised form of, moral reasoning, is true' (MacCormick 2007, 260).

> The law as it emerges from the interpretative process addresses its demands to us subject to a 'claim to correctness', making claims about the practical and moral justifiability of the duties or other legal relations it asserts. (MacCormick 2007, 260)

Indeed, 'the attempt to do justice in the legal forum, but always justice-according-to-the-law, must clearly come under the guidance of some conception of justice which is always a moral, or morally defensible, conception of justice' (MacCormick 2007, 260). This connection however does not imply equivalence: 'law and morality are conceptually distinct' (MacCormick 2007, 261), since their phenomenology is different, the one (law) being heteronomous, the other (morality) being a precinct of autonomy.

An institutional perspective concerning law should, therefore, be complemented through a reconstruction of social practices in terms of their implicit normative claims and of the moral implications of such claims. MacCormick seems to perceive this need, and this is why he openly subscribes to Jürgen Habermas's and Robert Alexy's discourse theory, at least in so far as their reconstruction of the morality of discourses and basic human intercourse is concerned.

Here we find an important difference between MacCormick's neo-institutionalism and traditional institutional theories of law, the latter not being interested or able to detect a strong normative dimension laying ground to the factual and communitarian ethicity of institutions. This point also marks MacCormick's distance from Weinberger's approach. The Czech scholar remains strongly anchored in the meta-ethical non-cognitivism of the neo-empirist philosophical tradition. Institutions' claims to justice seem to him to violate the iron logical law that forbids prescriptive implications from descriptive sentences. MacCormick first opens up to this possibility by means of his notion of 'orderliness', which is seen as the very basic feature of law. Now, 'there is order', he says, 'wherever people conduct themselves in relation to others on the basis of an opinion concerning the right thing to do' (MacCormick 2007, 18). And when thinking or reasoning about orderliness and its implications for our conduct, and especially about or conformity to social and legal rules, we revert to the notion of *reasonableness* (see, *inter alia*, MacCormick 2003, 789 ff). (Logical and instrumental) rationality is not all we need to be reasonable, and reasonableness can lead to moral considerations within what might seem, *prima facie*, a descriptive perspective. The hermeneutical point of view (Hart's internal statements about rule following) is indeed more reasonable than rational, and cannot always avoid or askew a moral undertone or some strong normative consequence. Rule application takes place through internal statements and these, a point MacCormick stresses greatly, are 'reasoned' statements. Individuals as subjects of the law do not move, and are not moved, like billiard balls, by mechanical touch and compulsion; rather, their conduct is based on reasons and arguments.

7. Beyond institutions

In conclusion, I could sum up this final section and the gist of these short considerations of mine in the following way. MacCormick's latest notion of an institution (especially as this is presented in *Institutions of Law*) runs the danger of downplaying institutions' special normative core in two respects. The first and most important is the attempt to conceptually reconnect institutions to co-ordination problems, thereby giving up the special ontological thickness of institutional experience and reality. Being within an institution, to use Cornelius Castoriadis' words, 'c'est litteralment voir dans ce qui est ce qui n'y est absolument pas' (Castoriadis 1975, 364); it is, in other words, to take an empirical 'x' for and ideal status-ascriptive 'Y'. This has also to do with the self-referential character of institutions much stressed by both Searle and Castoriadis. 'L'institution se presuppose', wrote the latter (Castoriadis 1975, 367). I am sure MacCormick's institutional theory would profit very much by pressing this point and developing it further.

On the other hand, some kind of substantive, though thin moral theory needs to supplement the notion of an institution. MacCormick's acknowledgment of the importance of Habermas's and Alexy's view in this respect might be expanded and made an integral and fruitful part of his concept of law. If, however, I were to be in the unlikely position of having to choose between MacCormick's post-positivist and neutral normative reading of law as institution and a highly moralised concept of law, as the one, for instance, offered by the old German institutionalism, or for that matter by the French (see Hauriou 1933), I would not hesitate to put myself on the side of the post-positivist neutralist. Paradoxically, the thick, strong institutionalism pre-empts any serious moral discourse about an institution which is considered to offer its own justification, while the post-positivist will have to complement a cognitive internal perspective with an explanation and a justification of what normativity means for the holder of the normative internal point of view. In fact, and it is MacCormick himself that stresses this point, a cognitive internal perspective is just parasitical on a (strong) normative internal point of view.

References

Arendt, H. (1978), *Crises of the Republic* (Harmondsworth: Penguin).

Atria, F. and MacCormick, N. (eds) (2003), *Law and Legal Interpretation* (Aldershot: Ashgate).

Castoriadis, C. (1975), *L'institution imaginaire de la société* (Paris: Seuil).

Gehlen, A. (1997), *Der mensch. Seine Natur und seine Stellung in der Welt.* (Stuttgart: UTB).

Hauriou, M. (1933), *Aux sources du droit: le pouvoir, l'ordre, et la liberté* (Paris: Librairie Blond & Gay).

Llewellyn, K.N. (1991), *The Bramble Bush* (New York: Oceana Publications).

MacCormick, N. (1973), *Law as Institutional Fact* (Edinburgh: Edinburgh University Press).

MacCormick, N. (2003), 'Reasonableness and Objectivity', in Atria and MacCormick 1978. Originally published in (1999) *Notre Dame Law Review* 74, 1575.

MacCormick, N. (2007), *Institutions of Law* (Oxford: Oxford University Press).

MacCormick, N. and Weinberger, O. (1986), *An Institutional Theory of Law* (Dordrecht: Kluwer).

MacCormick, N. and Weinberger, O. (1990), *Il diritto come istituzione* (Milano: Giuffrè).

March, J.G. and Olsen, J.H. (1989), *Rediscovering Institutions: the Organisational Basis of Politics* (New York: The Free Press).

Renard, G. (1933), *L'institution. Fondement d'une renovation de l'ordre social*, Paris: Flammarion).

Romano, S. (1977), *L'ordinamento giuridico*, (Firenze: Sansoni).

Romano, S. (1983), *Frammenti di un dizionario giuridico*, (Milano: Giuffrè).

Schmitt, C. (1934), *Über die drei Arten des rechtswissenschaftlichen Denkens*, (Hamburg: Wisseschaftliche Buchgesellchaft).
Stahl, F.S. (1830), *Die Philosophie des Rechts nach geschichtlicher Ansicht,* Vol. 1 (Heidelberg: J.C.B. Mohr).
Stahl, F.S. (1833), *Genesis der gegenwärtigen Rechtsphilosophie,* Vol. 2 (Heidelberg: J.C.B. Mohr).
Stahl, F.S. (1837), *Christliche Rechts- und Staatslehre*, Vol. 3 (Heidelberg: J.C.B. Mohr).
Zagrebelsky, G. (2006), *Essere delle istituzioni* (Napoli: Editoriale scientifica).

Chapter 6
Institutions and Aims

Victor Tadros[1]

In *Institutions of Law* Neil MacCormick outlines not only an institutional theory of law, but also a theory of law's institutions. One focus of the book, outlined particularly in chapters 1 and 2, is a claim about the concept of law, an institutional theory of law. Law, MacCormick thinks, is an institutional normative order. It is institutional because its rules and norms rest on authority and convention. The institution of law is normative, in that it is expected that the world will conform to the law, rather than it being expected that the law will conform to the world, what we might call its 'direction of fit'. And it is an order in that it expects to order conduct, not only in the sense that it allows us to predict behaviour, but also in the sense that it attempts to order behaviour by appealing to the human will. In other words, we can have expectations about what people will do in response to the law, not only in the predictive sense, but also in the normative sense.

The other aim of the book is to develop a theory of law's institutions. MacCormick's project is to defend a particular account of the institutional theory of law, but also of the institutional divisions that occur in the law. This project is normative: it is an attempt to outline the institutional divisions that there should be, or at least to see them in a morally plausible light. The institutional divisions in the law, MacCormick implicitly thinks, rest on values or aspects of values that the law is warranted in protecting or promoting.

It is not obvious that the normative project rests on the conceptual project. A natural lawyer, who thought that at least some legal facts are derivable from some moral facts, would be happy to pursue MacCormick's normative project. The disagreement between those who claim that law has conventional foundations and those who claim that it necessarily has moral foundations seems to have little impact on this latter question in MacCormick's own book. And it seems, to me at least, that there is little reason why it should. After all, conventionalists are answering a descriptive question about what the distinctive, or the necessary, features of law are. But that, of course, leaves open the normative project of what institutions of law we ought to have.

What institutions of law we ought to have, and what values they protect or promote, seems to me a much more interesting question, and probably also a much more difficult one, than the question about whether law is, conceptually

1 Thanks to the comments and criticisms of the participants at the Edinburgh workshop.

speaking, institutional. To say that law is an institutional normative order might be true enough, but I am not quite sure how important it is to say it. It is hard to care much about the nature of law, and it is a bit puzzling why legal philosophers have spent so much time on that boring question. What kinds of institutions of law we should have, and what principles should govern them is, in contrast, obviously an important question. It is a question that will determine whether our institutions are just or not. MacCormick, I suspect, also has some lingering doubts about the importance of his institutional theory, as he devotes much more of the book to discussing law's institutions and the values that underpin them than he does to the conceptual question.

A further thing to note is that discussing the institutions of law, in general terms, in the way that MacCormick does, is quite novel. There are few legal academics who could hope to develop a theory of law's institutions; to outline what their different roles and functions should be. Though he is not entirely clear about his methodology, MacCormick attempts to go about developing his theory by investigating the values underpinning law's institutions by something like a rational reconstruction. I think that his method is to attempt to make rational sense of the institutions of law by attempting to discover the values that those institutions purport to protect or promote, and to try to make best sense of them. I think that about the book in part because of the way it is written in itself, and partly because elsewhere MacCormick has outlined the approach of rational reconstruction as appropriate to legal theory (see MacCormick 1990).

I doubt that this is the right approach. My approach will be to suggest that we can pursue the project that MacCormick wants us to pursue only in the light of principles to be developed from a more fully worked out political theory than we are likely to find in the law itself. The reasons for this are twofold. The primary reason is that rational reconstruction will tend to suffer from conservatism. It will tend to defend the values that the law in fact adopts. But there is little reason to be confident that those values are motivated by justice. Rather they are likely to favour those who have had the most influence in shaping the law, or who would have the power to advocate change when they disadvantaged by it. Unlike typical critical legal scholars, I am not a sceptic about moral values. But I am sceptical about seeking them within rather than outside the law.

But secondly, the process of rational reconstruction assumes that distinct elements of the institutions of law rest on distinctly valuable practices. Perhaps there are different elements of justice that are served by different aspects of law's institutions. I doubt very much that this is true. I suspect, rather, that different elements of law must be understood to be in the service of a more general theory of justice, and that how institutional divisions can serve justice will be fraught with empirical difficulties that cannot be answered philosophically.

So the approach I will adopt will be to outline some more foundational questions about justice and to see how the institutions of law can best meet the demands that justice makes of them. Of course, I should say at the outset, this is a rather grand enterprise. Consequently, I will outline what I see as the best approach to the question of law's institutions rather than providing any determinate answers, and even there I will make relatively little progress. But even the little progress that I make will be sufficient to reveal some of the difficulties with MacCormick's approach.

1. Justification and justice

In order to begin the discussion, I will need to sketch out a theory that links together (1) the justification for having a state at all, (2) the proper aims of the state if we are justified in having one, and (3) the institutions of the state. The central point that I want to make in this section is that we should distinguish between the reasons why individuals who are not in a state might be justified in forming one and the reasons that ought to guide states once they have come into existence. These latter reasons guide the institutions of law.

To see the distinction between the reasons to bring something into existence and the reasons that guide one once one has brought that thing into existence, compare children. That it will make me happy is a good reason to have children, and that it will make me unhappy is a good reason against having them. But once one has children, one cannot regard them as *for* one's happiness. One's happiness tends to be a very strong consideration when deciding whether to have children, but a relatively weak consideration in deciding what to do with, or about, them once one has them.

It is sometimes assumed that the reasons that ought to guide states ought to be traceable back to the reasons why citizens would accept having the state. Imagine we are in a state of nature, it is suggested. What would we, in that situation, have good reason to accept from the state? That which cannot be justified to all individuals in a state of nature cannot be justified at all. I doubt that this is true though. I think that the reasons that ought to guide states may be distinct from the reasons that ought to guide stateless citizens in forming a state. Citizens who form a state owe more to each other than could be justified to citizens in a state of nature. They owe more to each other because they agree to be bound by a law that purports to speak for all of them. Because MacCormick is insufficiently sensitive to this, he tends not to grasp fully the implications of the demands of justice for the institutions of law.

Let us start with the justification of the state. One Hobbesian thought, which plays a role in *Institutions of Law*, is that having a state is justified because a state is required to achieve peace. Perhaps it is only because a sufficient state of peace is unattainable without a state that forming a state, and through it the coercion of the state's citizens, is justified. The plausible thought here is that, in the state of nature, we all face high risks of death as a result of conflict. Each citizen will then have an overriding interest in developing a mechanism for co-ordinating their activities that will tend to reduce, if not eliminate, conflict. The state is necessary for achieving this aim. Furthermore, all individuals have an interest in having the degree of social stability that allows them to keep the fruits of their labour, and, Hobbes plausibly thinks, only states can achieve this.

One problem that Hobbesians typically face is that there is no obvious motivation to subject our will to a sovereign who would have absolute power over our lives. How could that secure peace, when the sovereign himself might have violent inclinations? Surely we would have good reason to submit to the sovereign will only if we were confident that he would be more likely to preserve our lives and provide us with greater stability than we would have in the state of nature. But it is difficult to see how a sovereign with absolute power can guarantee that (see Hampton 1986, ch. 7).

Even if this problem can be overcome, however, the Hobbesian view faces a different concern. Even if Hobbes can provide a justification of our *subjecting* ourselves to sovereign will, grounded in our interest in not being killed, it does not seem to provide an obvious mechanism for generating principles to *guide* the sovereign will. Hobbesians face a concern that they are indifferent to what the sovereign does. As long as he can secure a degree of peace, it seems, he can do what he wants. The sovereign must make people better off than they would otherwise have been had they remained in the state of nature, for it is only if he does this that he can enjoy political legitimacy. But if he meets that test, the sovereign can act for his own benefit. As they are better off than they would have been had they not submitted to his will, citizens would appear to have no grounds to complain about the commands that he issues.

Perhaps it might be argued that if people sign up to the state in order to provide peace, it is peace and nothing more that the state must deliver. On this view, *all* the state can do is to provide peace. A contract to provide peace, it might be argued, is a contract for that and nothing more. To provide more involves coercing citizens to provide goods to each other that they haven't agreed to provide. Citizens *can* form agreements with each other to benefit each other to a greater degree than that. But they have no obligation to do so.

Here is one familiar way in which this broadly libertarian claim can be challenged, as developed by the modern social contract tradition that was invigorated particularly by John Rawls. The argument is as follows. The imposition of coercive rules is justified in order to achieve peace. Everyone has a reason to have a state over the state of nature, because in the state of nature we are all faced with too great a chance of death (or other severe suffering) due to an absence of adequate mechanisms to resolve conflict. The creation of a state, to prevent fundamental conflicts resulting in the threat of death, requires a set of rules backed up by coercion. But it does not require the adoption of any particular set of rules.

However, once we authorise the creation of a set of rules backed up by coercion, we must ensure that those rules can be justified from the perspective of each citizen treated as an equal. The reason is derived from the fact that the law is expressed in a public voice. It is a voice that purports to be spoken by citizens collectively. If it is to speak in this way, it must be capable of being spoken by each citizen. And it can do that only if each citizen has reason to endorse its rules. So a state which coerces its citizens must do so in terms that they can accept from their own perspective, and this creates demands that the laws that the state passes are just.

This, it might be suggested, is why states have special obligations to their citizens which they lack to non-citizens: it is only citizens who are coerced by state laws, so there is a special obligation on the state to justify those laws to its citizens in terms that each can endorse.[2] The problem of peace, on this view, is an enabling condition for the pursuit of other aims of justice. If the state is required to solve the problem of peace, it then triggers other aims that the state might legitimately pursue. In the absence of the problem of peace, there is no other way to trigger the just pursuit of those other aims.

This seems at least plausible to me. It is the thought that motivates social contract theorists, and is to be contrasted with libertarians such as Robert Nozick.[3] For Nozick, the justification for *having* a state also plays an essential role in determining what the state can legitimately do. For John Rawls (1999), and other social contract theorists, in contrast, whilst the pursuit of justice amongst a group of people who are not already governed together by a state is not a sufficient reason to *form* a state, the principles of justice do apply once a state has been formed. That is why Rawls is concerned with the principles of justice that ought to guide those who have already agreed to co-operate with each other for social advantage. In contrast, Nozick attempts to derive the principles that govern the state by attempting to determine what those in the state of nature would have reason to endorse, assuming that they haven't agreed to co-operate with each other. Nozick traces the limits of the state for those who have not agreed to co-operate. Rawls traces the rules that ought to guide co-operating citizens.

So the state will have a range of aims directed towards justice rather than mere peace. But what justice requires is hotly contested. Think about the question of unequal wealth. As will be familiar to many, there are heated debates both about what we should be trying to distribute (wealth, or resources or capabilities) and about what distribution we should be aiming for (whatever maximises, or equality, or a distribution which prioritises the worst off either absolutely or to a degree). Many (although not all of course), who engage with such debates, assume the basic contractualist idea that the distribution of wealth must be done according to rules which all can endorse in forming an unforced agreement with each other.

To see the significance of this for MacCormick's project, consider the claim that MacCormick makes about peace in the criminal law. In MacCormick's view peace plays an important role not only in justifying having a criminal law, but in justifying the content of particular sets of laws that we have. In chapter 12 of *Institutions of Law* MacCormick develops his account of the function of the

2 For a clear explanation of justice along these lines, see Nagel 2005. We need not endorse Nagel's scepticism about global justice to accept this idea.

3 Nozick 1974 is commonly regarded as the most important libertarian foil to the social contract tradition. However, it should, of course, be remembered that Rawls was not responding to Nozick, but the other way round.

criminal law by alluding to the important role that the criminal law has had in ensuring that peace is maintained. 'If everyone were in the position of having to defend her or his own rights against all comers', MacCormick rightly notes, 'and having to take his/her own steps to obtain some remedy from, or to punish, anyone who invaded their rights, the prospects of civil peace would be slim' (MacCormick 2007, 207).

This is right insofar as it goes, but it only provides a justification for *having* criminal law at all. Perhaps it does not even do that. Perhaps we should rather say that it provides a justification for having mechanisms through which the state can enforce rights. But there are different mechanisms that might be used for enforcing rights, and it is at least not obvious that the criminal law is the only one. The state might, for example, simply eject all citizens who interfere with rights. Such a system is not obviously a system of criminal law.

But whilst it is true that the necessity for peace is a good reason to establish a set of rules that are backed up by coercion in order to ensure that rights are adequately protected, that need not play *any* role in justifying a specific set of criminal laws. If social contract theorists are right to resist libertarianism, the specific set of criminal laws that we have is to be determined by requirements of justice, rather than by ensuring a minimal level of peace. And if that is true it is not obvious what role peace should play in a theory of just criminal law.

The reason for this concern is that peace is a threshold concept. Either we have civil peace or we do not. However, the principles of criminal law are not exhausted by getting us over the threshold. For a start, criminal law should aim at an appropriate distribution of *security*, to be determined in relation to other goods that it pursues. If peace is a threshold concept, security is not. We can, as individuals and collectively, be more or less secure above the threshold of peace. Criminal law might aim at maximising average security, or it might aim at a fair distribution of security that is concerned particularly with the security of the worst off.[4] But whatever the right view about that, in a peaceful state it is plausible that peace plays a very limited role, or perhaps no longer plays a role at all, in justifying the particular set of rules and principles of criminal law.

So now we have a more complex theory of the institutions of law. We distinguish between the justification of *having* a state with some laws, and the justification for the particular set of laws that we have. When thinking about the institutions of law, we are at the second stage of analysis rather than the first. We are concerned with what justice requires with respect to citizens rather than the motivation for having a state. Whilst the second question is important, it should be thought of as a ladder to get us to circumstances in which we are required to develop a comprehensive set of rules aimed at justice, but which, once we are there, plays no role in determining what actual rules we are to adopt, at least if social contractarians are right and libertarians wrong.

---

4 For more on this, see Tadros 2008.

2. Kinds and institutions of justice

Now that we have the distinction in place between the justification for having a state and the theory of justice that underlies the particular set of laws that the state should have, we can also get clearer about how we might go about distinguishing different aspects or institutions of law. The idea here is that different institutions of law each reflect aspects of a theory of justice.

I begin by outlining an account which is crude, but I think reasonably influential. I call it the *Simple View.* I will then show why I think that view is defective. A theory of justice can be divided into four parts. One part is concerned with democracy. A system of rules is just only if that system of rules is developed through democratic institutions properly understood. Another is concerned with distributive justice: the distribution of goods, resources, capabilities or welfare (or some combination of these). A related, and perhaps dependent part, is concerned with corrective justice: the rectification that should follow breach (or wrongful breach) of rights. A final part is concerned with criminal justice, which is concerned with condemnation and punishment for the commission of public wrongs.

This division tracks divisions in the institutions of law. Public law, on this view, might include two aspects. There is what we might call procedural public law, which is concerned with the constitutional and administrative rules that institute a proper theory of democracy, and which is therefore concerned with democratic justice. There is what we might call substantive public law, which is concerned with the distribution of resources, and which is therefore concerned with distributive justice. This includes tax law, but also the laws which substantively govern the provision of public goods, and perhaps the regulation of public services and goods. There is private law, which is concerned with corrective justice, and there is criminal law which is concerned with retributive justice.

This theory suggests that there is a division of labour, whereby each institution of law can be concerned with ensuring that a particular kind of justice is achieved. Separating out spheres of justice in this way might be thought necessary in order to ensure that any one aspect of justice is pursued adequately. So, for example, substantive public law ensures a just distribution of goods, resources and so on. Corrective justice ensures that the distribution is maintained when wrongs are perpetrated. Corrective justice need not itself be concerned with the distribution of resources because the appropriate distribution is already ensured by substantive public law. Criminal law is concerned with retributive justice and security, so other areas of law need not be directed towards these issues, and so on. If each area of law pursues its own justice goal perfectly, it might be argued, the system will be perfectly just. The justice of the legal system overall is simply the aggregate of its achievements in each sphere of justice. And each sphere of justice can best be pursued independently from the others through a different institution of law.

One way in which this idea might be thought obviously simplistic has to do with the role of constitutional (or human) rights. The idea here is that constitutional or human rights provide restraints on the pursuit of policies in other areas of law. But they are rights which (at least normally) apply to all legal institutions. For example, civil and political rights apply both to courts and to parliaments as restraints on their pursuit of other goals. This shows that the pursuit of each aspect of justice might be constrained. But the fact that there are constraints on the pursuit of any particular area of justice does not in and of itself undermine the claim that each institution of law has a specific justice goal. A constraint on an institution's pursuit of justice is not a new goal. There is then a question about whether we should see constitutional rights as derived from, integrated into or independent of a theory of justice, something that I will not have space to explore here.

The problems with the simple view are different. They are to do with the independence of the spheres of justice from each other. The best overall conception of justice cannot regard these aspects of justice as equals to be pursued independently. Rather, there is a complex relationship between them, and some are either less important than, or to be derived from, others.

3. Private law and substantive public law

The assumption, on the *Simple View*, is that justice will best be pursued through an institutional division of labour. I doubt that is true. Take the relationship between private law and substantive public law. The thought earlier was that substantive public law institutes the distribution of the relevant object of distributive justice (resources, welfare, capabilities). Private law then corrects for distributive distortions that result from wrongdoing. Let us develop this idea in more detail.

We begin with an idea about the relevant distribution. Let us assume, for the sake of argument, that justice requires conformity with Rawls's difference principle. Inequalities between citizens are justified, then, only if they are to the greatest benefit of the least advantaged group. Consequently, we design our substantive public law to deliver that distribution. Wrongdoing, however, will distort with the distribution, and private law is required in order to rectify the position of the person who has been wronged in order to ensure that justice is maintained. So, for example, the system of tax and the distribution of public goods are intended to ensure that the worst off are as well of as they can be, and the distribution that achieves this is protected by the rules of private law.

But that is quite the wrong way to see things. It proceeds as though the rules of private law are not themselves to be developed in service to the difference principle. But that is quite wrong. The rules of private law themselves have economic consequences, and they might or might not be in service to the difference principle overall. Consequently, there is no reason to think that the difference principle will best be complied with through the division of labour between taxation and private law advocated by the *Simple View* (see especially Kordana and Trabachnik 2005).

The *Simple View* supposes that substantive public law has the primary role in establishing the just distribution of goods that private law then plays a secondary role in maintaining. But why should we think that this is the best way of tracking the difference principle? It may be that some other combination of roles tracks the difference principle more closely. We attempt to identify the best combination of rules of substantive public law and private law that realise the difference principle, rather than assuming a division of labour into primary and secondary roles that may be suboptimal. It may be that the difference principle is best realised, for example, if disproportionate damages are sometimes introduced to those who exploit a very powerful economic position in contract formation to compensate for real world limitations in implementing an adequate tax system. Or it may be that some kinds of wrongdoing, such as some breaches of promise, ought to be tolerated because that is to the advantage of the worst off group. These are empirical questions which normative theory has little to contribute to. But they do suggest we should not make assumptions about a neat division of labour in attaining the aims of justice.

From this we can see a further problem with MacCormick's view about the relationship between public and private law. MacCormick thinks that a fundamental difference between public and private law is that public law powers are typically powers which can be exercised only for the general good whereas private law powers are powers that can be exercised for P's particular benefit.

The former claim must be right, but only for the reason that the state does not *have* a private good. The goodness of the state is dependent entirely on the goodness it does for others, and especially its citizens. The state, unlike individuals, is not an end in itself. So how could it be that public powers can be exercised for the benefit of the state? Of course, they may be exercised in order to preserve, improve or further empower the state, insofar as that is good for further individuals. Powers, it is reasonable to suppose, are only to be conferred in order to advance interests, and states do not have interests. MacCormick also suggests that public powers are conferred in a way that the exercise of them must be unbiased. That also seems right. In some cases, private individuals can act for agent-relevant preferences to advance the interests of friends and relatives. But the state does not have such preferences, (though, depending on how cosmopolitan we are and why, we might think that there is a similar relation that holds in the exercise of public powers, with respect to the distinction between nationals and non-nationals).

Private powers, on the other hand, might or might not be exercisable only for the good of the person exercising them. Think about two models of the relationship between contract law and taxation. On one model, contractors are entitled to think only about whether the contract formed will benefit them, regardless of any economic disadvantage the person that they are contracting with will suffer as a result of the contract. Taxation will ensure that the difference principle is nevertheless satisfied. On another model, contractors must have adequate regard for the interest of those that they are contracting with. In each case, taxation will have a significant role in ensuring that distributive justice is achieved. Which model we think preferable is dependent on which system is likely to achieve distributive justice overall. That is an empirical question, to which jurisprudence has little to contribute.

Furthermore, there will likely be private powers where individuals are constrained from exercising those powers in favour of some kinds of private interests. It is uncontroversial that employers cannot exercise private powers sensitive to the preferences they have to work with those of the same race or gender as they are. The extent to which we create further constraints on employment law for favouring friends, for example, depends on an underlying theory of justice. It might be argued that equality of opportunity to positions of advancement requires that firms hire only on the basis of merit and not on the basis of friendship, and, in that case, private powers, like public powers, cannot be exercised for at least some agent-relative preferences that the employer might have. That is important, it might be argued, in order to protect fair equality of opportunity, which, for Rawls at least, takes priority over the difference principle.[5]

In the light of this, MacCormick's claim that there is some important difference between public and private law in this regard seems problematic. It may in fact be the case that private powers tend to be exercisable for self-interest, as the system is set up at the moment. But if MacCormick's institutional theory is normative, then it is aimed at defending an account of the *appropriate* institutional divisions in law. This also shows up a weakness in the method of rational reconstruction. We may show that a reconstruction of the legal system as it is preserves the idea that private powers are exercisable private motives. But that is not to say that this would conform to what justice requires, and it is surely the latter that must be our priority in a normative institutional theory of law.

Other claims that MacCormick makes about the distinction between private powers do not track the law clearly, and it is hard to see how they could. Take his claim that private powers tend to be exercisable only bilaterally where public powers are exercisable unilaterally. Powers exercisable bilaterally are powers that require the consent of another whereas powers exercisable unilaterally do not. This just doesn't seem to track the public law / private law divide at all. The power to contract is the central bilateral power in law, but that is a power that can be exercised by the state as well as by private individuals. And it is part of public law to regulate state contracts. There are a host of private powers that are exercisable unilaterally: the powers of parents with respect to the education of their children; the power to own and divest of property; the power to make a will, and so on. Again, to establish what powers we ought to give to whom and whether they are to be exercised bilaterally or unilaterally requires us to understand the basis of the distribution of power in a theory of justice; something that MacCormick fails to provide. There is no reason to think, without argument, that powers of particular

---

5 Fair equality of opportunity is the first part of the second principle of justice, according to Rawls. A fully adequate scheme of basic liberties takes priority over fair equality of opportunity, which takes priority over the difference principle. See Rawls 2001, 42–43, for Rawls' final rendition of his two basic principles of justice.

kinds should be distributed in any particular way across the public law/private law divide in the way suggested by MacCormick.

4. Criminal law and distributive justice

MacCormick's idea in chapter 12 of *Institutions of Law* is that criminal law is primarily concerned with peace and civil society. I have already had cause to doubt whether that is true. I now want to question whether criminal law does have any specific aims, and how those aims should be integrated into a more general theory of justice. It might be thought that criminal law is a genuinely separate sphere from distributive justice, and that it ought to be developed according to independent principles of retributive justice. For Rawls, considerations of criminal justice were separate from distributive justice. One way to interpret this is that whereas distributive justice is concerned with desert only in a 'post-institutional' sense, criminal justice is concerned with moral desert. The idea of criminal justice, we might think, is that those who do wrong suffer for the bad moral character they have shown through their actions. This is entirely distinct from, rather than the opposite of, that which, for Rawls, is not aimed at ensuring that the good receive the benefits they deserve for their goodness (see Rawls 1999, 276–7).[6]

Unlike other areas of law, criminal law does more obviously have an independent aim; independent in the sense that it is not normally to be pursued through other areas of law: retributive justice. The criminal justice system has the exclusive function of investigating, prosecuting, condemning and punishing crimes. But that is not to say that its *sole purpose* is to prosecute, condemn and punish crimes, or that punishment for crimes ultimately serves a retributive rationale. There are two things to say about this, one of which is relatively uninteresting and the other is more interesting.

The uninteresting thing is that in deciding whether to investigate, prosecute, condemn and punish crimes, aims other than retributive justice must be taken into consideration. It must at least sometimes be true that retributive justice ought not to be pursued for cost reasons, or because it will be too distressing to the victim, or for a range of other reasons. However, this suggests that there are extraneous constraints on the pursuit of retributive justice, just as there may be constitutional or human rights constraints, and that is not news.

The more interesting thing is that the rules of the criminal law themselves might be sensitive to other ambitions in justice over and above retributive justice. The point here is that the definition of wrongs themselves, wrongs which can then be investigated, prosecuted, condemned and punished, may be dependent on other features of justice, and must therefore be integrated into a more general conception of distributive justice.

6 For an account of why this might be a plausible interpretation of Rawls, see Scheffler 2000.

There are some crimes where this account seems implausible. We do not decide whether rape or murder should be criminalised on the basis of the distributive effects of calling those things crimes. With respect to those crimes we can simply say that they are fundamental wrongs that the state has a central role in condemning. But with respect to at least some non-consummate crimes that is not the case. A non-consummate crime is a crime the commission of which does not normally, in itself, constitute the harm which it is designed to prevent.

Some non-consummate crimes, such as attempts, seem obviously wrong independently of any calculation with respect to the distribution of benefits and burdens. But there are other crimes, such as knife possession, where this is not so obviously true. Whether criminalising knife possession is justified is dependent upon the distribution of liberty and security that is achieved through criminalisation. Furthermore, the relevant calculation must be made in relation to a scheme of law that overall has distributive effects. So, for example, suppose in two different states that criminalising knife possession tends to reduce valuable liberty of those who are, in state 1, in the worst off group overall, with respect to liberty and other goods; and, in state 2, in a better off group overall. Criminalising knife possession, however, will benefit only a better off group with respect to security in both cases. It might be that criminalising knife possession will be justified in state 2 but not state 1. Or it might be that deprivation of liberty to possess a knife for the worst off group in state 1 is justified only if there is some kind of compensation with respect to another kind of liberty.[7]

Consequently, I am tempted to reject Rawls's view that criminal justice should be considered independently of a more general theory of distributive justice. We should be looking for a more unified account than that (see Scanlon 1988). Criminal law imposes burdens on citizens, and it should do so only if that is justified to serve some important aims of the system. I doubt that desert, considered pre-institutionally, is suitably determinate or transparent to be worth pursuing by the state, if indeed it has any merit at all. Criminal justice should ultimately be justified in the same kind of way as distributive justice.

Of course, I do not have space to establish any of this now. But even if it is false, the more general point is true: that we cannot entirely separate the aims of criminal justice from the aims of distributive justice. The distributive effects of criminalisation need to be integrated into a general scheme of distributive justice. The appropriate set of rules and policies in one area of the law may be dependent on the rules and policies adopted in another, and that is even true of the area where that is least true: criminal law.

7 See further Tadros 2008.

5. Democratic justice and the division of labour

Let us take another kind of division that is sometimes supposed to obtain with respect to the relationship between law and justice: the role of the courts in a democratic society. Here we will see that there is a further deeper question about the division of labour that rests on explicating a theory of justice.

How should we understand the relationship between the structure of our political and legal institutions and their aims in a democracy? Here is how this will be seen within the *Simple View*. The purpose of democratic politics is to decide what should be done by the state. Suppose that what should be done by the state is that which best reflects the preferences of citizens. The role of political institutions is to determine what preferences citizens have. So designing political institutions involves determining which institutions will tend to make decisions that track citizens' preferences. A central way in which political decisions are made effective is through law. The law should be designed in a way that tends to be most effective in realising political decisions. The quality of a legal system is to be determined by the degree to which it makes effective political decisions.

This simple model raises a number of questions with respect to our democratic institutions. Here are two. First, what do we mean by preferences? Do we mean simply the preferences that citizens in fact have *prior to* the political process? Surely we cannot mean that. Politics has an important role in influencing the preferences of citizens. So how do we ensure that our democratic institutions play a proper role in shaping citizens' preferences? Here we draw ourselves into the large and contested literature about deliberative democracy. Second, as preferences conflict, how are we to calculate what to do, given a set of citizens' preferences? As there is normally a range of options, what calculation of preferences dictates what we should do?[8]

On this simple model, what we might call normative institutional legal theory need not be troubled with questions of this kind. Normative institutional legal theory is the element of legal theory that is concerned with how legal institutions should be designed. There is a division of labour between normative institutional legal theory and normative institutional political theory. Normative institutional legal theory, which is MacCormick's focus, is concerned with effectiveness. It can leave to political theory the task of determining how to answer the questions about preferences.

This still leaves open a number of questions in normative institutional legal theory. One concerns the interpretation of legislation. When legislation is created through a democratic decision, should that legislation be interpreted according to the words of the statute, given their ordinary and natural meaning, or should

8 In Robert Goodin's terms, we should be interested in both the *inputs* into democracy (the reflective processes that contribute to ensuring that decisions reflect the considered view of citizens) and the *outputs* of democracy (to ensure that, when a vote is required, the weight given to each vote is appropriate). See Goodin 2003.

the courts attempt to determine the underlying preferences that motivated it? Within the *Simple View*, we might answer that question by determining which approach is more likely to reflect the preferences of citizens. The second is the role of the common law. What should the role of the courts be in deciding cases where no legislation has been passed to determine the issue? Should failure to pass legislation be taken to indicate endorsement of the common law position?

The *Simple View* suggests a division of labour between normative institutional political theory and normative institutional legal theory. It also suggests another division of labour: between normative institutional political and legal theory and normative substantive political and legal theory. There is no plausible sharp division to be drawn between normative political and legal theory. Normative substantive political and legal theory is about determining the aims of the law, and of other policies of the state. Normative substantive political and legal theory is about the set of rules and principles that citizens *should* prefer.

The idea is this. Political institutions reflect the preferences of citizens. But the preferences of citizens should be to have just policies and laws. Substantive legal and political theory is about the just aims of the state, and the laws and policies that best realise those aims. As the state is democratic, the aims of the state should only be institutionalised through just democratic processes, but that does not render substantive legal and political theory redundant: they have a role in attempting to shape citizens preferences, which can then properly shape democratic decisions.

The *Simple View*, though unreflectively endorsed by many, is not the best theory. It supposes a division of labour in institutional design that, I will suggest, is not plausible. What we need, I argue, is an integrated theory of justice, one in which institutional design is not independent, or at least not completely independent, from the aims of justice. The institutions of law, then, should be justified not by considering their nature or role, but by considering the part that they play in a broader theory of justice. The first thing that I want to say, then, is that we should develop an integrated account of normative institutional political theory, normative institutional legal theory, and substantive legal and political theory.

Democracy might have instrumental and intrinsic value. Its intrinsic value consists in it ensuring that the laws of a state are articulated in the name of citizens. In order for this to be the case, it might be argued, those citizens ought to have power over political decisions. So, one important aspect of democracy will have to do with the appropriate definition and distribution of political power. Power might be divided, in keeping with Ronald Dworkin, between influence and impact (see Dworkin 2000). The impact that a person has is dependent on the extent to which his vote counts in determining the outcome. The influence that he has is dependent on the extent to which he affects the decisions of others with respect to their votes. So a person with one vote, in a very simple voting system of 'one man one vote,' has an impact proportionate to the number of people that votes. But his influence may be great in that he may, through free expression, greatly alter the way others vote. Deliberative and reflective schemes of democracy are designed in order to ensure that influence is properly regulated, and have less concern with impact.[9] In *Sovereign Virtue*, Dworkin aims to show that we should not pursue either equality of influence or equality of impact as a goal (see Dworkin 2000, 211).

But democracy might also have instrumental effects, and we might evaluate different distributions of power on the basis of these effects. Suppose, again, that we endorse the difference principle. It may be that different distributions of power will tend to get us closer or further away from the difference principles. Considered with respect to its intrinsic value, a democratic system may look very attractive, but considered instrumentally it may be less attractive. Consider a system with more or less referenda. From an intrinsic point of view it might be that more referenda are desirable. But from an instrumental point of view, this may tend to erode rather than enhance distributive justice: for example, it might be overly sensitive to the desires of the group that is currently worst off at the expense of that group overall in the long term. This might be because, for example, those without assets will tend to care less about the long-term stability of the economy if they have mouths to feed now. But the long-term stability of the economy may best serve the interests of those who have the greatest need.

Now, the degree to which democratic systems should be evaluated according to their instrumental effects is a controversial question. For Rawls, for example, there will be a range of acceptable democratic systems available, and selection between these is dependent on the extent to which they will tend to deliver aspects of substantive justice, including the difference principle. For Joshua Cohen, on the other hand, this tends to undermine the significance of democracy: democracy is supposed to *work out* what distribution citizens consider just, and the system should not be stacked in favour of one distribution over others (see Cohen 2003).

I think that institutional design must at least to a degree be sensitive to the results of the design. One plausible way to see this is to consider, as Dworkin does, the various intrinsic values that there are in democracy itself and integrate them into a more general theory of justice. Democracy needs to be justified in the light of a substantive distributive theory that includes democratic values rather than the other way round. Below a certain democratic threshold, it might be argued, laws lose legitimacy altogether (see Tadros 2008). But beyond that threshold, symbolic and other values of democracy need to be weighed in the balance with other substantive outcomes of the system.

Now consider the impact that this idea might have for, for example, the division of labour between courts and parliament, and the kinds of empirical investigations that might be relevant in determining how to model the role that constitutional rights and judicial activism might have in the context of a general theory of justice. MacCormick's view, a familiar view in a heated debate, is that judges should not be directly influenced by politically contentious issues in a theory of justice, but should rather treat the legal system as a more or less independent and self-standing set of rules and principles. I do not want to take a stand on what view we should

9 See, for example, Goodin 2003, though these are not quite his terms.

endorse here. Rather, I rather to take a step back from that debate, and consider what theoretical and empirical questions are relevant to answering that question.

One initial question is the *possibility* of judges taking an apolitical view in coming to their decisions. MacCormick seems right, here, to indicate that judges can take such a view. However, this is not quite for the reasons that MacCormick suggests. He thinks that this is a consequence of the independence of the legal system. But it is not for *that* reason that judges are capable of deciding independently of their own political views. It is rather that individuals are capable of imagining that they hold to moral views, and even to accept a moral language, that they do not endorse (see especially Williams 1985, ch. 8). Hence, they are capable of imagining what someone who is committed to those views or to that moral language would decide about an issue regardless of their own preferences. So they can see the moral point of legislation, if that legislation has some putative moral basis, even if that moral basis is not one they endorse.

Now, we must face the question of whether they *should* be so independent. MacCormick's view is that there is a political value in judicial impartiality. Here is an outline of MacCormick's view:

> The very idea of a polity under the rule of law, a constitutionalist state, or law-state, is that of one in which there is a successful separation of powers such that different functions are carried out by different agencies. It is not then the case that judges and courts are in every sense non-political – of course they ought to be non-partisan, refraining from taking sides overtly in matters of inter-party dispute in the ongoing political struggles of the day. But achieving non-partisan impartiality is itself a particular political role, one of inestimable value in securing constitutional balance. It is by participating in this way that judges contribute most to sustaining the common good of the polity. (MacCormick 2007, 181)

This passage suggests two things. One has to do with the concept or idea of a constitutional (or I would rather say democratic) state. The other has to do with the consequences of a particular separation of powers with respect to the common good. These two things are somewhat related, but they are also independent.

To begin with, we should be suspicious of MacCormick's invocation of the *idea* of a constitutional state. If the separation of powers, and non-partisanship of judges, is part of the idea of a constitutional state, we should question whether such a state is a very *good* idea. The better approach, I think, is to treat the idea of a democratic state interpretatively, requiring us to argue on normative grounds that a politically independent judiciary is the best instantiation of the democratic state.

There are two ways in which we might do that, and that should be clear from the previous paragraphs. One has to do with the nature of democracy: we might say that judges who make politically partisan decisions flout democracy properly understood. We will then need to know something more about how to understand democracy. Alternatively, we might say that allowing judges to make politically partisan decisions has consequential advantages or disadvantages, which, I take it, is the point of MacCormick's reference to the way in which a politically independent judiciary can advance the common good. But in order to answer that question, (1) we will have to know something about the proper conception of the common good; and (2) we will have to investigate empirically how that good can best be advanced.

The answer to (1) is by no means straightforward. Is the common good to be determined by the best available moral theory? Or is there a conception of the public good that is political, that it is the role of political institutions to advance, a conception that is independent of any particular comprehensive moral position? Furthermore, we might say that it is not the common good at all that we should seek to advance, but rather justice. Finally, we might debate about whether it is the good of citizens or residents that is to be advanced or also, and equally, the good of others. I am not sure whether MacCormick, in this passage, intends something specific or something very general with the term 'common good', or whether there are goods to advance that fall outside justice, or whether the common good is to be interpreted in national or international vein. However, all of this is within the purview of philosophers.

Philosophers, I suspect, can contribute much less to (2). Once we have determined what should count as the common good, we want to know what procedures are most likely to advance it. Compare two systems, one that allows judges to make some decisions in a politically partisan way and another that requires them to adopt a politically neutral stance. Which system is most likely to advance the common good? I am just not sure. The debate has been focused mostly on the area of fundamental or constitutional rights. Waldron, in contrast with Dworkin, has argued both that decisions by legislatures are important for reasons of authority, but also that fundamental rights will most likely be promoted by restricting the role of judges (see Waldron 1999). For him, it is not just that democratic decision-making is more authoritative when compared with judicial decision-making. It is that legislatures are more likely to produce good outcomes.

Whatever the merits of the normative claim about authority, however, the empirical claim is contentious, and MacCormick does much too little to support it (see also Sadurski 2002). Surely much depends upon the kind of issue that we are considering, the extent to which political decision-making is likely to be sensitive to the interests of all citizens regardless of their tendency to participate in the political process, and so on. For example, in the context of criminal justice, those who are most likely to be oppressed, discriminated against, or otherwise treated unjustly are precisely those who are least likely to participate in the political process.

Furthermore, that is probably not just true of *our* political process, but of *any plausible* political process. That has an impact not only on the authority of political decisions about criminal justice, but also on their tendency to adequately track the interests of those to whom they apply. If courts are more involved in testing the legitimacy of decisions about criminal justice, would our policies be more likely to be fair and just? It is difficult to know, of course, but I suspect that a court that is given the role of scrutinising criminal justice legislation to ensure that the interests of the worst off are adequately addressed might make such legislation more just.[10]

We may well not want courts to have the power to *strike down* legislation, but we might want them at least to have the role of critically scrutinising legislation as it operates in practice, perhaps providing a declaration of incompatibility[11] with the right to a fair criminal trial (or even a newly fashioned 'right to a fair criminal law') to press the legislature to reconsider its policy. A system where courts had such a role may well do better in terms of the quality of legislation than a system where courts fail to engage with the political principles that ought to underpin criminal justice altogether.

Furthermore, it should be noted that the key, in institutional design, is to be imaginative about reform of the executive and the legislature *and* about reform of the courts. To develop our best conception of a system overall, in terms of outcomes, we should avoid the common mistake in the literature on fundamental rights of holding one aspect fixed and focusing on its faults and then recommending that it is the other area where reform will tend to deliver justice. Institutional design must be undertaken in a comprehensive way in ideal theory to provide a horizon for reform in a non-ideal world. I doubt that the current debate on the separation of powers takes this point seriously enough.

6. Conclusions

What I am advocating in this chapter is that legal theorists engage more closely with political theory than many of them have done to date. Whilst two of the most influential legal theorists in recent times, Ronald Dworkin and Joseph Raz, are also two of our most respected political theorists, much that has been developed in legal theory has been detached from the ambitions of political theory. That is in part because legal theorists have tended to be interested in the relatively uninteresting conceptual question that I began this chapter with.

MacCormick, to his credit, devotes relatively little attention to the conceptual question in his book. *Institutions of Law* is a book primarily about the institutional arrangement of law rather than a book about why law is best understood as institutional, and, for me, that is where its main interest lies. It is to his credit

10 Doug Husak, in his recent book, *Overcriminalization*, advocates a constitutional right not to be punished, and draws on constitutional theory to structure scrutiny of criminal legislation. See especially Husak 2007, ch. 3. However, he does not think that the courts are the appropriate body to do that. I would like to see more argument as to why not.

11 Under the *Human Rights Act* 1998, courts have the power to make a declaration of incompatibility where legislation cannot be 'read down' to make it compatible with the European Convention.

that MacCormick has brought to light a question of fundamental importance, and one that can only be answered in general jurisprudence rather than by specialists. But in order to complete that project, the first chapters of the book should have outlined in some more depth MacCormick's commitments with respect to justice rather than his views about the institutional character of law. Whether the character of law is institutional is neither here nor there as far as justifying or critiquing its institutional arrangements is concerned. To answer the question that MacCormick raises, jurisprudence must become a branch of political theory.

References

Cohen, J. (2003), 'In a Democratic Society' in Freeman 2003.

Dworkin, R. (2000), *Sovereign Virtue* (Cambridge, Mass. Harvard University Press).

Freeman, S.R. (ed.) (2003), *The Cambridge Companion to Rawls* (Cambridge: Cambridge University Press).

Goodin, R. (2003), *Reflective Democracy* (Oxford: Oxford University Press).

Hampton, J. (1986), *Hobbes and the Social Contract Tradition* (Cambridge: Cambridge University Press).

Husak, D. (2007), *Overcriminalization: the Limits of the Criminal Law* (Oxford: Oxford University Press).

Kordana, K.A. and Trabachnick, D.H.B. (2005), 'Rawls and Contract Law', *George Washington Law Review* 73:3, 701.

MacCormick, N. (1990), 'Reconstruction after Deconstruction: A Response to CLS', *Oxford Journal of Legal Studies* 10, 539–58.

MacCormick, N. (2007), *Institutions of Law: An Essay in Legal Theory* (Oxford: Oxford University Press.

McMurrin, S. (ed.) (1988), *The Tanner Lectures on Human Values*, Vol. 8 (Salt Lake City: University of Utah Press).

Nagel, T. (2005), 'The Problem of Global Justice', *Philosophy and Public Affairs* 33, 113–47.

Nozick, R. (1974), Anarchy, State and Utopia (New York: Basic Books).

Rawls, J. (1999), *A Theory of Justice* (Oxford: Oxford University Press).

Rawls, J. (2001), *Justice as Fairness: A Restatement* (Cambridge, Mass.: Harvard University Press).

Sadurski, W. (2002), 'Judicial Review and the Protection of Constitutional Rights', *Oxford Journal of Legal Studies* 22:2, 275–99.

Scanlon, T. (1988), 'The Significance of Choice' in McMurrin 1988.

Scheffler, S. (2000), 'Justice and Desert in Liberal Theory', *California Law Review* 88, 965–90.

Tadros, V. (2008), 'Crimes and Security', *Modern Law Review*, 71, 940.

Waldron, J. (1999), *Law and Disagreement* (Oxford: Oxford University Press).

Williams, B. (1985), *Ethics and the Limits of Philosophy* (London: Fontana).

that MacCormick has brought to light a question of fundamental importance and one that can only be answered in general jurisprudence rather than by specialists. [illegible]

References

Cohen, [illegible]
[illegible]

Chapter 7
What is a Legal Transaction?

Jaap Hage[1]

1. A first impression

The notion of a legal transaction (legal act, act-in-the-law, *Rechtsgeschäft, acte juridique*) does not play an important role in the common law tradition, but in the civil law tradition of the European continent it is one of the basic legal notions. Legal transactions are the means by which legal subjects can change the legal positions of themselves or other persons intentionally. Examples from private law are: contracts; terminations of contracts; last wills; transfers of rights; and the creation of rights in rem, such as usufruct and mortgage. Examples from public law: are legislation; and dispositions.

The notion of a legal transaction was probably abstracted from the more specific notion of a contract. In connection with contract formation, an elaborate doctrine has developed in the course of many centuries. The observation that a contract is normally formed on the basis of will (intention) and declaration of it turned out to be useful for understanding other transactions in private law, and then also in public law. And this has lead to a general doctrine about legal transactions, which on the continent plays a crucial role in the doctrines of private law and a somewhat less central role in those of public law. In the relatively recent civil codes of Germany and the Netherlands, legal transactions appear explicitly, with the Dutch code even containing a special part about legal transactions (sections 3: 32–59 of the *Burgerlijk Wetboek*). Although this regulation is mainly intended for application in property law, it can be applied analogously in other fields which lend themselves to it.

In the common law tradition, the notion of a legal transaction was not well developed, but obviously the phenomena that count as legal transactions in the civil law tradition also occur in the common law countries. What seems to be lacking is the general notion of a legal transaction and rules and doctrine that deal with legal transactions in general, rather than with specific phenomena such as contracts

---

1 I want to thank Andrew Halpin and the other participants in the Edinburgh symposium on Neil MacCormick's *Institutions of Law* for their comments on my presentation and an earlier version of this chapter. They made it possible to express my views on legal transactions more clearly. I also want to thank Neil MacCormick for inviting me to his symposium, thereby stimulating me to write this chapter in the first place. Email: Jaap.Hage@METAJUR.unimaas.nl.

and transfers, which count as legal transactions on the continent.[2] In legal theory, however, the idea of a legal transaction has received ample, although implicit, attention in the work of W.N. Hohfeld, who distinguished between a group of legal concepts centred around duties and rights and a group centred around powers and liabilities. This second group derives its relevance for this chapter from its close connection with legal transactions.

The Hohfeldian distinction was repeated by H.L.A. Hart, who emphasised the distinction between duty-imposing rules and power-conferring rules. And the still implicit theory about legal transactions was further developed by the distinction, made by MacCormick, between, on the one hand, institutive and terminative rules, which deal mostly, but not exclusively, with legal transactions, and, on the other hand, consequential rules, which deal with legal consequences that are not attached to events (MacCormick and Weinberger 1986, 52–53).

Although there is a lot of legal doctrine about legal transactions, especially in the continental doctrine of private law, a general theory of legal transactions that abstracts for the specific regulations of the subject in national law still seems to be lacking. In this chapter I try to make a start with remedying this shortcoming and, in doing so, I will take my starting point in the institutional approach to law[3] and will compare my view with the strongly related views of MacCormick on powers and validity, as presented in his *Institutions of Law*.

2. The world of law

We are all familiar with the physical world. It consists of a large number of 'things'[4]: big things, such a stars, galaxies, somewhat smaller things, such as seas and mountains, and small ones, such as viruses, molecules, and quarks, and very much in between, including human beings. These things have characteristics and stand in relations to each other. That things have these characteristics and stand in these relations to each other, are *facts*. The facts in the physical world obtain to a large extent independent of human beings. Think in this connection of the existence on earth of seas, mountains, and many kinds of living things, including those who appeared on the surface of earth before there were humans. And where the facts depend on humans, this is because of the physical interaction between

2 Arguably, the notion of (the exercise of) a legal power takes the place, in the common law doctrine, which is taken by the notion of a legal transaction in continental doctrine. See, for instance, the analysis of such exercise in Halpin 1996 and Spaak 2003.

3 This approach is described in, amongst others, MacCormick and Weinberger 1986; Lagerspetz 1995; La Torre 1999; Ruiter 1993 and 2001; and MacCormick 2007.

4 Intuitively, 'things' may be taken to be everything denoted by nouns (e.g. 'table', and 'rule'), proper names (e.g. 'Jane'), or identifying descriptions (e.g. 'the mayor of New York', 'the rights of minorities').

the human body and other physical things.[5] Think, for instance, of the existence of buildings, roads and artefacts. The social world, or social reality, does not only depend on what is physically the case, but also – and to a large extent – on what people believe the social world is. A fact in the social world can obtain because sufficiently many members of a social group believe it obtains and also believe that (sufficiently many) other members of the group have the same belief, both about this fact and about what the others believe.[6] Jane may, for example, be the leader of an informal group, because most members of the group take her to be the leader and believe that the others take her to be the leader too and believe that the other members do the same. Some rules exist as legal rules because sufficiently many people that participate in a legal system accept these rules as legal rules and believe that others do the same.

In modern societies, however, most legal rules derive their existence and status as *legal* rules from being made in accordance with rules that specify how to make legal rules. They exemplify a second way in which facts in social reality can obtain, namely through the operation of social rules, including legal rules. Social rules deal with how people should behave towards each other, but also with the proper use of language, with the definitions of games, and with the membership of socially defined sets, such as the set of legal rules. If the conditions of these rules are satisfied, their consequences hold in social reality. The part of social reality that is the result of the application of social rules is called the *institutionalised part of social reality*. Typical phenomena within the institutionalised part of the social world are: the existence of money; promises; the law; and everything created through the law, such as officials, legally defined organisations and most legal rules. Let us call the mode of existence in the institutionalised part of the social world *existence as institutional fact*.[7]

The two modes of existence in the social world do not exclude each other. On the contrary, the point of existence as institutional fact is that it generates acceptance. For instance, if somebody is appointed to prime minister, this person derives her status as prime minister from the appointment and the rules that deal with it. To this extent, her status of prime minister belongs to the institutionalised part of the social world. The point of the appointment, however, is that she will be

5 That the physical world is in part the result of causal interaction with the human body does not exclude that the same holds for the social world. The difference that I want to point out is that the social world is not exclusively the result of physical interaction with the human body, where the physical world – to the extent that it depends on humans – is.

6 This theme is extensively elaborated in Tuomela 2002, ch. 5. See also the discussion in MacCormick 2007, ch. 1.

7 This expression is somewhat infelicitous in the case of 'things' (instead of facts) that exist in the institutionalised part of the social world. I take it that the advantage of having a simple expression for this mode of existence outweighs the disadvantage of imprecision.

recognised and accepted as prime minister, and if this point is realised, her status will be based on social acceptance too.[8]

The world of law is part of the social world. In fact, most of the world of law belongs to the institutionalised part of the social world. The existence of large parts of the law is based on the operation of rules which lead to the existence of these facts as result of legal transactions and other events with legal consequences.[9] However, the law also contains parts which only exist because they are believed to exist.[10] Judge-made law in the civilian tradition, customary law, and other unwritten parts of the law, including many legal principles,[11] illustrate that not all of law is institutionalised.

3. Changing the world of law

An illuminating way to look at legal transactions is to see them as intentional modifications of the world of the law. Changes in the world of the law can come about in two main ways, related to the two ways in which this world exists, namely acceptance-based and as institutional fact. Changes in acceptance-based facts cannot be brought about merely by the (expression of the) intention to do so; changes in the set of institutional facts can, but not all of these changes are the outcome of intentional action. To see things in a proper perspective, it is useful to divide up the institutionalised part of the law in subsets, depending on the ways in which these institutional facts come about.

A first division is between facts that are the immediate result of changes in the world and facts that supervene on other facts. An offer and the acceptance thereof

8 In fact, there is a problem if the institutional mode of existence is not matched by the acceptance-based mode of existence. The discussions about the validity of unjust legal rules can well be interpreted as dealing with this very issue. For more on the relation between acceptance-based existence and existence as institutional fact see Ruiter 1993, 52–54.

9 As is well known, this is one of the major themes of Hart's conception of law. See Hart 1994, 77–96.

10 An interesting illustration of this phenomenon is that judge-made law plays a role in civil law systems that is quite similar to that in common law systems, although the former, in contrast to the latter, do not have stare decisis. The fact that a judge has adopted a particular rule in her decision is in the civilian tradition no legal reason why this rule has become a legal rule. But it is, under suitable circumstances, surely a cause why such rules are accepted as legal rules, and it is perhaps also a non-legal reason to accept such a rule as a legal rule.

11 That legal principles are part of the law, but nevertheless do not belong to the institutionalised part of it because they cannot be identified by means of their pedigree, is the main point of Dworkin's initial criticism of Hart's version of legal positivism. See Dworkin 1978, ch. 2.

are events, in the sense of changes in the world. These events normally[12] lead to the existence of an institutional fact, namely a contract between the two parties. That is why the existence of a contract exemplifies *event-based institutional facts*. If there is a valid contract, the parties are legally obligated to do what they agreed to do. This legal obligation does not follow from an additional event, but supervenes on the presence of the valid contract. Therefore, the obligations from a valid contract are *supervening institutional facts*. As will be clear from this example, supervening institutional facts may be the indirect result of events. Contractual obligations are the result of the offer and acceptance thereof that lead to the valid contract. The reason why these obligations are nevertheless categorised as supervening institutional facts is that their relation to the offer and acceptance is mediated by an intervening event-based institutional fact.

The events that lead to changes in the institutionalised part of the world of law can be subdivided into acts and non-acts. If the owner of a building dilapidates it, and the building collapses as a consequence, with casualties as a further consequence, the collapse is an event that leads the owner to event-based liability for the damages. This collapse is not an act. If the driver of an automobile causes an accident through his fault, he becomes liable for the damages too, this time as the result of an act. This act is not a legal transaction, however. It would still not be a legal transaction if the driver caused the accident on purpose, with the intention to become liable for the damages (cf. also MacCormick 1991, 74; and Spaak 2003). The reason why this is not a legal transaction is that the liability does not depend on the intention to create it. A legal transaction takes place, if somebody performs an act with the intention to create particular legal consequences (changes in the world of law), and the law attaches the intended legal consequences to this act precisely *because* they were intended.[13]

> Legal transactions are acts, performed with the intention to bring about changes in the world of law (legal consequences), to which legal rules attach the intended consequences because they were intended.

The schema in Figure 7.1 provides an overview of the division of institutional legal facts based on the different ways in which they come about.

---

12 Changes in the institutionalised part of the legal world are the result of the application of rules. Because rules are amenable to exceptions, not all changes in the world of law that would normally come about are actually realised. Hence the insertion of 'normally'. From now on, I will ignore the possibility of exceptions and skip the resulting use of 'normally'.

13 It may be argued that sometimes contracts are not based on offer and acceptance, but on reliance. In such cases there would, allegedly, be a legal transaction even though the relevant intention is lacking. I would say that in such cases, the legal consequences of a valid contract hold, but that these consequences are not the result of a legal transaction. See Hage 2007b. For a similar argument, but to the effect that these legal consequences are not the result of the exercise of a power, see Halpin 1996.

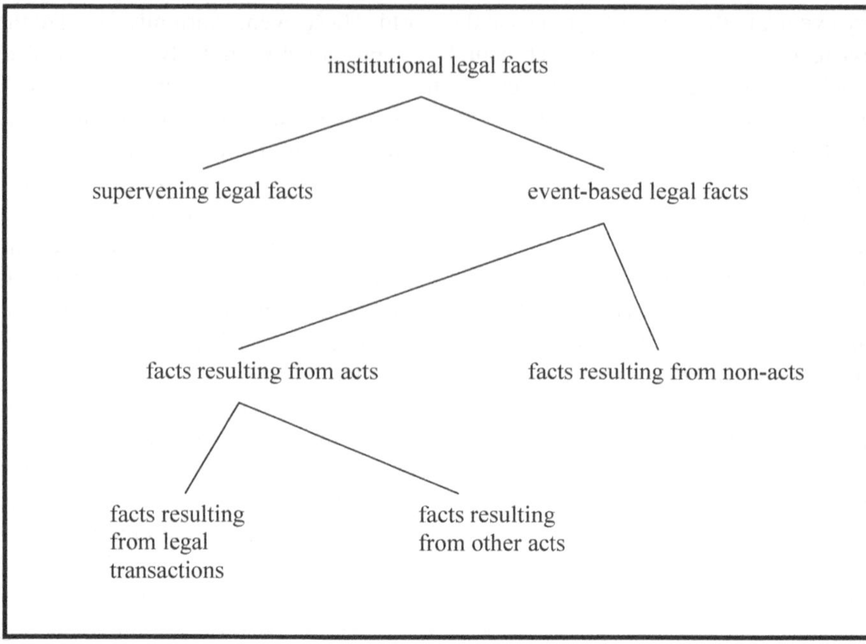

Figure 7.1 Institutional legal facts

4. Constitutive acts

In his paper, 'A Taxonomy of Illocutionary Acts', Searle (1979) made distinctions between types of speech acts which are useful for a better understanding of legal transactions. An auxiliary distinction in this connection is that between directions of fit. It is illustrated by the following example. Suppose I make a shopping list that I use in the supermarket to put items in my trolley. A detective follows me and makes a list of everything that I put in my trolley. After I am finished, the list of the detective will be identical to my shopping list. However, the lists had different functions. If I use the list correctly, I place exactly those items in my trolley that are indicated on the list. My behaviour is adapted to what is on my list. In the case of the detective it is just the other way round; the detective's list reflects my shopping behaviour. If we consider my behaviour as (part of) the world, we can say that my shopping list has the world-to-word direction of fit, because my behaviour must fit the words on the list. The detective's list, on the contrary, has the word-to-world direction of fit, because his list must fit the world (my behaviour).

The direction of fit holds between the propositional content of a speech act and the world. The illocutionary force of a speech act determines which direction of fit is involved. Searle distinguished five main kinds of speech acts:

- *Assertives* commit the speaker to something's being the case. For instance, the sentence 'It is raining' can be used for an assertive speech act. Assertives have the word-to-world direction of fit; they are successful if they are true.
- *Directives* are attempts of the speaker to get the hearer to do something. For instance, the sentence 'Give me your money' can be used for a directive speech act. Directives have the world-to-word direction of fit, and are successful if they are effective.
- *Commissives* commit the speaker to some future course of action. They also have, according to Searle, the world-to-word direction of fit. For instance, the sentence 'I promise to lend you my car' can be used for a commissive speech act. The difference between commissives and directives is, according to Searle, that directives direct the *hearer*, while commissives commit the *speaker*.
- *Declarations* bring about a correspondence between the speech act's propositional content and the world. They have, what Searle calls, a double direction of fit, because the world is made to fit the propositional content of the speech act, while that content comes to fit the world. For instance, the sentence 'I hereby give you my car' can be used for a declaration.
- *Expressives*, finally, express the speaker's psychological state. For instance, the sentence 'I thank you for lending me your car' expresses the speaker's gratitude. Expressives have no direction of fit, because they express, rather than describe the speaker's psychological state.

Searle's analysis of different kinds of speech acts by means of the difference in directions of fit provides a suitable starting point for the analysis of legal transactions. For that purpose it needs to be amended, however. My first amendment is merely terminological. Declarations in Searle's sense are speech acts by means of which facts are created. Searle's own examples include that somebody gets appointed as chairman and that somebody's position is terminated. Since these acts are constitutive (in the case of the termination in a negative sense), I propose to call these speech acts by means of which the world is changed *constitutive acts*, or *constitutives*.[14]

It should also be observed that it is not necessary for constitutive acts to be real *speech* acts. The only thing that is required is that constitutive acts have a propositional content, because that is what is to be made true in the institutional world. Moreover, this propositional content is always determined conventionally, which implies that in theory any event can be attributed any propositional content (cf. Ruiter 2001, 78–79; and Hage 2005, 168–70).

14 Constitutives as acts that bring about changes in the institutionalised part of the social world are made possible by constitutive rules. In a sense, both these rules and the constitutive acts based on them constitute the changes in the social world. Their roles are strongly related, mutually dependent, but nevertheless different.

The second amendment concerns the direction of fit of constitutives. According to Searle they have a double direction of fit, because the world is altered to fit the propositional content of the speech act by representing the world as being so altered (Searle and Vanderveken 1985, 53). This expression, 'double direction of fit', is somewhat misleading, because it suggests that both directions are equally important. If somebody copies the file which contains the text of this chapter, his file comes to be identical to mine, and mine comes to be identical to his. However, his copy of the file comes to be identical to my copy in a more basic sense than the other way round, because his copy of the file is adapted to my copy and not the other way round. Approximately the same holds for the double direction of fit: words come to fit the world only because the world has been adapted to words. Therefore I propose to speak, in the case of constitutives, of a world-to-word direction of fit.

However, the world-to-word fit of constitutives is not the same as the world-to-word fit of directives. An order is a typical example of a directive in Searle's sense. In the present context I use the notion of an order in a technical sense, which makes an order different from a command. Where a command requires a setting in which the commanding person has some authority over the person that is commanded, such a setting may be lacking in the case of orders. Everybody can order anybody. An order will normally exercise some psychological pressure on the hearer to do what he is being directed to do. However, there is no guarantee that the order will be obeyed and that the world will actually come to correspond to the directive's propositional content.[15] That is why Searle writes about the fit of *successful* directives, and 'successful' means in this context *effective*.

Constitutives also need to be successful to create the world-to-word fit, but their success is not the effectiveness, but rather the *validity* of the speech act. Searle correctly remarks that declarations (my constitutives) normally require an extra-linguistic institution, a system of constitutive rules, in order that the declaration may successfully be performed. For instance, there are rules that lay down how the appointment of a chairwoman should take place. If these rules are followed in a concrete case, the appointment in question is valid. The institution not only defines when constitutive acts are valid, but also connects consequences to valid constitutives, e.g., that somebody has become the chairman. These consequences

15 In fact, the very idea that an order, in the technical sense used here, has a propositional content, seems questionable. Suppose that somebody orders me: 'Shut the door!' According to Searle, this order has the propositional content that I shut the door. Going purely by the formulation, however, the order has only an action type (shutting of the door) in an imperative mood as its 'content'. If we interpret the imperative mood as a sign for the illocutionary force, the 'propositional content' would merely be 'shutting the door', not that I shut the door. Apparently the difference between orders and commands goes even deeper than what is suggested in the main text. Since orders do not belong to the set of constitutive speech acts in which I am interested in this chapter, I will ignore the issue.

are *changes* in the institutionalised world that account for the world-to-word fit of constitutives.

To distinguish between the world-to-word fit of constitutives and of directives, I call the world-to-word fit of constitutives *direct*, because these effects are the immediate consequence of the performance of the speech act. I call the world-to-word fit of directives *indirect*, because this fit only obtains if the speech act is followed by the behaviour that it directs the hearer to perform.

The third amendment concerns the analysis of commissives. According to Searle, commissives have the world-to-word direction of fit, which would – in my terminology – be the indirect world-to-word fit. This means that a commissive would only be successful if the behaviour to which the speaker committed himself was actually performed. However, if I make a promise, and nothing extraordinary is the case, I immediately come under the obligation to do what I promised to do. In other words, making a promise has a direct world-to-word fit. Therefore, I prefer to treat promises as a species of constitutives, rather than as a separate category of commissives. In general, it seems to me that commissives are a species of constitutives and therefore need not be a special category.[16]

Commissives have a counterpart in constitutives that impose obligations on others than the speaker. For instance, an officer in the army gives a command to a subordinate soldier. In that way, he imposes on the soldier the obligation to do what was commanded. Let us call these constitutives, which require a setting of rules, *commands*. Commands can then be opposed to orders that do not require such a setting. Anyone can order anybody, and the success of the order only depends on whether it is obeyed. Orders have an indirect world-to-word direction of fit. In opposition to orders, valid commands have the direct world-to-word fit. Their success lies in bringing about an obligation, and only in a derived sense in bringing about behaviour.[17] Where orders are directives, commands are constitutives.

5. Legal transactions as constitutives

Legal transactions can very well be taken as a special species of constitutive acts. They have the direct world-to-word direction of fit, meaning that if a legal transaction is valid, its propositional content becomes true in the world of law as a consequence of the transaction. It might be objected that the consequences of a legal transaction are 'really' brought about, not by the constitutive itself, which is merely an event, but by the constitutive rules that attach the consequences to the constitutive act. In a sense this objection is correct. However, it is correct in

16 Essentially the same point was made by Ruiter 1993, 67f. Notice, by the way, that a similar misguided difference between imposing duties on somebody else and on oneself is presupposed in the definition of a power as the capability to modify *somebody else's* legal position by (declaration of) will. Cf. Halpin 1996.

17 Ruiter 1993, 70f makes the same distinction.

the same way in which the breaking of the window is not caused by the brick that was thrown against it, but by the physical laws that made the window break when the brick was thrown against it. The brick made the window break because of the underlying physical laws. In the same way a legal transaction brings about its legal consequences because of the underlying legal rules.

The view that the legal consequences are 'really' caused by the exercise of the power to bring them about seems less persuasive to me. As I will argue in Section 6 'The rules that govern legal transactions', powers are not independent things, but rather supervene on the presence of a competence, of rules that attach legal consequences to a particular kind of act, and the capability to perform these acts. The exercise of a power is on this view nothing else than the performance of a relevant kind of act. It is this performance, the legal transaction, which, thanks to the underlying rules, leads to the legal consequences. The power has no independent explanatory force.[18]

Although it may seem obvious, at first blush, that if a legal transaction is valid, its propositional content becomes true in the world of law as a consequence of the transaction, the implications of this view are far-reaching. A couple of examples may illustrate the point.

Appointments

Legal transactions can be used to provide persons or organisations with a special legal status. A simple example would be the appointment, by means of a last will, of a person to be one's heir. The consequence of this appointment, if it is valid, is that the person in question has become an heir. The rules that define the consequences of this status – presumably that the heir inherits if the testator dies – become applicable to the appointed person.

In this connection, MacCormick has distinguished between three kinds of rules (see MacCormick and Weinberger 1986, 49–76; and MacCormick 2007, 49–50). *Institutive rules* define how a particular status (institutional fact) comes about. *Terminative rules* specify how the status is lost, or the institutional fact comes to an end. Finally, *consequential rules* attach further consequences to the existence of the status or the institutional fact.

The example about the last will illustrates two important phenomena in connection with legal transactions. The first is that a legal status, for instance that of an heir, by itself does not imply anything in the normative sphere, at least not immediately. Any normative consequences that are attached to this status are

18 It may be possible to take the notion of a legal power as a primitive and to define legal transactions and constitutive legal rules in terms of (the exercise of) powers. That would be comparable to defining causes and causal laws in terms of the power to bring about effects. As this comparison makes clear, I am not persuaded by this alternative way of conceptualising legal transactions and powers.

attached by consequential rules which make other institutional facts supervene on the fact that somebody is an heir.[19]

The second important phenomenon is already given with this last observation, namely that the impact of a legal transaction is very often defined by rules which do not refer directly to the legal transaction itself. The rules that determine the legal consequences of being an heir need not refer to the way in which one has become an heir. It is not necessary for the consequences of being an heir by last will to be different to those of being an heir by statutory provision.

Contracts

In the common law tradition, contracts are often seen as mutual promises.[20] With due respect to the common law tradition, that is a mistake. The point of making promises is to undertake obligations. Although it is possible to undertake obligations by means of contracts, contracts can be also used for other purposes that cannot be achieved by promises. It is for instance possible to appoint, by means of a contract, an arbiter who is empowered to adjudicate disputes that might arise in connection with the execution of (the rest of) the contract. Although it is possible to construct such an appointment as undertaking the obligation to do what the arbiter decides, this would misrepresent the nature of such an appointment.[21]

Although contracts do not necessarily lead to obligations, they often do. Surprisingly, few people see this as involving some variety of the naturalistic fallacy. Nevertheless, contracts bridge the 'gap' between is and ought, and the possibility to create obligations by means of a contract shows that this gap is not really there.[22]

It might be objected that contracts can only bridge the gap between is and ought because the obligation to do what was contracted is based on the rule that contracts ought to be followed. It is, however, questionable whether such a rule exists. The point of contracts is that the facts established by means of the contract hold between the contract parties. The rule that what parties agreed to holds

---

19 As Andrew Halpin pointed out to me, the rules that attach consequences to being an heir cannot have any content, on pain of the status not being the status *of an heir* anymore. I agree, but this shows that the nature of a *particular* legal status is strongly connected with a particular set of legal consequences (and possibly also with a particular set of institutive and/or terminative rules). It does not, however, show that consequential rules cannot or should not be marked off from institutive rules.

20 Cf. section 1 of the Second American Restatement on Contracts: 'A contract is a promise or a set of promises for the breach of which the law gives a remedy or the performance of which the law in some way recognizes as a duty.' Quoted in Beale 2002, 3. See also Fried 1981 and Kimel 2003.

21 Cf. Hart's discussion of the reconstruction of power conferring rules as duty imposing rules, in Hart 1994, 38–42.

22 In fact, Searle used the example of promises to argue that there is no such gap. See Searle 1969, 132–36.

between the parties, in itself does not impose any obligations. Obligations result from most contracts because by means of most contracts the contract parties *create* obligations between themselves. Note the emphasis on 'create'. The obligations were not yet there before the contract; they are the result of the contract. The presumed obligation to obey one's contracts is superfluous. If the contract does not create obligations then there is nothing to obey, and the rule would not make sense. If the contract does contain obligations, then the rule would be that one ought to do what one is obligated to do. That is a tautology which does not make much sense either. So there is no role for the rule that contracts ought to be obeyed, and the obligation to do what one contracted to do does not derive from such a rule. The obligation is created by means of the contract and it is a new obligation that did not yet exist before the contract, not even in the more abstract form of an obligation to obey one's contracts.[23]

Rule creation

In the next section we will see that legal transactions are governed by rules. An important point about legal transactions, however, is that they can also be used to create, derogate or modify rules.[24] To keep the discussion relatively simple, I will confine myself to the creation of new rules.

The first thing to notice is that newly created rules may be duty-imposing rules. The creation of rules can, therefore, lead to the creation of new duties. This should not come as a surprise after the discussion of the previous paragraphs because it is in a sense the same point that was made there.[25] Nevertheless, it may be worthwhile to notice that legal transactions can lead to new duties or obligations in more than one way.

The second thing to notice is that newly created rules very often are *not* duty-imposing rules. This means that there is nothing in the sphere of duties or obligations involved in the creation of rules as such. If the creation of new rules leads to duties, this is because the rules that were created impose duties, not because the creation of rules involves the duty to obey the newly created rules.

23 Some people, mostly logicians, make such a fuss about the gap between 'is' and 'ought' because they identify this gap with the impossibility to derive 'ought' from 'is'. It is impossible to derive 'ought' from 'is' indeed, at least if the only valid type of derivation is considered to be deduction. But, first, it is questionable to restrict valid derivation to deduction, even if this is done by definition. (See my 'Law and Defeasibility' in Hage 2005, 7–32.) And, second, there is no need to treat the constitution of new facts as a kind of logical derivation, so the impossibility of logical derivation does not prove the impossibility of constitution.

24 This is the central theme of Hage 2007a, 359–79.

25 The main difference is that contracts lead to duties for concrete persons or sets of persons, while rules impose duties abstractly specified, and therefore in principle open, sets of persons.

This is an extra argument, in addition to Hart's,[26] against the Kelsenian analysis of power-conferring rules as an oblique kind of duty-imposing rules.

The third thing to notice is that newly created rules may modify the institutional facts that supervene on other facts. As a result, the indirect legal consequences of legal transactions can be changed. For instance, if a new rule is created to the effect that the seller of a good with a price in excess of €1000 has to guarantee the proper functioning of this product during five years, the indirect consequences of a sales contract are modified.[27] It is even possible to make rules that redefine the ways in which legal transactions are to be performed and who has the capacity to perform them. In this sense, legal transactions can define themselves (see also MacCormick 2007, 155).

6. The rules that govern legal transactions

As discussed above, a legal transaction is an act with a propositional content to which the law attaches the consequence that the propositional content of the act is made true in the world of law. This does not sound very simple, but the practice of legal transactions is even more complicated. Not everybody can perform every legal transaction; not every legal transaction can be brought about in the same way; and not all propositional content can be made true. A legal system must have several kinds of rules in order to make legal transactions possible.

MacCormick discusses a number of these rules under the heading of legal powers. He distinguishes no less than nine kinds of rules dealing with the conditions of legal empowering, namely rules that specify (MacCormick 2007, 156):[28]

1. which person(s) have the power;
2. what capacity or competence they need;
3. what circumstances are required for the legal transaction;
4. what circumstances need to be absent;
5. which special procedures or formalities are required;
6. by means of which act the legal transaction can be performed;
7. which persons can be affected by the legal transaction;
8. which general capacity these persons should have;
9. which legal change is brought about by the legal transaction.

---

26 See note 21 above.

27 Remember that the direct consequence of a contract (in the sense of a special kind of constitutive act) is that a valid contract (in the sense of a 'thing' in the world of law) comes about.

28 I have rewritten the conditions to formulate them as conditions for valid legal transactions, rather than conditions for the exercise of legal powers. This difference in form should not make a difference in substance.

All of these factors are relevant, but perhaps they can be summarised under three headings:[29]

1. *Who* can perform
2. *which* legal transaction
3. in *what* manner?

Of these three questions, the second one is – not only literally – the central one. Every legal transaction has by definition a propositional content which indicates what change in the world of law the transaction aims to bring about. The nature of this change can be very diverse. Some changes affect the person who performed the transaction himself, e.g., if he waives a right. Other changes affect somebody else, e.g., if somebody is made an heir, or receives a licence. And there are also changes which do not affect anybody in particular, at least not directly. Legislation is a case in point, because the legal consequence of legislation is that one or more rules are created, modified or abrogated. These rules affect the legal positions of human beings and therefore legislation indirectly changes the legal positions of those humans, but this is an indirect effect of the legislation; the direct effect being 'merely' a change in the set of valid rules. It depends on the contents of these rules whether individual legal positions are thereby changed.[30]

For obvious reasons, the nature of the changes brought about by a legal transaction influences who is competent to perform this transaction. In general, changes that affect the public at large require a public competence, while transactions that only affect the persons involved in it usually merely require that the involved persons have sufficient mental capacities. Despite these differences, all legal transactions have in common the requirement that the persons who perform them have the competence to do so. This competence may be granted by private law – for instance to all human beings and some organisations – or by public law, and is (almost) always connected to a particular legal status, such as the status of a legal subject (the minimal condition), or a public officer.[31]

---

29 Obviously, these three questions are not directly related to the threefold division of rules into institutive, consequential and terminative rules. It looks as if both institutive and terminative rules deal with all of these three questions and that consequential rules are not directly related to legal transactions.

30 MacCormick makes a similar point when he writes that although power-exercising acts purport to change the legal position of some person in some way, it is not always necessary to have the relational character of power in mind. I would state it somewhat stronger: *powers need not be relational*. Brouwer and Hage 2007 argued, against Hohfeld, that duties are not relational either.

31 MacCormick 2007, 156–57, distinguishes in this connection between capacities, based on private law, and competences, based on public law. I agree that there are different grounds for capacities, but I do not see why this would lead to a difference between capacities and competences. Therefore, I use the word 'competence' to deal with the possibility to perform legal transactions as granted by the law.

The notion of competence is closely related, but not identical to the notion of power. A person P has the power to perform a legal transaction T if three conditions are satisfied:

1. There must be rules that make legal transactions of type T possible in general.
2. P is physically and mentally capable to perform the behaviour that counts as performing T.
3. P is legally competent to perform T.

On this analysis, competence is a necessary condition for having the power to perform a legal transaction. Since it does not make sense to confer this competence to somebody who is not capable to perform the required behaviour, or to perform the competence for a legal transaction that does not exist, competence will normally go together with the power to use this competence. Nevertheless, the notions of power and competence are different ones and it is possible to imagine cases where somebody is competent, but unable to perform the behaviour required for the legal transaction.[32]

Moreover, contrary to competence, which is a legal status conferred by competence-conferring rules, power is not a separate legal status, but rather something that supervenes on the presence of a set of rules. If the rules in the world of law are such that the three conditions for P having the power to perform legal transaction T are fulfilled, then P has the power to perform T. There cannot[33] be a separate rule that grants this power to P, although there must be a rule (or a set of rules) that confers on P the competence to perform T.[34]

32 An example would be a person who is unable to write and therefore cannot perform a legal transaction which requires writing performed in person. I would say that such a person has the necessary competence, but lacks the power to do what she is competent to do. Those who are attached to ascribing a power to such persons can use the notion of a legal power. Somebody then has a legal power to perform a particular kind of legal transaction if there are no legal hindrances for this person to perform that kind of legal transaction. I see no real advantage of distinguishing along these lines between powers in general and special legal powers, especially since I see a power as a status that supervenes on other facts and characteristics. See also note 34.

33 'Cannot', because it is not up to the law to grant physical or mental capabilities.

34 A similar point is made by MacCormick 2007, 160, who emphasises that powers are not based on a single power-conferring rule. My point would be that there cannot even exist such a thing as a power-conferring rule, although one or more rules together may have the supervening characteristic of creating a power. Moreover, this power is not a special legal status (like competence) but rather 'the ability to cause or prevent change in some prevailing state of affairs' (MacCormick 2007, 153). Apparently this ability is sometimes (partly) the effect of rules, but when this is the case, the *nature* of the power is not different from when this is not the case. Only the *grounds* of the power are different. So I see no need to make a principal distinction between on the one hand legal powers, or – more in general

Depending on the contents of a legal transaction, there will be demands on the form in which the transaction must take place. These demands may be minimal, like the demands made in the Dutch Civil Code that there is an intention and a form-free declaration thereof (section 3:33 *Burgerlijk Wetboek*), or more complicated such as the Dutch procedure for making a formal statute, which includes several steps, some of which involve group decision making (voting).

In this connection, it pays to notice that being a legal transaction is a legal status itself, which is assigned by the law to one or more events. The rules that assign this status make these events *count as* the performance of a legal transaction, and only in this status of legal transactions do these events have the intended legal consequences. These *counts-as rules*, as I will call them, specify what should be done in order to perform a legal transaction of the intended kind, and which additional circumstances are needed, or – on the contrary – should be absent, in order for this action to achieve the intended status of legal transaction.[35] If all the positive and negative conditions of the relevant counts-as rule are satisfied, the act in question counts as a *valid* legal transaction, and then it normally has the intended legal consequences. Validity in this connection does not mean anything more than that the act in question and its circumstances satisfy all the conditions required for a legal transaction of the intended kind.[36]

Arguably, the validity of a legal transaction not only depends on the underlying act and its circumstances, but also on the intended legal consequences. If these consequences are unlawful, or immoral, the legal transaction may be held invalid. For the evaluation of this view it is necessary to distinguish two questions. One question is whether a particular event counts as a valid legal transaction; the other question is what the legal consequences of the transaction are. If the intended legal consequences are unlawful or immoral, this might be considered as a reason why these consequences should not occur. There are at least two ways in which this result can be obtained. One way is to make the lawfulness and moral suitability of the intended consequences a condition for the validity of the legal transaction. The other way is to make these into conditions for the occurrence of these intended consequences as the result of an otherwise valid legal transaction. Take, for

– powers to modify the institutionalised part of the social world, and, on the other hand, purely physical or psychological powers, such as the power to influence somebody else's behaviour, or to break a brick with one's bare hands.

35 These are the conditions c–f mentioned by MacCormick.

36 Validity in this sense is a potential characteristic of all rule-governed activities, including goals in soccer and arguments in logic. It should be distinguished from validity as the mode of existence of rules. Confusingly, this latter kind of validity often depends on the validity in the first sense of legislative acts. A similar point is made by MacCormick 2007, 160–61, although MacCormick hesitates to use the word 'valid' for the mode of existence of rules, because of the (wrong) Kelsenian association of this kind of validity with bindingness. Rules do not bind, and neither do obligations. Obligations do not bind, unless this bindingness only means that the obligation is an obligation. Rules do not bind, unless this means that they have effects upon social reality (that they are operative).

instance, a contract in which A hires B to commit a murder. Let us assume that this 'contract' does not impose the duty on B to commit the murder. One way to reach this result is to declare the contract invalid; the other way is to say that the contract is valid, but nevertheless does not lead to the duty to commit the murder. Under the first construction the contents of a legal transaction are a factor that determines whether the transaction is legally valid. Under the second construction, the general rule that legal transactions make their propositional content true in the world of law has exceptions.

If the two issues, validity of the legal transaction and occurrence of the intended legal consequences, are clearly distinguished, as they should be, it seems strange to make the validity of the transaction dependent on the desirability of its intended consequences. From a conceptual point of view, the construction that the transaction is valid and that its intended consequences do not follow seems more attractive than the construction that a legal transaction is not valid if its consequences would be undesirable. At the same time, the idea that a legal transaction is valid, although its main objective does not succeed may seem to have drawbacks too. The intermediate 'solution' that a legal transaction is invalid if its main objective is not acceptable, while it is valid if only a detail does not impose duties because of its undesirable nature, seems to suffer from inconsistency.[37] I prefer the view that:

- the desirability of the intended consequences should normally not influence the validity of a legal transaction;
- the validity of a legal transaction provides a contributory reason why its intended legal consequences hold;
- the undesirability of the intended legal consequences provide a contributory reason why these consequences should not hold;
- whether the consequences hold should be the outcome of balancing the contributory reasons for and against.[38]

On this construction, there is no *rule* that brings about the world-to-word correspondence of legal transaction, or – more in general – of constitutives, but merely a 'principle' that leads to a contributory reason why the world should match the content of the constitutive. The implications of this view on constitutive acts go beyond a discussion of the nature of legal transactions.

37 And yet this is the 'solution' chosen in Dutch law.

38 For more on balancing contributory reasons and the logic that deals with it see Hage 2005, 69–86.

7. Conclusions

This chapter provides a first outline of a general theory of legal transactions. To this end, it abstracted from Searle's classification of speech acts to identify the category of constitutive acts. These constitutives operate within a setting of rules and are characterised by the facts that they have a propositional content assigned to them and that their purpose is to make this propositional content true in the institutionalised part of the social world.

Legal transactions are a special case of these constitutives. Their function is to provide participants in the legal systems with the power to bring about intentional changes in the institutionalised part of the 'world of law'. Since these consequences include the presence of duties, legal transactions, and – more in general, constitutives – make it possible to create duties where previously there were none. *In this sense*, they make it possible to bridge the alleged gap between 'is' and 'ought'.

There are several kinds of rules governing legal transactions. These rules specify who is competent to perform which kinds of legal transactions and by means of which acts, and under what circumstances, these transactions are to be performed. They operate against the background of the rule – or, as I argued, the principle – that the propositional content of a legal transaction becomes true in the world of the law. The *competence* to perform a particular kind of legal transaction should not be confused with the power to do so. Competence is a special legal status, usually attached to some other status (e.g., that of legal subject, or of public officer), which is a precondition for performing legal transactions of a particular kind. The *power* to perform a legal transaction involves a combination of factors, including the presence of rules that make a certain kind of transaction possible, the competence to perform this kind of transaction, and the physical and mental capability to perform the necessary act. The power to perform legal transactions is not assigned by some rule, but is a characteristic that supervenes on all the above-mentioned factors.

The above-mentioned subjects do not exhaust the subject of legal transactions. It seems particularly worthwhile to explore how legal transactions, as reasons for their intended consequences, play a role in the law as 'sources' of legal rules and obligations. Another interesting subject, which was only mentioned in passing, is the possibly conventional nature of the 'contents' of a legal transaction. Are these contents completely determined by the intention of the legal subject that performed the transaction? How, then, is the content determined in the case of collective intentionality, or in case the expression of the intention deviates from the 'psychological' intention? These subjects are not only relevant from the point of view of legal theory, but also play a considerable role in traditional doctrine.

References

Beale, H. (ed.) (2002), *Cases, Materials and Text on Contract Law* (Oxford: Hart Publishing).

Brouwer, P.W. and Hage, J. (2007), 'Basic Concepts of European Private Law', *European Review of Private Law* 1, 3–26.

Dworkin, R. (1978), *Taking Rights Seriously* (London: Duckworth).

Fried, C. (1981), *Contract as Promise* (Cambridge, Mass.: Harvard University Press).

Hage, J. (2005), *Studies in Legal Logic* (Dordrecht: Springer).

Hage, J. (2007a), 'Building the World of Law', *Legisprudence* 1, 359–79.

Hage, J. (2007b), 'De wondere wereld van het recht,' Inaugural Address, University of Maastricht 2007.

Halpin, A. (1996), 'The Concept of a Legal Power', *Oxford Journal of Legal Studies* 16, 129–52.

Hart, H.L.A. (1994), *The Concept of Law* (Oxford: Clarendon Press).

Kimel, D. (2003), *From Promise to Contract* (Oxford: Hart Publishing).

La Torre, M. (1999), *Norme, Instituzioni, Valore: per una teoria instituzionalistica del diritto*, (Rome: Laterza).

Lagerspetz, E. (1995), *The Opposite Mirrors* (Dordrecht: Kluwer Academic Publishers).

MacCormick, N. (1991), *H.L.A. Hart* (London: Edward Arnold).

MacCormick, N. (2007), *Institutions of Law*: An Essay in Legal Theory (Oxford: Oxford University Press).

MacCormick, N. and Weinberger, O. (1986), *An Institutional Theory of Law* (Dordrecht: Reidel).

Ruiter, D.W.P. (1993), *Institutional Legal Facts* (Dordrecht: Kluwer Academic Publishers).

Ruiter, D.W.P. (2001), *Legal Institutions* (Dordrecht: Kluwer Academic Publishers).

Searle, J. (1969), *Speech Acts* (Cambridge: Cambridge University Press).

Searle, J. (1979), *Expression and Meaning: Studies in the Theory of Speech Acts* (Cambridge: Cambridge University Press).

Searle, J and Vanderveken, D. (1985), *Foundations of Illocutionary Logic* (Cambridge: Cambridge University Press).

Spaak, T. (2003), 'Norms that Confer Competence', *Ratio Juris* 16, 89–104.

Tuomela, R. (2002), *The Philosophy of Social Practices* (Cambridge: Cambridge University Press).

PART III
Criminal Law

Chapter 8
A Comment on Personality and Corporate Crime

Nils Jareborg

I am quite often asked to give advice on what to read. If I had, a year ago, been asked: 'If I were to read only one book on general legal theory, which one would you recommend?', I would certainly have needed a day or two to find an answer. Today, I can answer the question before it is finished. *Institutions of Law* (MacCormick 2007) is a masterpiece. It is a rich and wise book, a classic already at birth.

Through the years I have found myself holding approximately the same views as Neil MacCormick. It was still a surprise that it was almost impossible to find something to disagree about. I came up with a list of two points.

One of them concerns the discussion on pp. 216–18 on crime as behaviour violating the conditions of civil peace. To be sure, such an explanation is very important in discussing why we have a system of criminal justice, or why we do not dismantle the criminal justice system. But it is of no or little help in deciding where to draw the line between crime and non-crime, that is, in discussing why some type of act or omission should or should not be criminalised. The concept of civil peace is simply too nebulous to be of guidance in such contexts. And I cannot see that the discussion on those two pages is fully coherent.

I leave, however, that topic to Magnus Ulväng – he too could not find much to disagree about. Consequently, I have chosen to say something about the other point on the list. It concerns personality (or personateness) and corporate crime. It is more a question mark than an outright disagreement. My reaction is a yes-but reaction.

1. Yes – an overview

The legal institution of personality is discussed in chapter 5. Juristic persons are discussed on pp. 83–86. From a legal point of view, natural persons (human beings) and juristic (artificial) persons are both persons because personality is defined by law. The ground for recognition is defined as 'capability to have interests and to suffer harm and capability for rational action' (MacCormick 2007, 83). There follows an explanation of why not only human beings, but also 'artificial' persons have such a capability. By the device of corporate personality:

> certain acts or events are recognized in law as bringing into existence a group that has its own personateness distinct from that of any individual human beings who are in law its members, servants or agents. The consequence is that certain acts, decisions and intentions can be imputed to the group as its acts, decisions or intentions. Further, certain states of affairs can be deemed legally relevant interests of the corporation. (MacCormick 2007, 85)

The capacities of corporations are dealt with separately in section 5.7 (MacCormick 2007, 95–96). In principle, there is no difference between natural and juristic persons. But some things that can happen to human beings cannot happen to corporations. And a corporation should not be appointed a judge, and so on.

In other words, personality is not a biological concept but a social concept. Here, one is reminded of the etymology of the word. The Latin word *persona* – in turn derived from the Etruscan word *phersu* – means 'mask' or 'character'.

As regards imputing criminal intent to corporations MacCormick argues that there are no theoretical problems. At p. 91 we read that

> it is possible to regard a corporation as *capax doli*, that is, legally capable of criminal wrongdoing in its own person, as distinct from having mere answerability vicariously for the wrongs of others. (MacCormick 2007, 91)

MacCormick returns to the issue in section 12.4, which discusses corporate crimes (MacCormick 2007, 218–21):

> We can ascribe intentions to corporations on much the same grounds as we can ascribe intentions to individual agents. Both deliberate about what to do. ... For both, deliberations may conclude in decision ... (MacCormick 2007, 219)

What has been established so far? MacCormick has convinced us that *prima facie* there is a basis for holding that corporations can be meaningfully considered morally or legally responsible for wrongful acts. But this is only a first step. So far, there seems to be little difference between the personateness of corporations and that of cats and dogs. These animals are certainly capable of intentional action, and they may even have an understanding of jurisdiction – in the case of cats, however, of feline jurisdiction over human beings.

The next step is to establish that corporations can be blamed. Crime presupposes blameworthiness. A crucial question is whether a corporation can be guilty of negligent omission. Indeed, one could say that all crime is a matter of intentional or negligent omission. A culpable action can be seen as an omission to control or supervise oneself.

In corporations, very often blame focuses on failure to control, supervise or counteract different kinds of activities and consequences of activities. MacCormick does not refer to such questions in terms of blameworthiness. But he does recognise their relevance in his discussion (MacCormick 2007, 220) of a ferry company operating a ferry service from England to Belgium in a way that involves obvious risks of death by drowning of passengers and crew. Of course, the company has a responsibility to ensure that unacceptable risks are neutralised, and there is no *theoretical* obstacle to finding the company guilty of negligent homicide.

The discussion of this case ends in a judgement that the view that corporations cannot commit crimes results in a 'retributive injustice unduly favourable to shareholder interests over those of travellers' (MacCormick 2007, 220). It could be added that there might also be other interests to consider, for example those of the employees. Such interests might work in both directions, but especially in cases of large companies, whose survival would be threatened by heavy sanctions, the result of prosecution might be serious unemployment in a community. Otherwise, up to this point, I agree completely with what MacCormick says. But as I said, my reaction is a yes-but reaction. I stumble on one sentence:

> In many systems, however, the law has groped only slowly and uncertainly to a clear and principled resolution of this matter. (MacCormick 2007, 91)

This is a description, but it must be read as implying criticism. However, I am far from sure that criticism is fully warranted. I would rather commend some cautiousness, some reluctance to impose responsibility for corporate crime – although mainly for practical reasons.

2. But – some problems

Some problems are connected with the question of *imputation of criminality*.

There are, of course, many offences that directly concern the, so-to-speak, normal life of a corporation. They may have to do with commerce and industry, ownership of factories, real estate or means of communication, and so on. It is obvious that corporations can do what amounts to crimes related to taxation, book-keeping, environmental protection, working conditions, export and import, building, transport, fishing, production of dangerous goods, and many others.

But what about offences of a more general character? Offences such as fraud, insider trading, industrial espionage, extortion, perjury, forgery, and so on. While a well organised corporation should regulate who is (primarily) responsible for matters of taxation, it would certainly be odd to have someone within, say, an ordinary transport company responsible for extortion matters. Extortion does not belong to the 'business' of the company.

On the other hand, there are, of course, corporations who make it their business to commit different sorts of crime. But this is no help. On the contrary, it makes everything more complicated.

Business-like criminality left aside, it is, for example, far from obvious that it should be possible for a corporation to commit murder, although there are good reasons to find it possible for a corporation to commit negligent homicide. Suppose a managing director of a car company hires someone to liquidate an overly successful salesman of a competing company. Or that – in an Agatha Christie scenario – six of the seven board members of a company kill the seventh, because she makes a lot of trouble for the company and is heartily disliked by everyone, in addition to being a foreigner. Can the company appropriately be said to have committed murder?

The point is that many types of crime can be committed by agents or employees of a corporation, in the interest of the corporation, in order to benefit the corporation, and even on behalf of the corporation, and it would still be odd to say that the corporation committed a crime. As suggested above, I think that has to do with the offence having no relation to the legitimate business of the corporation.

In other cases, one hesitates to impute responsibility, although it obviously is the business of the corporation to abstain from certain acts or omissions. State agencies, municipalities and other public organs have many duties, the neglect of which amount to criminal offences. One example is unlawful discrimination. Should municipalities and state agencies be capable of committing crimes? Or, since some state agencies are not corporations in their own right, but part of the state, should the state be capable of committing crimes? Should one state agency be capable of prosecuting another state agency? Again, we land in mild absurdity.

It must be concluded that general criminalisation of corporate crime is not something we would wish to have. In any case, there must be many exceptions, and I do not think that such exceptions can be formulated in a way that respects the principle of legality. So what a legislator can do, without endangering legal certainty, is to take small steps, consider one type of offence, or one group of offences, at a time, and take a stand on to what extent corporations should be held criminal. This calls for serious thinking, and it is a kind of task that most politicians and ministry people dislike.

I now turn to some problems concerning the *sentencing* of corporations.

First, the range of possible sanctions is quite limited. Normally, some kind of economic sanction is used, but death (liquidation) is a possibility. So is some kind of restriction of legal capabilities, such as suspension of a licence. In all cases, a disadvantage is that the sanction may seriously harm innocent people, mainly employees and creditors.

Second, dishonest corporations are suicide-prone. They simply disappear. There is nobody to punish. If there were any assets, they are now out of sight, and if they can be traced, it would often be unfair to deprive the present owners of them.

Third, there are problems concerning personal identity. On pp. 81–82, MacCormick discusses the implications of brain transplantation, not yet a problem as regards human beings. But among corporations brain transplantation is normal and frequent. Another difference is that the 'brain' of a corporation consists of a collection of human brains. A brain of a corporation, say the board members and the managing director, can thus be transplanted in pieces which can be put into different corporations. If the pieces are not transplanted, they simply live on as human beings.

All this has implications for the question of personal identity. The analogy between individual persons (human beings) and artificial persons breaks down. It is impossible to let personal identity be tied to the brain. One could, of course, let personal identity be tied to the body. But beyond confiscation of illegal gain this could be unfair. Suppose that a minor negligent company has scrapped its brain and installed a new one that has done what was needed to do to avoid further negligence. In one sense, it is the 'same' company, in that it has similar activities and the same name, say Acme Ltd. But if we take personateness seriously, in an important other sense it is not the 'same' person. We cannot now reasonably blame the company for what was done by another corporate brain. In its present 'personality' the company is innocent. Of course, it takes a lot more than a change of government or board to make United Kingdom or Exxon a 'new person'. All I want to say is that sometimes we encounter serious problems concerning personal identity.

Finally, the law of complicity may also create problems. In some countries, criminal investigation and prosecution are obligatory (if the evidence is sufficient) unless a statutory exception clause is applicable. A prosecutor is not free to pick out one or a few of the perpetrators for prosecution. So normally both the company and some natural person or persons would be prosecuted, although nothing is done by the company that is not done by a natural person. An act or an omission committed by a natural person is what counts as an act or omission by the company. Are both to be regarded as main actors, or is the natural person perhaps a kind of accomplice? Is it fair to hold both persons criminally liable?

The last problem can be solved by creating rules of priority. And certainly, the other problems, too, can be solved by creating detailed rules.

In short, what I want to say is that wholesale recognition of corporate criminal responsibility will probably create immense confusion. Progress in this area of law can proceed rationally only in small steps, and a lot of creative thinking must be invested.

References

MacCormick, N. (2007), *Institutions of Law: An Essay in Legal Theory* (Oxford: Oxford University Press).

different conditions. If the pieces are not transplanted, they simply live on as human beings.

All this has implications for the question of personal identity. [illegible]

[illegible]

Chapter 9
Criminal Law and Civil Peace

Magnus Ulväng

1. Introduction

This article is a response to Neil MacCormick's discussion on criminal law in chapter 12 of *Institutions of Law* (2007). I will focus primarily on MacCormick's definition of *crime* as 'behaviour violating the conditions of civil peace.'

MacCormick introduces his standpoint by stating that there is a convincing argument in John Locke's assumption of the existence of a universal right to punish, and

> if everyone were in the position of having to defend her or his own rights against all comers, and having to take her/his own steps to obtain some remedy from, or to punish, anyone who invaded their rights, the prospects for civil peace would be slim. (MacCormick 2007, 207)

Hence, civil society is dependent on states establishing a system of criminal law (including criminal and procedural institutions) in order to secure civil peace and, consequently, the state claims to exercise a monopoly over physical force and coercion.

Concerning the questions 'What is a crime?' and 'What differentiates a crime from other wrongdoing?' MacCormick follows his line of reasoning by establishing that crimes are species of punishable wrongs, and – further – that punishment ought only to be applied to 'serious and wilful wrongdoings' (MacCormick 2007, 209–10). These stipulations, taken together with the constraints stemming from the principle of a law state (rule of law), guarantee some form of acceptable justification for a criminal law system.

MacCormick's reasoning initially seems indisputable, but it rests on the assumption that Locke is right in his postulation that there is a 'universal right to punish'. As a criminal lawyer, I am somewhat hesitant to accept this assertion a priori, at least if one takes it as a *normative* statement. As a descriptive or empirical statement it is probably true that a 'right' to punish (or rather a practice of punishing) exists, but this is somewhat different from a normative justification. Certainly, if there is anything that is fundamentally problematic with criminal law, it is finding adequate answers to the questions concerning:

- why we punish at all (i.e. what is the purpose of intentionally inflicting some sort of pain or harsh treatment);
- what gives us the right to punish; and
- what are the functions of punishments.

My discussion is not to be understood as a critique of McCormick's analysis in chapter 12. On the contrary: it is difficult to disagree with anything MacCormick says in *Institutions of Law*. However, I think it is important to further elaborate the assumption of a universal right to punish, and I want to address some questions concerning the relationship between criminal law and interest in preserving civil peace. I am somewhat inclined to think that there is – or at least ought to be – more to the question of why we have a criminal law system (at all) than simply the empirical evidence provided by certain features of criminal law systems. In other words, I do not believe it is sufficient to adhere to a universal right to punish in order to offer a general justification for the existence of criminal law. Furthermore, depending on how we formulate a general justification for imposing punishment, I want to examine what the effects are on the principles of criminalisation and the permissible scope of the criminal law.

The remarks made here should be regarded as supplementary to MacCormick's discussion on the normative boundaries of criminal law. In order to make any sense of my comments it ought to be observed that I assume that there is a clear distinction between the following questions:

1. *Why* do we punish (at all)?
2. *What* do we (ought we to) punish?
3. *How* are we to punish (in terms of rationales for sentencing)?

These questions – which represent crucial distinctions in criminal law – are often treated as one and the same. But the answer to a 'why'-question differs from the answer to a 'what' or a 'how'-question. In recognising these distinctions it becomes obvious that criminal law has a more complex structure than might appear at first sight. The distinctions reveal a multi-layered normative structure, and different types of reasons are relevant on each level.[1]

---

1 An important contribution to the illumination of this structure was made by Hart. By separating 'General Justifying Aim' from 'Distribution of Punishment', he made it clear that the question of why we have a criminal law system could have a utilitarian explanation, whereas the question of how we ought to punish is dependent on retribution (Hart 1968, chs 1, 7 and 9). This distinction has later been developed in the doctrinal writings of criminal law. For further reading see Roxin 1966, 377 ff, Jareborg 1992, ch. 7, Honoré 1999, and von Hirsch & Ashworth 2005, ch. 2.

2. General justification of criminal law and civil peace

The practice of punishing 'wrongs' by imposing sanctions which cause pain or suffering has a very long historical tradition. Punishment can be described as a social institution, which has existed – and still exists (in some form) – in every society.

Discussions about the reasons for having a criminal law system and institutions of criminal sanctions are probably as old as the tradition of punishment itself. In modern writings on the general justification for criminal law it is naturally assumed that the criminal law and sanctions referred to are imposed by *states*. This has, however, not always been the case, and it should be remembered that state-controlled (modern) criminal law is a rather recent phenomenon. It was not actually until after the Enlightenment that, at the beginning of the 19th century, states monopolised criminal law. The fact that the roots of the practice of punishing lie so deeply in history complicates its adaptation to its present functions.

In the distant past, and for most of the Middle Ages, criminal sanctions were predominantly a matter between the parties involved and their families (relatives, clans etc.). Vengeance, blood-feuds or mere financial settlements were the normal means of settling disputes where 'wrongs' or 'crimes' had been committed. It is, therefore, probably true that when nation states evolved in Europe, and legislative power was allocated to a single sovereign, one of the aims of a centralised criminal law was to minimise the effects of uncontrolled feuds, which caused much disturbance in fragile and largely non-institutionalised societies.

As a starting point, we can thus conclude – with MacCormick – that a definition of crime as 'behaviour violating civil peace' is one important answer to why we have a criminal justice system at all. It seems to be true that criminal law – on an overall level – seeks to preserve civil peace and avoid private justice by criminalising specific deeds and monopolising violence within an institutionalised system. The idea behind this is to remove control over these kinds of conflicts from the citizens. Such a viewpoint is neither controversial nor new.

So far we have only established that punishment and criminal law are deeply rooted historically, and that monopolisation of criminal law seems to have something to do with sovereigns taking de facto control of the tradition of punishing in order to guarantee stability.

My point now is that an overall description stating that criminal law seeks to ensure 'civil peace' is too simple if we examine the criminal system and its functions in a modern and institutionalised state. Criminal law is thus (and perhaps first and foremost) an institution for distributing instrumental censure within a regulated practice of sentencing. I would, therefore, like to raise the question of whether McCormick's definition (mentioned above) really is helpful when it comes to defining criminal law and its boundaries today.

It is important to note some obvious features of criminal law as an integrated institution of society which concern the task of preserving stability and the conditions for civil peace. It should be remembered that criminal law is never the only solution, and that maintaining or preserving 'civil peace' is not a matter exclusively reserved to criminal law and its institutions. Societies have an interest in upholding civil peace and this aim is expressed in many ways, e.g., by promoting social welfare, economical stability, education, democracy, plurality etc. The creation of a tolerant, decent and peaceful society is thus the product of a vast number of factors.

In this context criminal law differs from all other types of law since it is purely repressive. It does not seek to solve conflicts or promote welfare or social values. The repressive nature of criminal law and punishment gives its practice a negative character, and it is acknowledged by many criminologists and criminal lawyers that punishment is not a particularly efficient way of solving conflicts or maintaining peace and stability. On the contrary: punishment (and especially imprisonment) actually causes instabilities in societies, and it is open to dispute whether it is a fair method for upholding a civil society. At best criminal law can function as a safeguard protecting the interests of individuals, or public interests, or collective interests. Many would argue that criminal law actually aims to *protect individuals from the state* (in the form of abuse of power). By formalising the practice of punishing, it becomes possible to at least control and constrain the institutional causing of pain, thus indicating that criminal law (and the state in itself) actually poses a threat to civil peace. Regardless of whether or not one accepts this description, we can at least conclude that any society ought to be careful in its use of criminal law, and sceptical of a public activity which causes so much harm and has such contested results. It also reminds us that there is a normative problem concerning punishment and the mere existence of criminal law.

So far, very little has been said about why we punish. Is preserving civil peace the ultimate general justification and, if so, what makes us believe that by punishing someone we will preserve civil peace?

In modern writings one finds two different justifications for preserving a criminal law system. The first is based on utilitarian concerns, i.e., the justification for having criminal law is the prevention of crime. The second focuses on the retributive aspect of punishment. This justification is not deduced from any consequences (in terms of positive or negative general prevention) but is instead based on the concept of deservedness, i.e., wrongdoing deserves punishment, and since punishment connotes 'blame', criminal law is justified as a way of communicating censure (von Hirsch & Ashworth 2005, 12). In its purest form, sheer wrongdoing justifies retribution.

Both the utilitarian/instrumental and the retributive/deontological theory can be criticised. The following questions reveal simple, but important, examples of the difficulties:

- Why must wrongdoing invoke (state sanctioned) harsh treatment?
- Why must punishment be imposed by the state?
- Why is punishment deserved?

- Must criminal law be effective (in preventing crime) in order to be justified?
- Are there any moral/ethical limits to punishments, and, if so, what are they?

Most criminal law theorists today find neither purely utilitarian nor purely deontological justifications to be fully satisfactory. Instead, the tradition of upholding a criminal law system (with its institutions) is usually justified using reasons derived from both of these theories, thus acknowledging that criminal law has many aims or functions.

I believe that the purpose of criminal law is most closely connected to some idea of crime prevention. It is through prevention that criminal law seeks to protect certain important interests. The assumption then is that the state (sovereign, democratic state etc.) wants to influence people to act in a certain way. This purpose can also – and ought to – be supported by retributive arguments (censure) in order to separate punishment from other measures and criminal wrongs from 'other wrongs'. At the same time it is necessary to give proper consideration to the fact that punishment involves censure and blame; criminalising acts and distributing punishment is part of institutionalised moral communication, which differs from other forms of government steering. One justification for criminalising an act is that it causes harm, and harmful behaviour deserves blame, and must be met with some sort of harsh treatment.

If this is what MacCormick means by invoking the aim of civil peace as justification, then he – just like Hart or the German school of positive general prevention – partly advocates the consequentialist point of view. I do not in any way disagree with such a position. On the contrary – one way to preserve conditions of civil peace is to *prevent harm*. On the other hand, if MacCormick accepts that punishment and criminal law (as an institution) are equally concerned with questions of desert, then the interest in preserving civil peace can hardly be the sole reason why someone deserves censure, blame and punishment.

However, 'civil peace' is a broad concept and there are, of course, many ways of preserving stability in societies. Regardless of whether criminal law is justified by utilitarian or deontological arguments, or a combination of both, I believe it is a mistake to assume that criminal law can take as its starting point the assumption that the right to punish is universal. Empirically this might be true, but within a normative theory of the (institutions of) law we must constantly ask why we choose to maintain a system which causes so much pain and whether or not it is justified. Locke's assertion ought, therefore, to be abandoned in favour of a justification of punishment and the institution of sanction that is morally acceptable.

If the aim of a criminal law system is to preserve something (civil peace) or avoid a threat to civil peace, then one has to be concerned with questions as to whether the system is effective (enough), what ethical limitations on punishments exist, what behaviour really entails harm, whether civil peace overrides other interests (such as fair imputation), and whether it is morally justifiable to punish a person (A) in order to prevent others (B, C or D) from committing crimes.

As a preliminary conclusion I think MacCormick is certainly correct in underlining the interest in peaceful civilian coexistence when seeking an *overall aim* for the organisation of society and thus the acceptance of coercive measures such as punishment. But I believe that it is necessary to emphasise that the justification for criminal law is much more complicated than simply concentrating on a single – though necessary – aim. Perhaps 'civil peace' could be labelled an 'umbrella concept', which could serve as a necessary ulterior condition for any interference on the part of the state to limit freedom or security. The concept, however, needs substance; otherwise it becomes empty and thus subject to possible exploitation by either unlimited utilitarianism or legal moralism.

3. Criminalisation and civil peace

Let us now turn to the 'what'-question, and the justification of criminalising certain acts or omissions. As pointed out above, this question is different from the 'why'-question (even though the justifications in answer to the 'why'-question will have implications for answering the 'what'-question).

When it comes to the questions of 'what is a crime' and 'what ought to be a crime', using the concept of 'civil peace' to make these distinctions becomes even more problematic. The question of what needs to be criminalised in order to secure civil peace is essentially empirical. If someone were to ask whether or not a certain act (X) ought to be a crime – or why an act (Y) is or is not a crime – one would find little guidance in the concept of civil peace. The only feature common to crimes is that – according to the legislator or the courts – they are in some way assumed to cause some relevant (risk of) harm. Yet this leaves unanswered both the questions asked above; the distinction between what 'ought to be crime' and 'ought not to be crime' remains to be made.

Given these limitations, I think it is necessary to supplement the overall purpose behind having a criminal law system with a normative theory of criminal law which could offer some guidance as to why some behaviour (act or omission) is wrong, and when it is justifiable to criminalise such behaviour (and perhaps most importantly – when it is *not* justifiable). When someone commits a crime, this becomes a reason for *condemning* or *blaming* the person and for *imposing censure.* This is what distinguishes crimes from other actions, and therefore necessitates the inclusion of a moral component in every decision to criminalise an act.[2] This is not, of course, to say that a moral consideration is sufficient grounds for criminalisation, or that all inherently immoral conduct ought to be a crime (see also Feinberg 1984, 27). The moral consideration serves only to ensure that there are good reasons for criminalising an act and imposing censure.

2 In this sense we are (perhaps) all 'soft legal moralists' (see also Duff 2007, 84 ff).

Assigning blame is complex and the fact that criminal law – the only legal institution to do so – imposes censure explains the somewhat exclusive character of this discipline. A normative theory can (and must) supply reasons why certain behaviour is considered wrong, and why it deserves censure. MacCormick, thus, quite rightly says that to punish becomes 'unintelligible without some proposition about the moral character of the act in respect of which the punishee is punished' (MacCormick 2007, 211).

So how could the concept of civil peace be of any guidance? It is obvious that crimes that are *mala in se* constitute moral wrongs which deserve blame and censure, but not primarily because they violate civil peace. The fact that certain acts, e.g., murder or rape, violate civil peace is a (i.e., *one*) reason to have a criminal law system (on the basis that punishment might prevent future crime or because the murderer or rapist deserves censure). But to state that such behaviour is a violation of civil peace tells us little about why the deeds are blameworthy. Blameworthiness is connected with harming a protected interest, and the justification for censure is derived from a moral principle that we ought not to harm others.

Moving over to *mala prohibita*, one can of course – with MacCormick – argue that prohibitions of this kind can be justified because '(e)ach act of wilful non-compliance weakens a scheme from which all, including the violator, draw benefit' (MacCormick 2007, 214) and that 'no individual would have sufficient reason to act in ways that counter the disadvantage or procure the positive value, save in the context of a relevant, universal, and reasonably well-enforced prohibition' (MacCormick 2007, 213).

MacCormick presents an excellent depiction of the reasons behind prohibitions expressed as *mala prohibita*, recognising that the justification depends on the context and the relation between the behaviour and either greater harm (in the future) or the fostering of a prized element in the common good (MacCormick 2007, 214).[3] But it becomes problematic when MacCormick concludes that 'what is wrong about committing crimes is that it involves some wilful form of behaviour that violates civil peace' (MacCormick 2007, 216).

This is – again – a descriptive argument. It probably fits well with most *mala in se* crimes, but it does not explain *mala prohibita*, and or why crimes are wrongs or what kind of acts ought to be criminalised. If one were to answer this question by saying 'any behaviour that violates peace', the argument becomes circular.

Explaining the wrongfulness of committing crimes in terms of their effect on civil peace has further implications. If we take this requirement that an act disturbs the civil peace seriously, we run into problems if, on the one hand, we

3 It should be noted that it is impossible to draw a clear or sharp distinction between *mala in se* and *mala prohibita*. This makes this separation less illuminating and less helpful when we search for good reasons to criminalise an act. I will argue below that good reasons for criminalisation can only be found if the actual behaviour represents some sort of (risk of) harm to a specific interest, and that the offender can be held responsible for the consequences of his actions.

have very blameworthy acts and, on the other hand, no empirical evidence of the existence of this kind of behaviour. Consider, for example, insurrection. Could we refrain from criminalising such behaviour simply because there is nothing to support the assumption that it actually occurs and actually disturbs the civil peace? I presume not, since if someone were to start a revolt we would probably consider it dangerous, harmful and worthy of censure. But then, what is wrong with a crime is not the effects it has on civil peace but instead the harm, or presumed harm, the behaviour entails.

MacCormick's definition is not sufficiently inclusive: much behaviour that is morally abhorrent – and which could be said to empirically violate the civil peace to a greater extent than regulatory offences – is *not* criminalised. Consider for example acts such as not paying debts to creditors, ruining a company (or a country) through poor economic management, committing adultery, lying to your friends, providing insufficient access to medical care or education (thereby creating poor health and illiteracy), misusing power to degrade or humiliate employees, friends, fellow citizens, etc.

Further, many non-criminal disciplines also seek to preserve a peaceful and civilised society, e.g., fiscal law (allocating resources for the distribution of common wealth), property law, labour law, social law, public law, etc. Violations of rules of this sort are not often criminalised, but instead met with an *administrative sanction or tort liability*. What distinguishes criminal sanctions from other sanctions, then, cannot be the immanent threat posed to civil peace. Instead, the distinction is connected with the question as to whether there are good reasons for imposing blame.

One could of course argue that this is just a positivistic protest which only proves that criminal law can reflect conflicting values, and that we cannot ignore the existence of conceptual limits to what can be done using certain kinds of institutional means (MacCormick 2007, 211). But the point is that such a response only works if the criticism is directed towards the dichotomy of law/morals (i.e., is/ought). Here, the question concerns whether the ulterior and necessary common feature of any 'crime' (and what is wrong with a crime), is the fact that it violates civil peace. If there are too many exceptions from such a maxim, then the proposition must be false or at least incomplete.

All that has been said above would also be true for *mala prohibita*. Taken as a descriptive statement, MacCormick's depiction of crimes as wrongs that violate civil peace is over-inclusive. Many regulatory offences can scarcely be said to disturb civil peace in any sense. Consider, for example, smoking illegal substances, purchasing sexual services between consenting adults, not following EU-directives in the area of agriculture, possessing images of child pornography retained from internet websites etc.[4] It could be argued that a lot of the prohibitions (justified

4 If the counter-argument is that this kind of behaviour actually does disturb civil peace, it only proves my point – i.e., that criminal law without a normative theory becomes boundless, and that MacCormick's definition presumes the existence of a society that

as *mala prohibita*) could actually be removed from the register of 'crimes' and instead be dealt with in other areas of law, e.g., administrative law and sanctions. Examples of such acts of misdemeanour are: mild disturbance in public places; failing to deliver information to state agencies; and other petty offences that result in fines. Some criminal law scholars argue that such a separation is both possible and preferable, and an example of such a system which clearly separates crimes from regulatory offences (*Ordnungswidrigkeiten*) can be found in Germany (see, e.g., Eser 1961, Mattes 1977 and 1982, and Weigend 1988). According to this doctrine, it is possible to dismantle a major part of the criminal law and deal with many prohibitions within administrative law. In this case, it is not necessary to use criminal law in order to uphold civil peace; it is sufficient to have measures and sanctions of some sort in order to control threats to civil peace.[5]

Adding a normative framework to MacCormick's definition would offer a justification for making actions, such as insurrection, a crime (it violates or threatens a legitimate interest which causes harm to other people), and what would similarly justify criminalisation of many *mala prohibita* is, at least in my view, that behaving in the proscribed manner is blameworthy in itself, because *it creates a(n) (enhanced) risk of greater harm to some protected interest.* It may be justifiable to criminalise the violation of the prohibition in order to prevent the risk of harm.

Whether or not criminalisation is justified depends on the weight of the protected interest, the distance between the mere risk-taking and the harm and whether or not the offender can be held responsible for the consequences of his actions.[6] We can, for example, accept criminalisation of minor pollution caused by (many) people if in the end the aggregated harm is substantial and threatens

---

already recognises the moral boundaries that I think should be part of the foundations of criminal law.

5 As a counter-argument, and perhaps as a paradox, it could nevertheless be argued that regulatory offences ought to be dealt with as *criminal offences*, in order to create acceptable control of the state and its distribution of sanctions. In this case, what threatens stability and civil peace and legitimises criminalisation is actually the exercise of state power. In the interest of controlling the state in its practice it would be necessary (and justified) to criminalise behaviour, even though such behaviour merely constituted violation of a prohibition.

6 This is also true in cases of provocative behaviour that threatens civil peace (see and compare MacCormick 2007, 217 ff, 265). The reasons for invoking criminal law must be that the provocateur's behaviour actually represents some (risk of) harm to others. Regardless of whether or not acts like drawing cartoons with religious motives, intercourse between consenting adult siblings, etc., creates moral panic in society (or otherwise causes a threat to civil peace), it would not make it more or less justifiable to criminalise the act. In fact, the example with the reaction to the publishing of the 'Muhammad caricatures' proves that even though certain behaviour actually threatens civil peace, it is unclear that it would be justified to use criminalisation to prevent such behaviour. We still need an explanation to what is wrong with the behaviour and why it is justified to blame the provocateur and hold him criminally responsible for the consequences of his behaviour caused by *other* people.

the whole environment. We can also accept criminalisation of rather low-risk behaviour – e.g., a general prohibition on the possession of knives in public places or the use of defective cars – as long as the behaviour creates a potential risk of severe consequences of causing greater harm (bodily harm, etc.).

My point is that in neither of the examples mentioned above can the justification of (or the reasons behind) the criminalisation be that the behaviour 'violates civil peace'. The actual violation of the prohibition neither disturbs civil peace nor justifies punishment; instead it is the risk-taking (accumulated, aggregated or in form of abstract endangerment) that *can* be considered a sufficient reason for criminalisation.

Once again, I believe the concept of civil peace is of little use as a substantive part of criminal law theory. Taken as a normative statement, it tells us only that the avoidance of harm as an over-arching purpose helps to preserve conditions of civil peace. With crimes that are wrong in themselves, the two criteria correspond (avoid harm – violate civil peace), but as a tool for legitimising, or justifying, why something other than *mala in se* ought (or ought not) to be a crime, the instrument is too blunt. It works on a general level; but we are not solely interested in maintaining civil peace. We need a justification relating to the moral character of the behaviour which could explain: (1) why we chose to communicate the censure (to the offender as well as to community as a whole), and (2) how we publicly evaluate the conduct of the offender through punishing and imposing censure. It becomes virtually impossible otherwise to separate harmful acts that abuse other people (blameworthy acts which could be deemed criminal) from harmful acts that do not involve any reprehensible disregard of anyone's interest (accidents, etc.). Without such a normative theory, we lose the possibility of criticising the criminal law system and what is considered blameworthy by politicians, the legislator or the courts.

Perhaps all this only proves that criminalisation is just one way of internalising norms. Whether norms are, first and foremost, internalised through criminal law is highly disputable. What is considered to be blameworthy and reprehensible behaviour, posing a threat to civil peace, is usually determined through informal social control and conventional morality. Criminalisation is justified if, and only if, the conduct could be said to be blameworthy and represent some relevant form of harm (to others). Otherwise we risk treating people as a means to an end. There ought also to be a secondary requirement that the criminalisation is to some extent effective. Imposing pain and suffering without even the prospect of a preventive effect must be considered both meaningless and immoral. This position differs somewhat from a description where criminal law – through crime prevention – seeks to secure civil peace.

4. Conclusions

Nothing I have discussed in this article contradicts MacCormick's opinions as expressed in chapter 12. I have simply tried to supplement the description of the functions of criminal law, and thus argue that we need a normative theory of criminal law that would enable us to distinguish crimes from non-crimes, as well as what ought to be criminalised from what ought not to be criminalised.

I believe that MacCormick presupposes such a normative framework, in which case most of what has been said here is superfluous. But the *formulation* of the aim and purpose accorded to criminal law in *Institutions of Law* is somewhat unfortunate, since it may give the impression that the most important relevant framework is the interest in protecting civil peace. When we justify criminal law, we should never start with the assumption that something is necessary in order to preserve civil peace, and then ask whether there are any moral constraints. Instead we ought to begin with the normative element and ask why we think it is appropriate to intentionally inflict pain or suffering on someone. Just because we live in Scotland or Sweden, we should never assume that we have a universal right to punish. Such a starting-point can be very dangerous and our practice and institutions of criminal law should always be subject to moral deliberation. Empirical or instrumental justification can mask such an obligation.

Hence, the normative framework ought not to be a sub-principle constraining the use of criminal law. On the contrary, I think that the moral justification must come first. This is not to take a natural-law view or make any claims that criminal law must be consistent with morality in the sense that morally bad law cannot be valid criminal law. Nor have I tried to defend legal moralism in any strict sense. But criminal law, as an institution, is completely saturated with ethical/moral assumptions, principles, etc. Since punishment involves condemnation and blame, to ascribe to a crime a certain amount of 'moral wrongness' becomes a necessary condition of criminalisation.

The aim, or the function, of criminal law must, therefore, be derived from a rather complex normative order. In order to be able to answer the questions of what the purpose, function or aim of criminal law is, or what ought to be the permissible scope of criminal law, it is necessary to explore the institutions of criminal law and work out a (specific) normative theory that fits the specific criminal law system under investigation. Such a theory would no doubt differ widely depending on which system and what institutions were subjected to examination. At the same time, I am quite convinced that the concept of civil peace is too nebulous to provide any guidance in such contexts.

References

Duff, A. (2007), *Answering for Crime* (Oxford: Oxford University Press).

Eser, A. (1961), *Die Abgrenzung von Straftaten und Ordnungswidrigkeiten* (Würzburg).

Feinberg, J. (1984), *Harm to Others* (Oxford: Oxford University Press).

Hart, H. L. A. (1968), *Punishment and Responsibility* (Oxford: Oxford University Press).

Honoré, T. (1999), *Responsibility and Fault* (Oxford: Oxford University Press).

Jareborg, N. (1992), *Straffrättsideologiska fragment* (Uppsala: Iustus förlag).

MacCormick, N. (2007), *Institutions of Law* (Oxford: Oxford University Press).

Mattes, H. (1977 and 1982), *Untersuchungen zur Lehre von den Ordnungswidrigkeiten, Band I–II* (Berlin).

Roxin, C. (1966), 'Sinn und Grenzen staatlicher Strafe', *Juristische Schulung* 6, 377–387.

von Hirsch, A. and Ashworth, A. (2005), *Proportionate Sentencing* (Oxford: Oxford University Press).

Weigend, T. (1988), 'The Legal and Practical Problems Posed by the Difference between Criminal Law and Administrative Penal Law', *Revue Internationale de Droit Pénal* 59, 67.

PART IV
The Methodology of Jurisprudence

Chapter 10
Methodology and the Articulation of Insight: Some Lessons from MacCormick's *Institutions of Law*

Andrew Halpin[1]

1. Introduction

Neil MacCormick's *Institutions of Law* (2007) provides stimulating access to a rich range of issues to do with the law, as the variety of contributions to the present volume attests. Subtitled *An Essay in Legal Theory*, it is an intellectual inquiry on the nature of law, and alongside such insights it brings to our understanding of different aspects of the law, it illustrates and raises broader issues regarding the general enterprise of intellectual inquiry, the value of conceptual analysis, and the role of theoretical methodology. These broader issues form the subject for this chapter. They are made all the more attractive to pursue by MacCormick's own reflections within his book that relate directly to them.

It will be helpful to state some background assumptions to the particular study to be made here of themes that are in themselves open to considerable controversy. It will be assumed that the principal purpose of intellectual inquiry is to gain insight on a subject over which, prior to the inquiry, there existed a certain lack of understanding.

That is not to say, in general, that such insight must be of practical value, since the subject matter may be vastly removed from the world of practical endeavours or practical processes. Nor is it to say that the increase in understanding gained by the new insight corresponds to a greater grasp of how the world is or how something within it works. Intellectual inquiry may be undertaken into a subject that is itself a theoretical construct, which from the viewpoint of the inquirer is even regarded as presenting a false view of the world or how something within it works. For example, one may wish to gain a clearer understanding of Aquinas's view of natural law while utterly rejecting his natural law perspective.

It should also be noted in passing that the nature (as well as the fruit) of intellectual inquiry may be more or less theoretical. We tend to distinguish middle

1 I am grateful to Bebhinn Donnelly, Dennis Patterson and William Twining for helpful discussions on the topics covered here, as well as to participants at the Edinburgh Leverhulme Symposium in December 2007 for valuable comments on an earlier draft.

range theory which is more empirically grounded and focused, from the more abstract grand theory (Merton 1968; Skinner 1985); and when theorising about theory, we talk of meta-theory. On the other hand, some intellectual inquiry is barely theoretical at all, though strenuously intellectual in exercising the intellect (consider the translation of a newly found ancient text). For present purposes we shall assume that the kind of intellectual inquiry we are concerned with is theoretical in nature, but will not need to delve into the precise level of the theory involved.

Where the subject matter of an intellectual inquiry is a practice found in the world, such as law, and the principal purpose of the inquiry is to inquire into that practice, rather than to engage with the history of ideas on that practice, or a scholarly study of a particular intellectual outlook upon that practice, then a mutually reinforcing dynamic holds between theory and practice. Sound theory will yield practical insight; and, the experience of practice will form a testbed for the soundness of theory. These conditions are taken to apply to MacCormick's book (as well as to other significant works of legal theory).

It will also be helpful to introduce at this stage, the key relationships between the basic themes of intellectual inquiry, conceptual analysis, and theoretical methodology. The part to be played by conceptual analysis, and hence the value it may possess within an intellectual inquiry, will depend on how we regard the activity of conceptual analysis itself. This is far from being uncontroversial. Similarly, the questions what role methodology may play in a theoretical enterprise, and what value that role possesses, remain controversial. The relationship between theoretical methodology and conceptual analysis is a close one, so long as it is accepted that a theoretical intellectual inquiry will involve the development and use of concepts. This is to recognise nothing more than that intellectuals deal with ideas. From this it follows that a sound methodology of theory will incorporate an appropriate role for conceptual analysis. Whether a methodology of theory has anything to offer beyond that is a matter on which we will reflect further below.

The structure of the chapter is shaped by its subject matter. Due to the existence of controversy over the basic themes to be explored, it will be necessary to spend some time attempting to clarify them before locating the discussion more particularly within MacCormick's *Institutions of Law*. In the layout of the chapter, some general treatment of conceptual analysis and methodology within legal theory will, accordingly, precede an engagement with a number of relevant topics surfacing in the book. However, it should be stressed that the opportunity to engage with the book has beneficially preceded the development of the general treatment of the basic themes. In conclusion, I will offer an assessment of how MacCormick's book contributes to the way we should go about the articulation of insight on the nature of law. The fuller discussion of particular insights offered by the book are taken up within the other contributions to this volume.

2. Conceptual analysis – the broad picture

The underlying issue to be examined in considering the place of conceptual analysis is the relationship between our ideas or concepts and the acquisition of understanding. It can conveniently be approached by considering Brian Leiter's recent work (Leiter 2007) in following Quine's departure from the established philosophical priority of concepts into taking the naturalist turn.[2]

The position rejected by Quine and Leiter has been conventionally set in terms of recognising the *a priori*/*a posteriori* and analytic/synthetic distinctions. In both cases the distinction turns on there being a set of concepts or propositions that are derivable from reason without empirical study. This, in turn, promotes the possibility of first getting a set of valid concepts in place and then working out how they fit to the world we are seeking to understand. Here, conceptual analysis and more broadly, philosophy itself, is a more basic (prior, fundamental) enterprise than empirical or scientific inquiry.

If these postulated distinctions are shown to be a vain, empty artifice by Quine, then it would appear that everything is left to empirical inquiry, and that philosophy or conceptual analysis in the elevated sense has no special role to perform. Instead of being the Queen of the sciences ruling over what scientific inquiry can effectively engage with, philosophy becomes the domestic servant of Science tidying up the discoveries obtained through scientific inquiry. The naturalism espoused by Leiter captures this development by postulating a uniform approach to the acquisition of all understanding through a scientific-empirical study of the natural world.

The position favoured by Leiter takes for granted that there is an evident scientific approach, rather than the nature of scientific inquiry itself being contestable. It also assumes that there is a uniform character to the scientific-empirical approach, whatever it is applied to. This latter assumption is particularly strong when Leiter skates over the possible cracks in the ice between a natural-science approach and a social-science approach. He ignores the peculiar difficulties raised by seeing social science as hermeneutic or (subjectively) interpretive rather than (objectively) empirical.

The residual role for conceptual analysis, once it has been cast down from its elevated philosophical position, is limited to a basic stock-taking, or organising, of empirical discoveries, the domestic servant role. But this rides on the blurred vision of scientific inquiry just mentioned. Putting aside the distinctive problems of a social-scientific inquiry, the contestable nature of scientific inquiry in itself leaves open a preliminary (if not prior) role for concepts in undertaking scientific investigation. Given the contestable nature of scientific inquiry, there is an inevitable choice in that one must first choose a set of explanatory ideas/concepts with which to investigate the natural world before embarking on the empirical inquiry to test whether those ideas work, and provide further understanding of the phenomena under investigation.

---

2 For stimulating discussion of what precisely this may involve, see Haack 1993.

Conceptual analysis is not as Leiter would have it, a process of helping to display our best current empirical-scientific understanding of the world, even if we are restricting our gaze to the acquisition of scientific understanding. There is a process of choosing ideas prior to empirical testing; and a process of confirming ideas through empirical testing; as well as a process of producing (new) ideas as a result of empirical data (that may not sustain the ideas we first commenced with).[3] The domestic servant role for conceptual analysis cannot account for the first and second of these processes, and fits too loosely with the third process.

Tidying up empirical data does not adequately describe this third process, since in addition to tidying up the data obtained empirically any major scientific concept will seek to offer further explanatory insight on matters for which empirical evidence is not yet available. Moreover, the data presented is being viewed through the preliminary ideas (even though it may have failed to sustain them), and hence there is a skewed or limited perception of the data: other aspects of it pertaining to alternative explanatory ideas were ignored, not even tested for.

Although ideas may be regarded as loosely being brought in to tidy up the present data, the explanatory ideas are not relying fully and exclusively on that data. The ideas are not determined exclusively by a fit with empirical evidence, but require an imaginative leap or postulation on the nature of the natural phenomena under investigation and the significance of the evidence. This may, on further testing, become confounded by subsequent empirical data, or even subsequent perception of the present data taken from a different imaginative vantage point.

The ability to imagine beyond the constraints of a present conceptual apparatus must equally derive from something beyond the current scientific enterprise, if that present conceptual apparatus is something that is seen as reflecting present scientific understanding. Thomas Kuhn (1970) famously attempts to capture this abandonment and replacement of scientific understanding with his notion of a paradigm shift, but this contains two problematic aspects which reverberate around an account embracing naturalism and scientism. First, it underlines the contentious nature of the scientific venture – present scientific understanding may be about to be displaced by the next paradigm shift. Secondly, on Kuhn's account, the decision to change paradigm cannot be scientific; that is to say, it is not determined by scientific understanding. For it rejects the old scientific understanding based on the discarded paradigm, and only after the paradigm shift occurs is the new understanding based on the preferred paradigm deemed scientific. These two points combine to suggest that there is something at play in our acquisition of understanding which is not scientific.[4]

The implications of taking the naturalist turn, in terms of abandoning a priori analytical concepts, do not play out so easily as to provide a simple domestic

3 Reflecting the mutually reinforcing dynamic between theory and practice mentioned in the introductory section.

4 A more basic experience of nature (Kuhn 1970, 72, 77).

servant role for conceptual analysis. The role of concepts is to interact with scientific inquiry – seen as a dynamic combination (and recombination) of received scientific understanding, a broader experiential base which may call that understanding into question, and an imaginative faculty which may postulate other possible understanding. In this light, a concept does not merely relate received scientific understanding, but is also an agent for change and development of that understanding.

A fuller account of conceptual analysis can distinguish four different roles. The practice of conceptual analysis may allow these roles to overlap, and run into each other, but a failure to appreciate them all amounts to an impoverished account of conceptual analysis.

1. There may be *initial elucidatory expository* analysis in the sense of providing concepts in which different findings can be more clearly and effectively expressed (for example, power-conferring distinguished from duty-imposing). This role provides a conceptual apparatus in which raw data can be expounded and so is expository in a primary sense in relation to that data.
2. There may be *secondary expository* analysis of concepts that have already been provided (as in role (1)) within a particular way of understanding something, such as further work on Hart's internal aspect of rules, or the popular notion of sovereignty. Here, the exposition is only indirectly related to the raw data. In seeking to clarify Hart's concept of the internal aspect of rules, or the popular notion of sovereignty, the analyst may indeed be motivated by the ultimate desire to make that concept more useful in expounding the raw data, but may be motivated by a desire to shed greater light on that concept for quite different reasons. The ultimate objective may be to use the exposition as a means of arguing for the concept's inability to account for the raw data; or, it may be that the motivation is purely scholarly in attaining a clearer grasp of what is meant by the concept in question. In all these cases the primary subject matter of the analysis is the existing concept.
3. There may be *exploratory explanatory* analysis of concepts in the sense of the creation of concepts which have the potential for possessing explanatory power in an area of inquiry where understanding is lacking or can be readily challenged. This differs from role (1) in that the recognition of the fit between the raw data and the expository work of the concept is far more controversial and tentative, more suggestive of a not yet fully worked out approach rather than a clear depiction of a readily grasped insight. So, whereas the distinction between power-conferring and duty-imposing (the illustration of (1)) is uncontroversially grasped, Kelsen's *Grundnorm*, or Raz's concept of legal authority would fall under (3) as offering an approach with which to explore and seek further explanation of a subject which remains dense and complex.

4. There may also be *normatively exploratory* analysis where the concepts created are being used to promote an alternative (possibly idealistic) explanation of how things could be (differently) arranged. Rawls's concept of maximin, arranging distribution in a way which provides the greatest possible benefit to the least well off, would be an example of this role.

It is worth reiterating that these four different roles may overlap both in the practice of conceptual analysis and in the different perceptions of what a particular task of conceptual analysis is about or has achieved. So, (2) may be confused with (1), or easily run into it. An analyst may regard the work done as falling under (1) while a critic may place it under (3). A particular task of analysis may involve aspects of each of (1)–(3). And the mix of, or confusion between, (3) and (4) is too evident to need noting. The critical point to recognise is that all of these roles (and their contestable applications) can fall under conceptual analysis, and so what exactly is being undertaken within a particular sequence of analysis may vary immensely depending on the state of the subject under consideration and the motive of the analyst. For Leiter to limit conceptual analysis to an expository role in relation to received scientific understanding is to limit the expository role and to deny the exploratory role. Leiter leaves conceptual analysis stagnating with established understanding, and stifles the enterprise of intellectual inquiry.

The broader portrayal of conceptual analysis offered here is not restricted to natural science but pertains to any area of human intellectual inquiry (an inquiry understood as ranging over a possible field of understanding where the understanding is in some respects still incomplete, with a view to advancing understanding) and so encompasses natural science, social science, legal (doctrinal) science, legal theory, and so on. We do not need to take up a viewpoint on the relationship of philosophy to the sciences, or on the a priori/a posteriori or analytic/synthetic distinctions, or on the naturalist turn, in order to appreciate the broader portrayal of conceptual analysis. These can easily become distractions from considering the full scope of conceptual analysis. Nor does this broader portrayal of conceptual analysis lead us ineluctably to embrace either Platonic forms or scientism: it relates to the dynamics of intellectual inquiry, not to the static foundations of purportedly justified conclusions.

A digression on epistemology

This raises the issue of the relationship between conceptual analysis and epistemology. Two observations can be made. First, not all conceptual analysis need be concurrent with sound epistemology – we could use conceptual analysis to expound more clearly a position which we accept as epistemologically flawed (for example, we could accept that Kelsen's epistemology in establishing the *Grundnorm* is unsound, yet still use conceptual analysis to expound more clearly what to understand by Kelsen's idea of a *Grundnorm*). Secondly, not all epistemological concerns are expressible as involving conceptual analysis

– justified/sound understanding may require adherence to precepts such as, 'Consider all the evidence', 'Approach the issue with a clear mind'.[5]

It may be taking the point too far, but I am inclined to suggest that conceptual analysis seen as a key part of intellectual inquiry is a more basic endeavour than establishing a sound epistemology. That achievement, and the extent to which we consider it possible, may only be a further intellectual inquiry rather than the precursor of all intellectual inquiries. If so, the justification/soundness of our understanding is ultimately determined not by our epistemology, but by how far our intellectual inquiries succeed in bumping up against the world; that is to say, by the success and scope of our imaginative conceptual undertakings as measured by what the world throws back at us. Even in the case of conceptual analysis being used in an idealistic normative exploratory manner, there is the risk of our perceived idealistic possibilities bumping up against the realities of the world.

3. Conceptual analysis – particular problems

Recognition of an elucidatory role for conceptual analysis leads to a consideration of the way in which the provision of clearer concepts can assist in making sharper distinctions between different matters that are found within the subject matter of a theoretical inquiry. If we acquire a clearer concept of law, will we be able thereby to possess a clearer understanding of the distinction between law and morality?

Recognition of the differences between expository, exploratory, and normative-exploratory roles for conceptual analysis may alert us to the danger of conceptual analysis that is undertaken with an expository motivation, slipping into an exploratory mode, and then becoming entangled in a normative-exploratory purpose. If we commence with the task of producing a concept of law that reflects a common understanding of law, have we become more ambitious in proposing a concept of law in the absence of an established understanding, and do we end up with a concept of law which determines what can be (we think should be) recognised as law?

These remarks point to a deeper set of problems related to the different ways in which we use words and concepts both to *identify* something and to *convey understanding* of something.[6]

(1.) An idea or concept of something capable of identifying it in one context may not be able to distinguish it in a more subtle context from something else.

It may be possible for a concept of law to be used to distinguish law from morality in one context but not in another.

5 I refer here to understanding we can have grounds for knowing to be sound, rather than sound understanding we happen on by accident.

6 See further, Halpin 2001, chs 6–9.

(2.) A single word used as a label to identify a variety of different things may not be capable of being transferred to a common idea or concept equally applicable to them all.

All that we are prepared to call 'law' may not fit under a uniform concept of law.

(3.) Quite different ideas or concepts conveying different understandings may relate to what is commonly identified as the same thing.

Different concepts of law may provide different insights on our understanding of what is commonly agreed to be law …

(4.) It is another matter whether those different concepts are compatible or in conflict with each other.

…and may build up a richer understanding of law, or offer competing understandings of law.

(5.) The subject matter we identify for our inquiry may be in an unfinished state, and so a concept may appropriately convey an understanding of what it is that leaves that subject matter open to completion in possibly different ways.

Even with a concept conveying the fullest understanding of the nature of law, we may be left with no understanding on which way the law on a particular point will go – though we should have a greater understanding of the factors that will be involved in determining it …

(6.) More particularly, the subject matter we identify for our inquiry may be in an unfinished state due to it including contentious evaluative elements, and so a concept may appropriately convey an understanding of what it is that leaves that subject matter open to further evaluative debate and completion in different ways.

… or, we should have an understanding of where the arena for evaluative debate lies that will be involved in determining the law on a particular point.

Awareness of this set of problems may render the practice of conceptual analysis, and the enterprise of theoretical inquiry, more modest in its ambitions, but it is also likely to produce a more realistic picture of what can be attained. In particular, a fuller appreciation of the different ways in which we use words and concepts both to identify something and to convey understanding, sheds some light on the possibility of theoretical disagreement. This is a phenomenon often taken for granted, and alluded to throughout this chapter, but which on closer scrutiny can cause confusion.[7]

7 The confusion is worsened by Ronald Dworkin (1986) employing 'theoretical disagreement' to refer primarily to the *practical* disagreement by judges over the disposition of a case and then linking that to the alleged inability of some theoretical accounts (that is, positivist theories) to explain the disagreement. Confusion is worsened further by this attack on positivism blending into the semantic sting attack – if positivists rely on a criterial

The confusion can be dispelled by acknowledging that it is possible to *identify the subject matter* prior to working through (competing) approaches in undertaking conceptual analysis of the material, which aim to provide greater understanding of that subject. This common identification of subject matter may occur even if afterwards the breakdown of the material by different theoretical approaches into different concepts differs considerably.

So, we may agree on *identifying* the subject matter of state municipal law as encompassing legislative material, recorded judgments of the courts, and a process of authoritatively recognised reasoning over the determination of particular cases. This will be done without yet offering any significant understanding of the nature of these elements of the material. We may then advance, for the purposes of providing *understanding*, a concept of law, and this may or may not include an aspect of the reasoning element from the material that has been recognised. A concept of law which is limited to the rules found in statutes and precedents (leaving distinct a treatment of legal reasoning), differs from a concept of law that extends to the principles found in legal reasoning.[8] But they do not differ over the identification of the subject matter of the intellectual inquiry. The competing concepts each offer alternative understandings of state municipal law, and that field of inquiry is the location for their theoretical disagreement.

4. Methodology

In recent years there has been an explosion of interest on methodology in jurisprudence (Dickson 2004; Halpin 2006; Leiter 2003). I will not fully engage with the ensuing debate here, but seek to pick out some salient points. I shall make things more straightforward by adopting the strategy of first assuming sound methodology in jurisprudence does amount to establishing an appropriate role for conceptual analysis, and then consider whether there is a further separate role for methodology.

In parallel to the treatment of conceptual analysis above, we can identify distinct roles for (or types of) methodology in jurisprudence linked to conceptual

meaning of law both to identify and explain law, then disagreements over the understanding (explanation) of law must be disagreements over different subject matters, hence theoretical disagreement (on the same subject matter) is impossible. The approach developed here breaks Dworkin's grip on theoretical disagreement in both instances by insisting that the identification of law even by positivists differs from their understanding/explanation of law. It also allows a theory of law room to develop a theoretical account of where practical disagreements might lie in the law without insisting that practitioners must themselves act from a theoretical position on 'the grounds of law' in order to determine their response (practitioners' *awareness* of the grounds of law is another matter entirely).

8 Representing the different conceptual analyses from Hart (or subsequently Raz) and Dworkin.

analysis, dependent upon whether the theoretical inquiry is in nature: initial elucidatory expository, secondary expository, exploratory explanatory or normatively exploratory – or a combination from these. Without embarking on another digression here, it is worth briefly making two points regarding the familiar distinction between expository and censorial jurisprudence. First, expository needs to be broken down further into elements of elucidatory, secondary expository and exploratory explanatory. Secondly, the distinction between expository in that fuller sense and censorial as covering normatively exploratory becomes more fragile, precisely because of the ease with which one can pass between the descriptive exploratory explanatory and the normatively exploratory.

In responding to the contemporary debate, this more differentiated approach to methodology allows us to make a number of interjections. First, Ronald Dworkin's attempt to stage the debate as a contest limited to an external descriptive Archimedean methodology or an internal normative interpretive methodology[9] is flawed because it fails to discern the exploratory role on both the descriptive and normative sides of the inquiry. Since the descriptive side is not simply elucidatory, there may be competing descriptive-explanatory approaches within different exploratory explanatory efforts.[10] Also, there may be competing normatively exploratory approaches to the subject.[11] Furthermore, there can be not simply slippage between, but also the possibility of meaningful interaction between, descriptive and normative in the exploratory mode. These points can be illustrated by a careful examination of how Dworkin, in *Law's Empire* (1986), proceeds from an explanatory exploratory position purporting to describe the normative and argumentative features of law, to the normatively exploratory point that law should be understood as possessing the features of justifying state coercion in a manner that displays integrity.[12]

The second interjection that can be made affects Julie Dickson's suggestion of a three-way contest between descriptive, evaluative, and indirectly-evaluative types of methodology (Dickson 2001). This too overlooks the exploratory role within both descriptive and evaluative/normative theoretical inquiries. Since the exploratory role is fulfilled by taking what the theorist considers important as a means of providing descriptive-explanatory power or normative coherence to the subject matter under investigation, the characteristic that is meant by Dickson to mark out the indirectly-evaluative approach (what the theorist considers to be important about the subject matter) will already be catered for within the first two approaches and does not require separate recognition. The difficulty faced by

9 For detailed references to Dworkin's methodological approach, see Halpin 2006, 95 para. (V)(a).

10 Take the differences in approach between Hart, Raz and Coleman, to name obvious examples.

11 Obvious examples here are Dworkin and Finnis.

12 See Halpin 2006, 95–97 paras (V)(c)-(i).

Dickson in establishing a distinctive content for an indirectly-evaluative approach underlines this point.[13]

A third, more general interjection from the standpoint of linking sound methodology to an appropriate role for conceptual analysis while taking the broader portrayal of conceptual analysis developed above lies in the observation that the promotion of a particular methodology alongside a preferred theoretical approach does little to convince that the invocation of methodology is anything more than partisan support for the preferred theory. If the methodology is exactly coterminous with the theoretical or analytical approach adopted, then it stands or falls with the value of that theoretical approach in seeking to understand the subject in question, and adds nothing to it. If, however, it is wide enough to encompass alternative theoretical approaches, then we are open to the possibility of our theoretical tools, the modes of conceptual analysis, delivering other options – and if that is a possibility, what restriction should be placed on those other options? In short, why should we not embrace, in our methodology, the full range of conceptual analysis depicted above, while we remain unsure of how the subject of our inquiry is to be understood?

There remains the question of what role methodology might play outside its identification with the appropriate role for conceptual analysis. Having supported the broad portrayal of conceptual analysis, it is difficult to find one. Admittedly, the approach to conceptual analysis as the manner in which intellectual inquiry is undertaken, may well be amplified further, but only in the direction of contributing more to the general picture of the ways in which we can beneficially use conceptual analysis within intellectual inquiries. I avoid turning this into a set of epistemic values, as Leiter (2003) would have it, or meta-theoretical values, as Dickson (2004) prefers. Although such general precepts of sound analysis may play a part,[14] I have stressed above the significant part to be played by the particular experiential base relating to the subject matter under investigation, in working through an effective conceptual analysis yielding greater understanding of that specific subject matter.

This does, however, lead to another possibility. Instead of moving beyond conceptual analysis to find a wider role for methodology, we might instead use methodology to widen the range of effective conceptual analysis for a specific subject matter. That is to say, having found a particular deployment of conceptual analysis yielded benefits in providing greater understanding of that subject matter, we may be in a position to suggest how the working method we have successfully adopted might be deployed further in gaining yet more insights on the subject matter in question. This falls short of suggesting that a sound methodology is the arbiter of valid theory. The more limited claim for methodology is developed out of analytical insight upon a particular subject matter, rather than making methodology a prerequisite for such insight.

---

13 See the debate with Leiter, discussed in Halpin 2006, 97–98 para (VI)(b).

14 For further discussion, see Halpin 1998.

3. Engagement with *Institutions of Law*

In a number of ways the approach taken in *Institutions of Law* (MacCormick 2007) can be regarded as exhibiting aspects of the picture developed above. I shall seek to reveal in more detail where that is so, and where there is divergence from it, in considering the book's treatment of the following topics.

The role of methodology

MacCormick's approach to methodology sits easily in the picture presented here, in that he insists that 'methodology has its own importance, but only in relation to methods which generate interesting and significant findings' (2007: 7). This certainly suggests a priority to insight, but leaves open just where the importance of methodology resides. It would be possible to read into the general characteristics of law established by his theoretical approach that MacCormick lists at the end of his book (pp. 303–04), a limited role for methodology as suggested above. The suggestion is that further illumination will build upon these insights by adopting the working method so far adopted, encapsulated as treating law 'as institutional normative order' which encompasses both 'empirical understandings of legal activity' and acknowledgment of law as 'a category of human practical life' (p. 300).

Nevertheless, this would be to ignore the further discussion by MacCormick of his methodology, 'the methodology of interpretative analytical inquiry' (p. 242), in which he explicitly (pp. 299–302) detaches a conceptual understanding of law from its actual practice. This raises a number of points relating to the possibility of divergence between MacCormick's approach to methodology and the picture I have portrayed above.

At a simplistic level, there appears to be agreement between us, in accepting that any conceptual analysis of law, which aims to illuminate our understanding of law, must allow for the incomplete state of the practice of law, for the possibility of the actual practices of law to develop in different ways, and for some of those practices to be regarded as better or worse realisations of what is considered to be the underlying purpose of law (see pp. 287; 293; 296–98 and 298–301). The difference may lie in the extent to which MacCormick sees this as necessitating a gap between conceptual understanding and the observation of practice (pp. 298–99), whereas the picture I have portrayed above seeks to accommodate the possibility of understanding such divergent practices *within* the conceptual analysis undertaken.

There is in one passage (p. 300) an apparent vacillation by MacCormick over the precise relationship between sound theory and empirical fit: on the one hand, poor empirical fit does not refute a theoretical conceptual approach; on the other hand, good empirical fit makes a theoretical conceptual approach more persuasive. I would suggest resolving this by insisting more strongly on the link between sound theory and an experiential base, while allowing for the exploratory mode of the theoretical endeavour to place a more tentative grasp on both our theoretical understanding and the empirical understanding to which we seek to fit it. A further point to repeat here is that in identifying the normatively exploratory role for conceptual analysis, we have recognised that concepts may be created 'to promote an alternative (possibly idealistic) explanation of how things could be (differently) arranged.' Of course, the appropriateness of engaging in that particular role for the specific subject matter of law must still be linked to our experiential base. That is to say, we discern, from our experience of law, the potential for law to be different in the achievement of normative goals than what is currently found throughout its practice. And the appropriateness of that move in the conceptual analysis of law, although not earning universal acclaim is at the very least a serious issue to consider – in contrast to the conceptual analysis of other subject matter, such as subatomic particles.

Theoretical and practical questions

This leads on to the relationship between theoretical and practical questions, notably between 'What is law?' and 'What is the law on *x*?' (p. 284). MacCormick's emphasis here (p. 284 note 9) on the general theoretical question about the nature of law being a prerequisite to theoretical insights which may illuminate the possible range of responses to practical legal questions is important. As is his insistence (p. 284) that a good answer to the general theoretical question will not in itself provide a good answer to the practical question. My insistence elsewhere (picked up by MacCormick at p. 284 in note 9) on maintaining a link between theory and practice does not sufficiently acknowledge these points, which *Institutions of Law* richly demonstrates.

Nevertheless, the picture provided above of the theoretical enterprise maintains the essential link between theory and practice up to the point of sound theory offering adequate understanding of how there is the opportunity for various (competing) responses to be made to practical legal questions. And this I take to be an evident advantage of the theoretical approach adopted in *Institutions of Law*.

Explanatory definitions and conventionalist definitions

MacCormick points out (2007: 284–85) an important difference between definitions which rely on the conventional identification of something and explanatory definitions which provide an enriched understanding of something. This distinction can be related to the distinction made above between the use of words and concepts to identify something or to convey understanding of it. A possible minor point of divergence lies in MacCormick's use of definitions to capture this distinction. We may enrich our understanding of something through arriving at a clearer idea or concept of it, without necessarily providing a definition of it.

The process of moving from pre-understanding to possibly altered understanding referred to by MacCormick in this section (p. 285), is paralleled in comments made above on the dynamic nature of conceptual analysis.

The scientific character of legal theory

MacCormick's concern (2007: 304–05) to preserve the reputation of legal theory as a scientific enterprise rather than being in the business of purveying ideology is possibly assisted further by the picture drawn above which locates both scientific and legal-theoretical inquiries as intellectual inquiries, and suggests how the soundness of either can be similarly preserved.

The articulation of insight

The picture of intellectual inquiry provided above lays great stress on its success being dependent on the ability of the theory being developed to bump up against the world, to provide greater illumination of an experiential base. This may be contrasted with efforts to establish a strong methodology (or secure epistemology) with which to defend a theory – a methodology that may only amount to a partisan endorsement of the theory being promoted. MacCormick's concern with the confirmatory role of experience (2007: 286) and the copious demonstration of his own rich experience of the subject under investigation is central to his project. Moreover, his modest approach (as I have reconstructed it) to methodology, and, certainly, his answering to the charge of methodological syncretism (p. 303), reveal a lack of need to resort to strong methodology. In addition, he recognises the complexity of the subject matter (p. 5) and a proper openness (p. 305) to the elements and controversies it contains. *Institutions of Law* provides more numerous insights than could easily be catalogued. Significant among them are those which contribute to our understanding of the way we should go about the articulation of insight on the nature of law.

References

Dickson, J. (2001), *Evaluation and Legal Theory* (Oxford: Hart Publishing).

Dickson, J. (2004), 'Methodology in Jurisprudence: A Critical Survey', *Legal Theory* 10, 117–56.

Dworkin, R. (1986), *Law's Empire* (London: Collins).

Haack, S. (1993), 'Naturalism Disambiguated', in *Evidence and Inquiry: Towards Reconstruction in Epistemology* (Oxford: Blackwell).

Halpin, A. (1998), 'Concepts, Terms and Fields of Enquiry', *Legal Theory* 4, 187–205.

Halpin, A. (2001), *Reasoning with Law* (Oxford: Hart Publishing).

Halpin, A. (2006), 'The Methodology of Jurisprudence: Thirty Years Off the Point', *Canadian Journal of Law and Jurisprudence* 19, 67–105.
Kuhn, T. (1970), *The Structure of Scientific Revolutions* (Chicago: University of Chicago Press).
Leiter, B. (2003), 'Beyond the Hart/Dworkin Debate: The Methodology Problem in Jurisprudence', *American Journal of Jurisprudence* 48, 17–51.
Leiter, B. (2007), *Naturalizing Jurisprudence: Essays on American Legal Realism and Naturalism in Legal Philosophy* (Oxford: Oxford University Press).
MacCormick, N. (2007), *Institutions of Law: An Essay in Legal Theory* (Oxford: Oxford University Press).
Merton, R. (1968), *Social Theory and Social Structure* (New York: The Free Press).
Skinner, Q. (ed.) (1985), *The Return of Grand Theory in the Human Sciences* (Cambridge: Cambridge University Press).

Chapter 11
Is Bad Law Still Law? Is Bad Law Really Law?

Julie Dickson[1]

Neil MacCormick devotes part 4 of his rich and wide-ranging book, *Institutions of Law* (2007), to a discussion of correct jurisprudential methodology and of various issues regarding the relationship between law and morality. In this chapter, I wish to consider a cluster of issues to which he draws attention – especially in chapters 15 and 16 of the book – which we may begin to approach *via* the questions which form the title above. In legal philosophy, answering these questions is sometimes thought to be the special responsibility of natural law theory, long associated, rightly or wrongly, with the maxim *lex injusta non est lex*.[2] In the course of the following discussion, however, I wish to consider these questions in a broader way in the sense of exploring how various legal theorists from across the jurisprudential spectrum approach them, and by using the question of whether bad law is still and/or really law as a means to considering some important methodological issues regarding what is required in order properly to understand law's nature.

In the first section of this article, I explore some contemporary legal theoretical views on the issue of whether bad law is still, or is really, law. In the second section I then offer a more detailed comparative analysis of John Finnis's and Neil MacCormick's views on this question, and on related methodological issues. As this discussion proceeds, I develop and begin to defend a position wherein although it is necessary to understand law's aims, and the values which it ought to realise in order properly to understand its nature, the failure to achieve those aims or to realise those values does not thereby render something less than fully law.

1. Is bad law still law? Is bad law really law?: A cook's tour

Many prominent legal philosophers have devoted time and attention to considering whether bad law is still, or is really, law. John Finnis's take on this issue brings out the relevance of the 'still/really' distinction mentioned in the title to this chapter

---

1 I wish to extend my thanks to Neil MacCormick and Maksymilian Del Mar for inviting me to take part in this book project.

2 For discussion of this issue, and the extent to which it is and has been the proper concern of natural law thinking, see Finnis 1980, especially chs II and XII.

and in the present section header. In his seminal work, *Natural Law and Natural Rights* (1980), Finnis contends that bad laws are still laws in the sense that they pass the relevant tests of legal validity in a given legal system, but are not 'really' laws in the focal meaning or central case sense of the term because they go against the very point or purpose of having law, which is to secure justice by reasonably resolving co-ordination problems for the common good of a given community (see Finnis 1980, 266–70 and 276–81; and Finnis 2007, section 4). Finnis's position is also interesting in that he claims that the issue of whether unjust laws are still and/or really law is only of minor concern in natural law thinking (see Finnis 1980, ch. 12, section 1), and indeed at times in his writing he claims that the issue is lacking in importance generally (see Finnis 2007, opening of section 4).

These latter claims might seem counter-intuitive, on the grounds that Finnis's entire theory of law is premised on the idea that an adequate understanding of law must proceed from an adequate understanding of law's morally valuable point or purpose (see, e.g., Finnis 1980, ch. 1, especially at 14–15; and Finnis 2003, *passim*) and that in order for a legal theorist to determine what is to count as law for the purposes of his inquiry, he must take a stance on what that point or purpose is and understand the central case of law in terms of that which successfully achieves it *via* specific techniques (see Finnis 1980, *passim*, but especially ch. 1, e.g., 16). Finnis hence states that in his view law is by its nature morally valuable (see Finnis 2003, 111) which, one might have thought, would mean that he would regard the question of whether unjust laws are really law to be an important one, and, moreover, that he would be tempted to answer it in the negative. Sometimes, Finnis talks in exactly these terms: 'Unjust laws are not laws, though they may still count in reasonable conscientious deliberations, and certainly warrant attention and description' (Finnis 2003, 114), but taking his views as a whole,[3] this seems merely to be a dramatic way of stating the position summarised at the outset of this section, i.e., that there is a secondary sense in which unjust laws are still laws – they pass certain tests of legal validity in a given legal system – but they are not 'really' laws in the central case or focal meaning sense of the term because they do not contribute to realising the morally valuable purpose inherent in the nature of law.[4]

This approach, that of claiming that 'bad laws are still law in one sense but not in another, and the whole issue is not that important in any case', has certain affinities with Ronald Dworkin's stance on this topic. For Dworkin, we identify and understand what law is by constructively interpreting it, i.e., by finding its general justifying value or point, putting it in its best light with regard to that point, and working out which legal rights and duties flow from it thus construed (Dworkin

3 Including elsewhere in the article from which the above quote is taken, see, e.g., Finnis 2003, 108, 111 and 128.

4 Various issues raised by Finnis' stance on these and related issues are discussed further in section 2 below.

1986, *passim*).[5] In *Law's Empire*, Dworkin identifies properly constraining and justifying the employment of state coercive force as the most abstract point of law (Dworkin 1986, 93).[6] This being so, if, in the case of certain putative laws, it does not seem possible to interpret them in their best light as properly constraining and justifying state coercive force, the question of whether they are still, or are really, laws, arises. In this vein, in *Law's Empire*, Dworkin discusses whether the Nazis had law and contends that we can view them as still having had law in a sense, and that we know what someone is talking about when he says that the Nazis had law, i.e., that they had institutions, judges, directives etc., which are usually thought of and spoken of as legal in character (Dworkin 1986, 102–03). However, he contends, we also know what someone is talking about when he says that Nazi law was not really law or was less than fully law, i.e., they are making, 'a skeptical interpretive judgement that Nazi law lacked features crucial to flourishing legal systems whose rules and procedures do justify coercion' (Dworkin 1986, 104). Dworkin also seeks to demote the importance of the question of whether there is really law in wicked legal systems, at least in the form in which it usually appears in legal philosophical debates, and to replace it with various interpretive questions regarding the capacity of particular laws to justify state coercion in various circumstances (Dworkin 1986, 108).

It may seem somewhat ironic that two theorists who contend, albeit in very different ways, that in order properly to identify and understand law, we must take a stance on, and understand it in terms of, its morally valuable purpose or point, claim not to be terribly interested in the question of whether purported instances of law which fail to achieve that purpose – which do not contribute to securing justice *via* reasonably resolving co-ordination problems for the common good, or which do not properly constrain and hence justify the exercise of state coercion – are indeed still instances of law. By contrast, H.L.A. Hart, for whom law was to be approached *via* a non-morally evaluative methodology, and was to be understood as a social institution ultimately to be identified *via* a social facts test (conformity with a recognition rule in fact accepted and practised by officials in the relevant jurisdiction) rather than by evaluative argument (see Hart 1958, especially Introduction and sections I and II; and Hart 1994, especially chs 5 and 6, 207–12), thought it of vital importance that we face head-on the issue of whether the moral iniquity of rules of law renders them any less legal (Hart 1994, 207–12). Hart's view was that in the interests of intellectual clarity (Hart 1994, 209), and of subjecting law to appropriate moral scrutiny (Hart 1994, 210–11), we should not

5 For illuminating commentary on Dworkin's position as a whole, see Stavropoulos 2003.

6 Dworkin claims in *Law's Empire* that his ascription of this purpose to law is merely provisional and that the purpose itself, abstractly conceived, is uncontroversial. I have taken issue with these claims in Dickson 2001, ch. 6. For an insightful discussion of the role of law's general justifying value or point in interpretivism more generally, as opposed to in particular instantiations of that approach, see Stavropoulos 2003.

exclude from that which we count as law directives which are morally iniquitous. As regards the latter interest, this was because Hart believed that a sense that law must always be subject to appropriate moral scrutiny and that certifying something as law does not tell us whether or not it ought to be obeyed, was 'more likely to be kept alive among those who are accustomed to think that rules of law may be iniquitous, than among those who think that nothing iniquitous can anywhere have the status of law' (Hart 1994, 210).

In previous work, I have argued that Hart's arguments in favour of these points seem at odds with the methodology he implicitly adopts elsewhere in *The Concept of Law* (Dickson 2004, 149–50). In particular, Hart appears to present the issue of whether to classify morally iniquitous law as law or not as a choice, and to contend that the choice is to be influenced by the intellectual and moral beneficial consequences resulting from one way of classifying it over another (see Hart 1994, ch. 9, especially 209). This view (in ch. 9 of *The Concept of Law*) sits awkwardly with the approach taken to characterising law elsewhere in the book, where Hart appears to regard his task as being to explain the *nature* of law, and where he seems to view law as having a nature, and as having essential properties which make it into what it is, and which are capable of being ascertained.[7] If this is so, then it is incongruous to speak in terms of choosing to view law in one way or another depending on the beneficial consequences of so doing.[8]

A different approach to this issue is taken by Robert Alexy. Following and seeking to defend the views of Gustav Radbruch,[9] Alexy contends that although unjust laws are still properly classified as law and ought to be applied by courts in cases coming before them, when the injustice reaches a gross or radical level, then such laws cease to be law and must give way to the demands of justice in cases (Alexy 2002, especially 28–35 and 40–68). Such a view seems in some ways less equivocal than that offered by either Finnis or Dworkin: grossly unjust laws are not laws in one sense but not in another; they simply cease to be laws.[10]

---

7 For example, in arguing that law's essential properties include a union of primary and secondary rules wherein officials accept a secondary rule of recognition from the internal point of view, in Hart 1994, chs 5 and 6.

8 For further discussion of this issue, see Lyons 1984, 64; Soper 1987; Moore 1992, 203–40; MacCormick 1985, 7–11; Schauer 1996; Schauer 2005; Dickson 2004, ch. 5, section A; and Green 2008.

9 For the 'Radbruch formula', see Radbruch 1990, 89.

10 In an article discussing various aspects of Alexy's *The Argument from Injustice* (2002), Joseph Raz appears to find the Radbruch/Alexy position ambiguous between a claim that necessarily no grossly unjust law is law and necessarily grossly unjust rules ought to be set aside by judges even if they are law (see Raz 2007). In this same article (note 34), Raz mentions an attempted reconstruction of Alexy's argument in *The Argument from Injustice* offered by Andrei Marmor (in a private communication between Raz and Marmor). In this reconstruction, Marmor interprets Alexy as contending that necessarily, judges ought to interpret the law so that grossly unjust law is rendered invalid. My interpretation of Alexy proceeds along the lines Marmor suggests.

So where does Neil MacCormick stand on all this? MacCormick shares with Finnis the view that an adequate understanding of law must proceed from an adequate understanding of law's point or purpose, and of the values it ought to realise (MacCormick 2007, chs 15 and 16, especially 264, 293–98 and 305). Indeed, MacCormick approaches this issue in a broader manner than this, claiming that many concepts in the 'human social realm' (MacCormick 2007, 295) – including cars, paintings and geography lessons – have to be understood in terms of their 'focal meaning', i.e., in terms of how well they 'exemplify the values to which the enterprise is properly considered to be oriented' (MacCormick 2007, 295).[11] In the case of law, too, 'Our understanding of it has to be in terms of its functionality towards certain values' (MacCormick 2007, 297) and in terms of the aims it seeks to achieve, namely 'the realisation of justice and the common good, according to some reasonable conception of these' (MacCormick 2007, 304). This methodological approach appears, for MacCormick, to stem from something about the nature of law: that in his view law makes an implicit claim to justice, and that this sets the standard by which it ought to be judged (MacCormick 2007, 274–77). He argues that both legislative and judicial acts of law-making necessarily make such a claim, evidence for which may be found, for example, in the fact that, 'legislation often bears a title like "Administration of Justice Act"; but never "Administration of Injustice Act"' (MacCormick 2007, 275), and in the duty of judges to do justice according to law (MacCormick 2007, 276). MacCormick thus appears to regard law's implicit claim to justice as a necessary feature of law (MacCormick 2007, 274–76) and to view it as providing evidence that law ought to aspire to realising justice, and that success in this task sets the standard by which law should be judged. I thus understand MacCormick's position to be that, because it is in the nature of law to make a claim to justice, then, to understand it well, we must understand the character of that claim, and must view law as something which ought to live up to it, and which is to be judged according to how well it does so.[12]

---

11 MacCormick also regards his view as having affinities with Ronald Dworkin's idea of the need to understand concepts in the human social realm as interpretive concepts. However, as the discussion in this section and the next should make clear, I regard him as having more in common with John Finnis' and Robert Alexy's views than with Dworkin's as regards how to go about understanding law. MacCormick himself expresses doubts as regards aspects of Dworkin's views, especially the requirement that in interpreting law we should aim to put it in its best light, or make of it the best possible example of the form or genre to which it is taken to belong, in MacCormick 2007, 296–97.

12 I base this reading on MacCormick's views on law's implicit claim to justice in MacCormick 2007, 264 and 274–77, and on his remarks on why justice is to be privileged as a special virtue of law, and the methodological implications of this point, 298–99. It is an interesting question whether law ought also to be judged by standards which it itself does not claim to attain. As far as MacCormick's view goes, he does mention other moral standards which law ought to attain, e.g. that it should not be used to prejudice or violate

But what is MacCormick's view as regards how we are to view purported instances of law which do not make good on law's implicit claim to justice, and which do not realise those values law ought to?[13] Unlike Finnis and Dworkin, MacCormick does not attempt to claim that this issue is not important, and does not adopt an equivocal position on it wherein such purported instances of law are law in one sense but not in another. Rather, he espouses a view which is similar to Alexy's in structure. First of all, he notes that although an adequate understanding of law must include understanding it in terms of the distinctive values it ought to realise, in reality, actual law often falls short of realising those values (MacCormick 2007, 264, 297 and 298–302). The 'omnipresent possibility of failure, and the high likelihood that any real system will have serious blemishes' (MacCormick 2007, 297)[14] mean that we would do well to adopt, 'a critical attitude towards actual institutions of law and state' (MacCormick 2007, 264–65).

MacCormick further claims that, with regard to many instances of unjust law, they remain law nonetheless:

> There can indeed be unjust laws, and what is alarming about this is that they are perfectly genuine laws, upheld and enforced through the coercive power of the state. 'An unjust law is a corruption of law'[15] – yes, but it is real law that is thus corrupted. (MacCormick 2007, 271)

There is a limit to this, however, and when injustice reaches a certain point, then the resulting rules and attempts to govern would not properly count as law at all (MacCormick 2007, 271–73). How do we determine when that limit is reached? For MacCormick:

> ... if what is done cannot be accounted for under any possible conception of justice that could reasonably be adopted or advocated by a reasonable person willing to subject his or her beliefs to discursive scrutiny, then what is thus done by way of rules and practices of governance would not properly count as law. (MacCormick 2007, 273)[16]

MacCormick's views on these issues seem to be views about the nature of law, and hence to be views which presume that law has a nature which legal theorists can attempt to ascertain. For example, as was mentioned above, he seems to argue

individual autonomy (p. 265), but he privileges the realisation of justice as a 'special virtue of law' (p. 298).

13 I say 'values' and not 'value' here because at some points in his discussion MacCormick refers to 'the realization of justice and the common good' (MacCormick 2007, 304) as the relevant values, and elsewhere, too, he refers to values, plural, in this context.

14 Internal footnote omitted.

15 Internal footnote reference to Aquinas 1989.

16 Internal footnote reference to Alexy 2002 omitted.

that it is in the nature of law to make an implicit claim to justice, and that this provides evidence that justice is the distinctive virtue to which law should aspire, and by which it ought to be judged. Likewise, his claims that, in general, unjust laws are a corruption of law, 'but it is real law that is thus corrupted' (MacCormick 2007, 271), but that at some point a limit of injustice is reached beyond which putative legal standards would not properly count as law, seem to be claims about the nature of law, i.e., claims about which properties are necessary for something to be law, and about that something ceasing to be law when certain properties are absent. There seems to be no trace here of the kind of argument which Hart appears to flirt with in chapter 9 of *The Concept of Law* to the effect that we can choose to view law in one way or another, and that the beneficial consequences of so doing should guide the choice.[17]

So much for our Cook's Tour of some contemporary legal philosophical approaches to the issue of whether bad law is still, or is really, law. In the next section I submit some of those views – in particular, those of Finnis and MacCormick – to further critical scrutiny in order to examine their relation to some important issues in jurisprudential methodology.

2. Understanding law: Law's nature, and how law ought to be

Differentiating issues

As discussed in Section 1, John Finnis contends that unjust laws which do not contribute to the realisation of law's distinctive morally valuable purpose are not 'really' law in the central case or focal meaning sense, the explication of which lies at the core of Finnis's natural law theory. In his article, 'Law and What I Truly Should Decide' (Finnis 2003), he elaborates further on his reasons for holding this view, and, in so doing, reveals some interesting points regarding his stance on jurisprudential methodology.

In that article, Finnis argues that the concept of law shares certain features with the concepts of medicine and argument in that putative medicines or arguments which do not instantiate the values they ought to are not really medicines or arguments at all (although there is a secondary sense in which they can still be spoken of as such, for example, to provide information in textbooks or histories of lethal medicines or invalid arguments) (Finnis 2003, 108 and 114). In a footnote, he then mentions the following point which was raised during discussion of his

17 I am somewhat unsure of this point, however, owing to MacCormick's seeming support for the kind of argument Hart appears to run in chapter 9 of *The Concept of Law* in earlier work, e.g., MacCormick 1985, *passim* but see especially 10–11 and 37. His views in Part 4 of *Institutions of Law* (2007) discussed above, however, do appear to presuppose that law has a nature which legal theorists can attempt to ascertain, and that one important task of legal theory is to identify and understand law's necessary features.

paper (which was given as the 2003 Natural Law Lecture at Notre Dame Law School):

> On the occasion of the Lecture, Joseph Raz asked why law should be thought to be like argument, medicine or contracts, rather than like novels or paintings, or people, that are still novels or paintings, or people, even if they are bad. (Finnis 2003, 114 note 9)

Finnis's response is:

> One answer is that, like argument, medicines, and contracts, law has a focused and normative point to which everything else about it is properly to be regarded as subordinate. Novels and paintings, on the other hand, can have incompatible points, e.g. to entertain or arouse (like kitsch or porn) or to tell a truth with artistry. People exist in the natural order as living substances even if they are not functioning adequately or at all in the orders of logic and thought, deliberation, and/or exercises of skill. (Finnis 2003, 114 note 9)

These points give further insight into several interesting aspects of Finnis's position. First of all, while Finnis regards the formula 'a bad X is not really an X' as applying to several concepts and not merely to law, he does not see it as holding with regard to all concepts. Furthermore, he contends that the formula applies only to those concepts which have, 'a focused and normative point to which everything else … is properly to be regarded as subordinate'. Where a concept has such a point, it seems that, for Finnis, we must adopt a methodology wherein we understand it primarily in terms of that point, and must conclude that purported instances of it which do not serve that point are not really instances of it at all (see further Finnis 1980, ch. 1; and Finnis 2003, *passim*). But does this follow? In this sub-section, and the two which follow it, I discuss the relation between the claim that in order properly to understand law, we must understand it in terms of the point or purpose it ought to realise – a moral point or purpose according to Finnis and MacCormick – and the claim that instances of law which fail to serve that point or purpose must be viewed as not, or not really, law at all. In so doing, I will not offer any direct argument on the issue of whether law does have a distinctive moral point or purpose, and, if so, what that might be. For the sake of argument, I will follow Finnis and MacCormick in their views that it does have such a point, in order to consider further what follows from this as regards how we ought to go about understanding law, and as regards whether and in what sense bad law is still to be accounted as law. By so doing, I hope to isolate and discuss those methodological issues in which I am particularly interested in the present chapter.

Finnis and MacCormick strongly support the thesis that law has a moral point. They also characterise that point in the same terms: the realisation of justice and the common good. If it is true that law has a moral point or aim, what follows regarding how we should go about understanding it? Those aspects of Finnis's and

MacCormick's views discussed thus far can be cast in terms of a methodological insight that we must understand law in a way which pays adequate attention to law's aims and to those values it ought to realise. MacCormick's position brings this out very clearly in his discussion of law's implicit aspiration to justice (MacCormick 2007, 270 and 274–77, discussed in section 1 above).[18] His view appears to be that because law necessarily claims to realise a certain conception of justice, that hence, in order properly to understand it, we must understand the nature of that claim, what it would be for law to make good on it, and must understand law as something which, by its nature, has a distinctive moral task that it ought to perform. In my view this is very plausible: if it is part of the nature of something that it claims to serve a certain point or purpose, and that we ought to view it as having a certain task to perform, then in order properly to understand it, it would seem that we must understand that claim and what it would be for the thing in question to make good on it, and to successfully perform the task that it ought to. As an analogy: some would argue that the Oxford tutorial system has a distinctive educational point or purpose, perhaps to foster excellence and independence of mind in learning, through providing students with discussion-based, individually-tailored expert teaching focused on the student's own written work and oral contributions. However much experience may have taught us that actual tutorials do not in fact always fulfil their purpose or realise the values they are supposed to, we would miss something important about the Oxford tutorial system if we failed to understand what it claims to be, what its point or aim is, and what values it ought to realise. Likewise, if, by its nature, law has a moral point or task, and ought to realise some distinctive value or values, then in order properly to understand it, we must seek to understand that task and those values, and understand that they set the standard against which law ought to be judged.

This methodological insight instructs legal theorists seeking to understand the nature of law to direct their attention not merely towards what law is, but also to what law aims to be and ought to be, and to those standards by which it should be judged. It asks us to take seriously the possibility that it is part of law's nature that it ought to perform a certain moral task, and to realise a certain value or values, and that hence, if we wish to understand the nature of law, we must seek to identify and understand that task and those values.[19]

If law has a moral task to perform such that legal theorists should seek to understand that task, and to understand those values law ought to realise, does this point support the conclusion that purported instances of law which do not perform that task and do not realise those values are not, or are not really, law at all? On the face of it, the answer would appear to be no. This is because the methodological

---

18 For discussion of whether justice is the distinctive value to which law aspires, see Gardner 2000.

19 In a recent article, Leslie Green discusses the interesting idea that law has a distinctive way of failing that its nature makes possible – Green terms it 'legalism' – and which hence ought to be viewed as the vice internal to law, see Green 2008.

insight that we should pay adequate attention to law's point or aim, and to the values it ought to realise concerns a need adequately to understand law's *objectives*, and what law *ought to be*, rather than what it *must* be in order to be law. Of course, if Finnis and MacCormick are correct in those aspects of their views discussed above, then they are in a sense drawing attention to something that law *must* be in order to be law: it must be something which has the aim of realising justice and the common good, and it must be something which is to be judged according to how well it succeeds in so doing. It also seems plausible that law must be capable in principle of succeeding in achieving its aim and realising those values it ought to, as it would make little sense to understand and judge something in terms of a standard which it was incapable in principle of ever attaining. However, none of these things that law 'must' be in order to be law supports the conclusion that if law does not successfully achieve its aims or realise those values it ought to, then it is not really or fully law. On this view, failing to *have* the relevant point or aim and/or failing to be the kind of thing which in principle is capable of achieving it and which hence can sensibly be judged according to whether it does so would seem to render something not law, but failing *actually to achieve* that point or aim does not seem to, because the essential property of law in this case is not that law does realise certain values, but that it aims to, and that it ought to. The thesis that law has a moral point, and the methodological insight that we must try adequately to understand that point, and to understand the values law ought to realise, thus does not appear to support the conclusion that law which fails to realise that point, and fails to instantiate those values, is not, or is not really, law at all.[20]

Challenging Finnis's views

For John Finnis, however, there does appear to be an important connection between his claims that law has a focused and normative point and that in order properly to understand law we must understand this point and those values law ought to realise, and his view that instances of law which do not serve that point and do not realise those values are not really law. The character of that connection seems to be as follows. According to Finnis, law has the focused and normative point of realising justice and the common good *via* the reasonable resolution of societal co-ordination problems. This being so, legal theorists, in attempting to understand law, must come to differentiate concepts, and to determine what counts as law from the point of view of one who properly understands law's focused and normative point and who appreciates the way in which law distinctively contributes to the realisation of the common good and human flourishing. From that point of view, the central case of law is to be demarcated as that which serves that point successfully, and thus laws and legal systems which do not successfully serve that point, and do not realise the values they are supposed to, are not really law (Finnis

20 It would be interesting to discuss the above points in terms of my views of correct jurisprudential methodology in Dickson 2004, but this cannot be attempted here.

1980, chs 1 and 7; and Finnis 2003, especially 114). Of course, Finnis emphasises that it is possible to refer to unjust laws and legal systems as law in a subordinate sense, but as they are not, for him, central cases of law, hence we are entitled to say that they are not really, or not fully, law, and sometimes, more baldly than this, simply to say, 'Unjust laws are not laws …' (Finnis 2003, 114). Thus Finnis feels entitled to claim that, 'law is rightly conceived as *by its nature morally valuable*' (Finnis 2003, 114; original emphasis).

Finnis hence makes two additional moves which take him beyond the view discussed in the preceding section that if law has a moral point or aim, and ought to live up to certain values, then in order properly to understand it we must understand that point and those values, and what it would be for law to succeed in attaining them. The first move is his claim that this methodological insight requires legal theorists to adopt a central case vs. peripheral cases methodology, and to demarcate as the central case of law that which successfully realises law's moral point or aim and for that reason generates moral obligations to obey it (See especially Finnis 1980, ch. 1). Finnis' second move is to claim that a central case methodology leads to the view that peripheral cases of laws and legal systems are (depending on the way he chooses to formulate the point), not really law (Finnis 1980, 277–78), less than fully law (Finnis 1980, 279), law only in a secondary sense (Finnis 2007, section 4), or not law (Finnis 2003, 114).

Finnis' second move, and the 'two-tier' view of law it leaves him with, also explains his seeming espousal of incompatible statements about the relation between law and its moral point or purpose. Throughout his work, Finnis is at pains to emphasise that, necessarily, law has a distinctive moral point or purpose that it ought to realise.[21] However, at points he also seems to contend that, necessarily, law is by its nature morally valuable in the sense of *realising* a distinctive moral point or purpose.[22] As John Gardner has pointed out, if we read each of these statements as referring to necessary features of law then they are incompatible. In order for us to understand something as having a certain point or aim, then it must be possible for it to try to achieve that aim, and if it is possible for it to try to achieve that aim, then it must be possible for it to fail as well as succeed in the attempt. However, if something *necessarily* achieves a certain point or aim – i.e., if it must achieve it in order to be an instance of the thing in question – then it cannot fail to so do, and so cannot be understood as having that point or aim in the sense of trying to achieve it (see Gardner 2006).

In my view, Finnis attempts to 'dodge the bullet' of this incompatibility by using 'law' in two different senses: a central case sense, and a more general sense which includes both central and more peripheral cases. The relations between each of these two senses of law and law's moral point or aim are then as follows:

21 See those works referred to in this chapter so far.

22 I base this reading on, e.g., Finnis 2003, 111; and Finnis 1980, 14–15 and 276.

- Law#1 (general sense including both central and peripheral cases) necessarily has a moral point or aim which it should try to achieve (and which in some cases, central cases, it does in fact achieve).
- Law#2 (central case sense) necessarily achieves law's moral point or aim of serving justice by reasonably resolving co-ordination problems for the common good of a community.

Finnis moves between these two senses of law in his work, without always indicating clearly which he is using at any given time. Of course, this does not so much 'dodge the bullet' as multiply the target: the problem then becomes that there is an incompatibility between the two senses in which Finnis is using the term 'law', and they cannot both be true statements about the necessary features of law.[23] At times in his work, Finnis further claims that in any case it is a philosophical mistake to attempt to demarcate law's necessary features and hence differentiate law from non-law (Finnis 1980, 278–80).[24]

23 In my view, something of this character is also implicit in Dworkin's position which results in him sometimes appearing to claim that necessarily law has a moral aim, and sometimes appearing to claim that necessarily law is that which succeeds in successfully achieving that moral aim. I cannot explain or defend this further here, but it underpins my view that John Gardner is mistaken in attributing to me belief in incompatible statements about the nature of law in my interpretation of Dworkin's views in *Evaluation and Legal Theory*. Rather, in my interpretation of Dworkin's views, I was tracking this ambiguity in his position (admittedly not very clearly). See Gardner 2006, 216 note 32, referring to Dickson 2004, 106).

24 In a recent article, John Gardner argues that legal theorists ought to accept the methodological insight discussed above (i.e., that if law has a moral objective, then in order properly to understand it, we must seek to understand that objective and what it would be for law to attain it), and Finnis's first move with regard to it (i.e., that we should understand law in central case terms, and should regard as law's central case law which successfully realises those moral values it ought to), but reject Finnis's second move, i.e., that non-central cases of law are to be consigned to some grey area or not-quite-law status – see Gardner 2007. For reasons I cannot discuss in depth here, I have some qualms regarding Gardner's adoption and particular use of the 'central case' idea, and some doubts that his view is as 'Nearly Natural Law' as he contends. For example: Gardner is using the term 'central case of law' to mean something quite different from Finnis because Gardner rejects the view that non-central cases of law are less than fully law (Gardner 2007, 18–19) whereas Finnis embraces it; Gardner believes that the project of demarcating law from non-law and understanding the limits of law is valuable (Gardner 2007, 20) whereas Finnis views it as a philosophical mistake; Gardner believes that Finnis' claim that law has a moral nature boils down to the claim that we need to understand what law aspires to be, morally speaking, in order properly to understand it (Gardner 2007, 24), whereas Finnis intends both this and something more by his claim that law has a moral nature, i.e., that law in sense #2 mentioned above necessarily achieves its moral purpose, and that instances of purported law which fail to so do are for this reason not really law or law only in a secondary sense.

With Finnis's view more sharply in focus, we can consider again his reasons for contending that there is an important connection between his claims that law has a moral purpose or point and that in order properly to understand law we must understand that point and those values law ought to realise, and his view that instances of law which do not serve that point and do not realise those values are not really law at all:

> On the occasion of the Lecture, Joseph Raz asked why law should be thought to be like argument, medicine or contracts, rather than like novels or paintings, or people, that are still novels or paintings, or people, even if they are bad. One answer is that, like argument, medicines, and contracts, law has a focused and normative point to which everything else about it is properly to be regarded as subordinate. Novels and paintings, on the other hand, can have incompatible points, e.g. to entertain or arouse (like kitsch or porn) or to tell a truth with artistry. People exist in the natural order as living substances even if they are not functioning adequately or at all in the orders of logic and thought, deliberation, and/or exercises of skill. (Finnis 2003, 114 note 9)

As a first response to this it is tempting to ask: why does the fact that (according to Finnis) law has one focused and normative point (which legal theorists must seek to identify and understand in order properly to understand law) rather than several support the conclusion that instances of law which fail to realise that point are less than fully law? Whether law has one point or many that it ought to realise, such points would seem to denote standards to which law aspires, and which it ought to attain, and hence the successful realisation of that point would seem to belong to that aspect of law's nature concerning that which it should be, rather than that which it must be in order to be law.[25] Perhaps, however, the focus should be on the 'to which everything else about it is properly to be regarded as subordinate' part of Finnis's formulation. The contrast he draws between law and people may be particularly instructive. Presumably, for Finnis, people do not have the focused and normative point of rational thought to which everything else about them is properly to be regarded as subordinate because there is something else important about them – their embodiment as living beings of a particular kind – which persists even in cases where they are not functioning well or at all in terms of rational thought, and by reference to which they are still to be understood as being people. Law, then, must be different for Finnis in that it does not have equivalent other important properties which persist even in cases where its focused and normative point is not realised successfully, and by reference to which we should still identify and understand it as law.

Although I thus have qualms about several aspects of Gardner's view, his article has been extremely helpful in clarifying my thinking as regards several of the issues discussed here.

25 See the discussion of these points in the preceding section.

But is this true? In my view, there are good reasons to doubt that it is. Legal systems are institutionalised normative systems in which inter-related norms are created, modified, applied and enforced by social institutions such as legislatures, courts and tribunals, the police and other executive agencies. In any jurisdiction governed by law, some such institutions exist and they and the norms they interact with form part of the social reality of those living in the society in question. These features of the social reality of law as it actually exists and is and has been implemented in human societies have a deep and pervasive impact on the lives of people living under law, irrespective of whether it successfully realises its moral point or objective.[26] Such features of law are thus plausible candidates for the 'something else' important about it, in virtue of which it exists and is to be understood as law, even when it fails to realise the moral point or purpose it ought to. Law and people are not as disanalogous as Finnis claims: although the social reality of law is very different in character from the biological reality of people, both persist even when those entities fail to be as they ought to be, and both are properties of sufficient importance such that we should view phenomena exhibiting them as remaining instances of law or people respectively.

If it is in the nature of law that it has a distinctive moral point, and that it ought to realise certain values, then we will miss something important about the nature of law if we fail to understand that point and those values, and what it would be for law to realise them successfully. However, we will also miss something important about the nature of law if we do not understand those other properties of law which comprise its social and institutional nature, which have a deep and pervasive effect on the lives of those living under law, and which persist when law fails to realise its moral point and fails to instantiate those values it ought to. Instances of such law abound, as both MacCormick and Finnis make clear to us: MacCormick when he reminds us to 'Mind the Gap' between the values law ought to serve and the social reality of law as it is instantiated in human society (MacCormick 2007, 298–302), and Finnis when he tells us that although in his view law is by its nature morally valuable, he is talking about law in the abstract rather than in its historical implementation:

> Thus law is rightly conceived of as *by its nature morally valuable* – not in the sense that Joseph Raz attributes to that phrase, according to which the thesis would be making a claim about 'the way [law or the law] is actually implemented in history', the obviously false claim that law 'in its historical manifestations through the ages [ ] has always, or generally, been a morally valuable institution.' (Finnis 2003, 111; original emphasis)[27]

26 For further discussion of this point, see Dickson 2004, 59–60, 120–21 and 139–43.

27 The quotations within this quote are from Raz 2003, 13. This latter article has also been helpful in assisting my thinking as regards the issues discussed above.

However, although he recognises that the social reality of law as it has been implemented in human society includes law which fails to realise law's moral point, Finnis reduces those properties which make such law into law to a subordinate status as compared with those properties of the central case of law which does realise that point. Moreover, in insisting that the starting point and primary concern of legal philosophy must be consideration of law's moral point and why morally we ought to comply with law (e.g., in Finnis 2003, 115 and 129), and in recognising, in the above passage, that the statement that law is by its nature morally valuable is true only of law in the abstract rather than in its actual historical implementation in human societies, Finnis is prioritising understanding and explaining law in the abstract over understanding and explaining the social reality of law. But why should legal theorists be primarily interested in law in the abstract, and why should we grant explanatory priority to those aspects of law's nature which are concerned with how law ought to be, over the social reality of law as it has actually been implemented in our societies? As has been discussed above, in order to understand law we need to understand what it aims to be and what it ought to be, but it is the aims and aspirations of an existing social institution which we are seeking to understand. We must, therefore, grant adequate explanatory importance to the social reality of law as it has been realised in human societies. Law thus understood can fail and often has failed to realise those values it ought to, but it exists nonetheless in the reality of the creation, modification, application and enforcement of its norms by social institutions. It does not seem to make sense, therefore, to relegate such law to some grey area or not-quite-legal status. By so doing we fail to grant adequate explanatory importance to all aspects of law's nature: those concerning what it ought to be and any moral point it may have; and those concerning the social reality of law as it has actually existed and been implemented in human social life.

A further point can also be made in support of the view that morally bad law which fails to be as it ought to be, but which possesses those other important properties of law discussed above, should still be accounted as law. This point proceeds from the fact that we worry so much – and with specific concerns in mind – about the existence of morally problematic legal systems. We worry, for example, about how to understand them, how we ought to classify them, and what we ought to do in response to the practical problems that they generate (such as what to do with individuals acting in grossly immoral ways and relying for their defence on laws legally valid at the time of their actions permitting or requiring such acts), such that we debate and discuss such issues with urgency, in war crimes tribunals,[28]

28 For example, those which occurred at Nuremberg, Germany, between 1945 and 1949.

courts of law[29] and academic debate.[30] We do so, I venture, because it troubles us when something which by its nature ought to live up to certain standards, and which – according to Finnis and MacCormick – ought to realise a distinctive moral purpose or point, does not do so, and hence fails to be what it ought to be. However, the fact that we evaluate law in light of the distinctive values it ought to realise, and become concerned if instances of law do not realise those particular values, indicates that what troubles us about such instances is that they are failing precisely *as law*, for if it turned out that the thing doing the failing was not law at all, or was not really law, then why should it be held to the particular standards that *law* ought to live up to, and why would it trouble us if it failed to attain those particular standards? We evaluate law in light of the distinctive standards that law ought to attain, and are troubled in those cases where it fails to attain them because it is failing to be as *law* ought to be. It only makes sense to regard instances of morally bad law as subject to those standards, and to be concerned about their failure to be as law ought to be when they do not attain them, if they are indeed instances of law.[31] Once again, then, it does not make sense to relegate such instances to some grey area or not-quite-law status: they are law, and they are not as law ought to be – this is why we are troubled by them in the manner that we are.[32]

The discussion above attempts to challenge Finnis's view that endorsing the point that legal theorists must understand law's moral purpose or point and those values it ought to realise supports the conclusion that instances of law which do not achieve that purpose and do not realise those values are not really law at all. Insofar as it is successful in so doing, it should also indicate that, *contra* Finnis and Dworkin,[33] it *does* matter whether we understand morally bad law as remaining law nonetheless: it matters in terms of giving adequate explanatory emphasis to the social reality of law as it is actually implemented in human societies, and in order adequately to explain the sense in which we judge and are concerned about such instances in terms of their failure *as law*.

---

29 For example, Judgement of July 27, 1949, Oberlandesgericht, Bamberg; BVerfGE 3, 225 (232); BVerfGE 22, 98 (106) (cases arising in the wake of the Nazi regime), and LG Berlin, NStZ 1992, 492 (493); BVerfGE 95, 96 (97) (cases involving wall shootings at the former border between East and West Germany).

30 As well as the works by Alexy, Dworkin, Finnis, Hart and MacCormick discussed in this article, see, e.g., Hart 1958; Hart 1965; Fuller 1958; Fuller 1969; and Dyzenhaus 1991.

31 John Gardner makes this point, and illustrates it first with reference to the concept of a human being before applying it to law in Gardner 2007, 2 and 18–20. His illuminating views on this issue have influenced my thinking in the present chapter.

32 Once again, I am not mounting any argument here as to whether law indeed has a distinctive moral purpose or point or what any such point might be. I do, however, believe that there are certain values law ought to realise, and certain standards which it ought to attain, and by which it is to be judged, and that our worries and concerns regarding the failure of certain instances of it to do so are significant in the sense discussed above.

33 See the discussion in section 1 above.

MacCormick's stance reconsidered

As was discussed in section 1, MacCormick takes a rather different stance from Finnis regarding whether bad laws are still, or are really, law. His view is that although we must understand law's implicit claim to justice, and '[o]ur understanding of [law] has to be in terms of its functionality towards certain values' (MacCormick 2007, 297), it is not the case that law which fails to make good on that claim, and fails to realise those values, is not really law. Rather, unjust laws remains law in many instances:

> There can indeed be unjust laws, and what is alarming about this is that they are perfectly genuine laws, upheld and enforced through the coercive power of the state. 'An unjust law is a corruption of law'[34] – yes, but it is real law that is thus corrupted. (MacCormick 2007, 271)

In espousing this view, MacCormick recognises the importance of the points made in the discussion of Finnis's views in the preceding section. First of all, he acknowledges the point that although the law we encounter in human societies often fails to realise those values it ought to – justice and the common good according to MacCormick – it remains fully law – 'real law' to use MacCormick's term – nonetheless.[35] If it remains law despite failing to achieve its purpose of realising justice and the common good, then there must be other important properties about it which persist even when that purpose is not realised successfully, and in virtue of which it is to be accounted as law. *Contra* Finnis, then, MacCormick cannot regard those other important properties of law as subordinate to law's moral point or purpose such that instances of law which exhibit them but which fail to realise that purpose are not really law. From the quote above, and from his view throughout *Institutions of Law* that law is to be understood as 'institutional normative order',[36] it is clear that those other features of law include its norms, their formation into what MacCormick terms 'institution-arrangements' (MacCormick 2007, 35) (such as contract, property and trusts) and 'institution-things' (MacCormick 2007, 36) (such as stocks and shares, copyrights and patents), and the social institutions – 'institution agencies' (MacCormick 2007, 35), such as legislatures, courts and the police – *via* which those norms are created, modified, applied and enforced. It is thus evident that MacCormick's view of law grants adequate explanatory importance to the social reality of law as it is actually implemented in human

34 Internal footnote reference to Aquinas 1989.

35 See also MacCormick 2007, 264: 'Law ought to be just and ought to serve the common good for all within the jurisdiction. But law frequently fails to be as it ought to be. What law is and what it ought to be are different things.'

36 For MacCormick's account of law as institutional normative order, see MacCormick 2007, *passim*, but especially chs 1–2.

societies, i.e., to those social and institutional features of law *via* which it exerts a deep and pervasive influence over the lives of those living under it.

Secondly, in making the point that, 'what is alarming' about unjust laws 'is that they are perfectly genuine laws' (MacCormick 2007, 271), MacCormick also recognises the further point I made in the preceding section, i.e., that we judge such examples in terms of their failure *as law*, and are alarmed by and concerned about them precisely because they are law, and are hence to be judged according to whether they realise the values law ought to, but they do not in fact realise those values.

In these respects, then, MacCormick's view better captures certain important facets of law and of our understanding of it as compared with Finnis's. However, as was also noted in section 1 above, there are circumstances in which, according to MacCormick, the *radical* injustice of a given law or set of laws renders it/them not law at all (MacCormick 2007, 271–73). This raises the question: if 'non-radically' unjust law remains law nonetheless, then why does radical injustice require the different response that such law is not properly viewed as law at all? As was pointed out above, if 'non-radically' unjust law is still law, then it must be so in virtue of possessing important properties other than successfully realising its moral point or purpose. If law is law, then, in virtue of its possessing properties other than successfully realising justice, why can we not account radically unjust law as law too, in virtue of those same properties? I am not entirely clear on the answer to this from the chapters on methodology in *Institutions of Law*, but would suggest that MacCormick's claim that radically unjust law ought not to be viewed as law is linked to his claim that it is in the nature of law that it makes an implicit claim to justice (MacCormick 2007, 274–77). This thought springs from the way in which MacCormick defines radically unjust law:

> if what is done cannot be accounted for under any possible conception of justice that could reasonably be adopted or advocated by a reasonable person willing to subject his or her beliefs to discursive scrutiny, then what is thus done by way of rules and practices of governance would not properly count as law. (MacCormick 2007, 273)[37]

It is clear that radically unjust law does not succeed in realising a conception of justice. But is it MacCormick's view that it is impossible for those creating and administering such law even to make a *claim* to justice, and, as making such a claim is part of the nature of law,[38] thus radically unjust law cannot properly be accounted as law (MacCormick 2007, 271)? This interpretation seems plausible. In general, unjust law remains 'real law' for MacCormick, and so, *contra* Finnis, he does not claim that whenever law fails to realise those values it ought to it should

37 Internal footnote reference to Alexy 2002. See also MacCormick 2007, 277.

38 See MacCormick 2007, 274–77 and the discussion of MacCormick's views in section 1 above.

be regarded as less than fully law. Rather, it is only when law fails so radically in its aspiration to realise justice and the common good, such that it becomes impossible even to *claim* that it realises a vision of justice, that MacCormick regards such purported law as not really law at all. As, for MacCormick, making a claim to justice is part of law's nature, then law in respect of which no such claim can be made cannot properly be understood as law.

Questions remain, of course. Is it true that a claim to justice is a necessary feature of law? Is it impossible for those creating and administering law to make such a claim (at all? Or is it that such a claim must be made sincerely?) in the case of radically unjust law? Do the answers to these questions lead to the conclusion that radically unjust law is not to be understood as law? As these issues are not the main concern of the present article, which focuses instead on jurisprudential methodology, and on the relationship between certain methodological claims and various theorists' views regarding whether bad law is still and/or really law, I leave them to one side for the moment.[39] However, the points made above do reinforce my earlier claim that MacCormick's views are more successful than Finnis's as regards giving adequate emphasis to the social reality of law as it is actually implemented in human society, and to the fact that we worry about law which does not realise those values it is supposed to precisely because it is law, but it is law which fails to be as law ought to be. Unjust law which fails to be as law ought to be remains law nonetheless for MacCormick, thus reflecting the social reality of law, which often does so fail,[40] and which concerns us precisely because it is law, but it is failing to live up to those particular standards by which law ought to be judged. The only point at which unjust law is not to be understood as law at all is when it cannot be construed as making a *claim* to justice which, for MacCormick, is one of law's necessary features. Thus if I am correct in my interpretation of MacCormick, in his view it is not that radically unjust law ceases to be law because it fails to possess a necessary feature of law *as it ought to be* (although it does so fail: it is radically unjust), rather, it ceases to be law because it fails to possess a necessary feature of law *as it is* and must be in order to be law, i.e., that it makes a *claim* to justice.[41]

For all this, however, I do have doubts regarding an aspect of MacCormick's methodological approach. At one point in *Institutions of Law*, MacCormick formulates his position thus:

---

39 My instinct, however, is, *contra* MacCormick: (1) that it is possible for those creating and administering radically unjust law still to claim that it fulfils certain purposes and lives up to certain values, and (2) that radically unjust law is still to be accounted as law. I cannot further explain or defend these views here.

40 This point is noted at several points in MacCormick 2007, e.g., 264, 271 and 298–99.

41 I do not know whether MacCormick would agree with the interpretation of his position offered here.

> 'Mind the gap!' is the moral of the story so far. It is hardly disputable that a conceptually satisfactory understanding of law that looks to its focal meaning and acknowledges the character of an interpretative concept like law must take fully into account the values to which legal activity is essentially oriented. But this makes urgent attention to the gap between law grasped conceptually and law in its actual social implementation and impact. (MacCormick 2007, 299)

As has been discussed in the two preceding sections, I support the point that in order properly to understand law we must understand its aims and the values it ought to realise. However, the final sentence of the passage quoted above strikes me as mysterious. MacCormick draws a distinction between law grasped conceptually on the one hand, and law in its actual social implementation and impact on the other. Moreover, in this passage, 'law grasped conceptually' would appear to mean law in its focal meaning, i.e., for MacCormick, law which both aspires to, and realises, justice. Law in its actual social implementation and impact, on the other hand, would appear to mean law which, although it may aspire to justice and make a claim to realise it, may or may not in fact succeed in its aspiration. I am puzzled by this because of MacCormick's views, discussed above, that bad law remains law nonetheless when it fails, in a non-radical way, to realise justice, and that even in the case of radically unjust law, the reason that it is no longer to be understood as law is not because it lacks a necessary feature of law as it ought to be (realising justice and the common good) but because it lacks a necessary feature of law as it is (making a *claim* to justice). If this is so, then how can 'law grasped conceptually' be law in its focal meaning, which succeeds in realising justice, and how can 'law grasped conceptually' be viewed in contradistinction to law in its actual social implementation? If, for MacCormick – as my above analysis claims – there is some way of still accounting something as law despite its failing to realise its aspiration to justice, then surely whatever properties in virtue of which such law is still law are part of the concept of law, i.e., are part of 'law grasped conceptually'. For MacCormick, as was noted above, such properties include aspects of law as 'institutional normative order' other than successfully realising those values to which law aspires. This being so it does not make sense to view 'law grasped conceptually' as law in its focal meaning, or to view 'law grasped conceptually' in contradistinction to law as it is actually implemented in society: those properties of law 'in its actual social implementation and impact', in virtue of which it is law, and remains law, despite its sometime injustice must be properties picked out by the concept of law, otherwise we would not account things possessing such properties as law (and MacCormick does count them as law).

3. Conclusion

In this chapter, I have tried to explore the idea that we need to understand law's aims and what law ought to be, in order properly to understand it. I have also discussed the link between this methodological point and the claim that law which fails to realise the values it ought to is not really or not fully law. In my view, legal theorists should endorse the methodological insight that in order properly to understand law we must understand law's aims and the values it ought to live up to, but reject the further point that instances of law which fail to be what they ought to be are not really law. The position I have outlined stands opposed to various aspects of John Finnis's views, as Finnis believes that the methodological insight, together with some other points regarding the nature and status of law's moral point or purpose, supports the conclusion that instances of law which fail to realise the ideals they ought to are not really law at all. I tried to challenge this view by arguing that it results in legal theory failing to grant adequate importance to the social reality of law as it is actually implemented in human societies, and that it fails to do adequate justice to the sense in which our concerns and worries about morally bad law stem from the fact that they are failing precisely as instances *of law*.

Neil MacCormick subscribes to the methodological point that we need to understand law's claims, aims and the values it ought to realise in order properly to understand it, but rejects the view that law which fails to be what it ought to be thereby ceases to be law. Rather, purported law ceases to be law only when it is radically unjust, to the point where it cannot possess one of the properties which, for MacCormick, is a necessary feature of law as it is rather than of law as it ought to be, i.e., that it makes a *claim* to justice. Although I disagree with certain aspects of his views,[42] I have argued that this stance is more successful than Finnis's in that it grants adequate explanatory importance to the social reality of law as it actually exists in human society, and that it better captures the sense in which we are concerned about morally bad laws precisely because they are law, but are failing to be as law ought to be.

Writing this article has afforded me a welcome opportunity for further reflection on aspects of Neil MacCormick's views. What emerges clearly from such reflection is that, as regards his stance on jurisprudential methodology, as with so many other aspects of his work, Neil MacCormick's views are subtle, thought-provoking, and enduring.

References

Alexy, R. (2002), *The Argument from Injustice: A Reply to Legal Positivism* (Oxford: Clarendon Press).

---

42 See e.g., note 39 above, and the conclusion to the preceding section.

Aquinas, St. T. (1989), *Summa Theologiae*, McDermott, T. (ed.). (London: Eyre and Spottiswoode in association with Methuen).
Cohen, M. (ed.) (1984), *Ronald Dworkin and Contemporary Jurisprudence* (London: Duckworth).
Coleman, J. and Paul, E.F. (eds) (1987), *Philosophy and Law* (Oxford: Basil Blackwell).
Dickson, J. (2004), 'Methodology in Jurisprudence: A Critical Survey', *Legal Theory* 10, 117–56.
Dickson, J. (2004), *Evaluation and Legal Theory* (Oxford: Hart Publishing).
Dworkin, R. (1986), *Law's Empire* (London: Fontana Press).
Dyzenhaus, D. (1991), *Hard Cases in Wicked Legal Systems: South African Law in the Perspective of Legal Philosophy* (Oxford: Clarendon Press).
Finnis, J. (1980), *Natural Law and Natural Rights* (Oxford: Clarendon Press).
Finnis, J. (2003), 'Law and What I Truly Should Decide', *American Journal of Jurisprudence* 48, 107–29.
Finnis, J. (2007), 'Natural Law Theories', *The Stanford Encyclopaedia of Philosophy*, available online http://plato.stanford.edu/archives/spr2007/entries/natural-law-theories.
Fuller, L. (1958), 'Positivism and Fidelity to Law – a Reply to Professor Hart', *Harvard Law Review* 71, 630–72
Fuller, L. (1969), *The Morality of Law* (New Haven: Yale University Press).
Gardner, J. (2000), 'The Virtue of Justice and the Character of Law', *Current Legal Problems* 53, 1.
Gardner, J. (2006), 'Law's Aim in *Law's Empire*', in Hershovitz 2006.
Gardner, J. (2007), 'Nearly Natural Law', *American Journal of Jurisprudence* 52, 1 (pagination references from http://users.ox.ac.uk/~lawf0081/progress.htm).
George, R.P. (ed.) (1992), *Natural Law Theory: Contemporary Essays* (Oxford: Clarendon Press).
George, R.P. (ed.) (1996), *The Autonomy of Law: Essays on Legal Positivism* (Oxford: Clarendon Press).
Green, L. (2008), 'Positivism and the Inseparability of Law and Morals', *New York University Law Review* 83, forthcoming.
Hart, H.L.A. (1958), 'Positivism and the Separation of Law and Morals', *Harvard Law Review* 71, 593–629.
Hart, H.L.A. (1965), 'Lon L. Fuller: *The Morality of Law*', *Harvard Law Review* 78, 1281–96.
Hart, H.L.A. (1994), *The Concept of Law* (Oxford: Clarendon Press).
Hershovitz, S. (ed.) (2006), *Exploring Law's Empire* (Oxford: Oxford University Press).
Lyons, D. (1984), 'Moral Aspects of Legal Theory', in Cohen 1984.
MacCormick, N. (1985), 'A Moralistic Case for A-Moralistic Law', *Valparaiso Law Review* 20, 1–41.
MacCormick, N. (2007), *Institutions of Law: An Essay in Legal Theory* (Oxford: Oxford University Press).

Moore, M. (1992), 'Law as a Functional Kind', in George 1992.

Pavlakos, G. (ed.) (2007), *Law, Rights and Discourse: The Legal Philosophy of Robert Alexy* (Oxford: Hart Publishing).

Radbruch, G. (1990), *Rechtsphilosophie III, Vol. 3 of the Gustav Radbruch Gesamtausgabe*, Kaufmann, A (ed.), (Heidelberg: C.F. Mueller).

Raz, J. (2003), 'About Morality and the Nature of Law', *American Journal of Jurisprudence* 48, 1–15.

Raz, J. (2007), 'The Argument from Justice, or How Not to Reply to Legal Positivism', in Pavlakos 2007.

Schauer, F. (1996), 'Positivism as Pariah', in George 1996.

Schauer, F. (2005), 'The Social Construction of the Concept of Law: A Reply to Julie Dickson', *Oxford Journal of Legal Studies* 25, 493–501.

Soper, P. (1987), 'Choosing a Legal Theory on Moral Grounds', in Coleman and Paul 1987.

Stavropoulos, N. (2003), 'Interpretivist Theories of Law', *The Stanford Encyclopaedia of Philosophy*, available online http://plato.stanford.edu/archives/win2003/entries/law-interpretivist.

PART V
Reply

Chapter 12
Concluding for Institutionalism

Neil MacCormick

The chapters in this book make a cumulatively powerful case for taking seriously, though not uncritically, the claims of institutionalism as a profitable approach to understanding human law as an omnipresent feature of human society and societies. It is profitable because it is broad and inclusive of law in all its forms. 'Institutional normative order' affords a comfortably broad explanatory definition of law. William Twining justly surveys here and elsewhere in his own books the multiform and yet pervasive character of law, both in history and in the contemporary globalised world of planet Earth. He places this in the context of wise advice to legal thinkers to eschew narrowness of mind and of vision, and to avoid the stato-centrism that has been characteristic of all too much 'Western' legal thought. Law takes many forms, and pluralism ought to prevail in jurisprudence. One may add that there are interesting forms of law, notably moral law and scientific law that are not institutional (moral law) nor indeed normative (scientific law), but that help in the ordering of the way we mutually understand each other, and in the way we understand the character of the universe around us.

Recent work in institutional theory of law, particularly by Ota Weinberger, Dick Ruiter, Jaap Hage, Eerik Lagerspetz and myself, has owed a good deal to reflection on the philosophy of language and the theory of speech acts. This has been done in interaction with attempts to develop legal theory beyond the modern legal positivism of the 'pure theory of law' advocated by Hans Kelsen, Frantisek Weyr and others or the 'analytical positivism' of Herbert Hart and his numerous school of admirers and followers. In the present volume, Massimo La Torre helpfully labels this recent work as 'neo-insitititutionalism' to mark it off somewhat from the earlier twentieth-century flourishing of institutional theories about law such as those of Santi Romano, Maurice Hauriou and (on the very dark side) Carl Schmitt. A great debt is owed to La Torre for his searching scholarship into the overall history of jurisprudential institutionalism and to the relationships as well as differences between older and newer versions. What this makes clear is that there is most certainly an institutional aspect to law that invites attention through the prism of some appropriate philosophical methodology.

How much attention the institutional aspect deserves is controversial. Ronald Dworkin, target of the chapter here by Fred Schauer, has dismissed this 'sociological' feature of law as being of no real interest to philosophers of law. Within the present volume, Victor Tadros makes a similar point. He argues that the vital underpinning of any attempt to produce a comprehensive understanding of law must be a grand theory of justice in which are integrated sub-themes such as those concerning distributive justice, retributive justice, corrective justice and justice in exchange. Substituting for this an explanation or analysis of the concept of institutional normative order is opting for what is boring and rather obvious, and omitting what is exciting, in need of explanation, and fundamental to understanding law as a whole or any particular branch of it.

While I agree with Tadros about the need for a broader theory of justice than that which I included in *Institutions of Law*, I can fall back on the excuse always open to the author of a multi-volume series on a single theme. ('Law, State, and Practical Reason' is my overall theme.) My theory of justice, or account of the space to be filled by a full-blown such theory, is now stated in my forthcoming *Practical Reason in Law and Morality* (MacCormick 2009). On the other hand, for reasons similar to those tellingly deployed by Schauer in critique of Dworkin, I reject the proposition that explanatory work on the institutional nature of law – and what we mean by 'institutional nature' – is either pointless-because-obvious, or indeed boring. To support this claim, it is perhaps appropriate to turn at this stage to accounting for the approach I took in writing *Institutions of Law*. I shall also use this context as one in which to respond to the brilliant essays prepared by colleagues and friends for inclusion in the present book, for each of which I give unstinted thanks.

Institutions of Law is a work in four parts. The first ('Norm, Institution, and Order') has an explanatory purpose; the second, ('Persons, Acts, and Relations') an analytical one; the third ('Law, State, and Civil Society') a synthetic one, and the fourth ('Law, Morality and Methodology') an evaluative one in various dimensions of value.

So far as concerns the explanatory part, one can safely say that very few people who have though or written about law in at any rate the last hundred years have been at all inclined to deny that it has an institutional aspect (in perhaps more than one sense of the term 'institutional'). But most have either thought this too obvious to need any explanation, or, perhaps, have thought it already adequately explained via Hart's 'union of primary and secondary rules' or Kelsen's theory of 'legal dynamics' or something of the kind. For me, however, much as I have learned from both Hart (especially Hart) and Kelsen, I do not find their explanations satisfactory. Pressed to the point of explaining actual cases and situations, they break down. We do need something better than either finally achieved.

Starting from the idea that human beings are norm-users (since they are speaking animals) before they can possibly become norm-issuers or norm-analysts, and developing thus the Hartian insight about the 'internal aspect' of human rule-oriented behaviour, one can explain what norms are and what 'normative' means. Considering possible human conduct (e.g., standing in a spontaneously formed queue) where people interact on the basis of mutual beliefs about each other's behavioural orientation, one can understand how each thinks others ought to, and probably will, behave. From this also, we can construct an idea of 'orderliness' in conduct as distinct from disorder, orderliness that results from reciprocal observance of essentially similar beliefs and dispositions of different persons. Hence one can understand normative order, in this case of a purely customary or conventional kind.

Next, however, one may consider how in some social setting the management of some service may include management of the queuing behaviour of (for example) customers in a railway station or airport or delicatessen. (Perhaps there is a numbered roll of tickets and each new arrival takes a fresh consecutively numbered ticket and waits for the number to be called or electronically displayed.) This involves an at least two-tier normative practice, one that authorises queue-managers to tell people the rules they must follow here, and to enforce them by only serving those who observe the rules. The normative order of the queue is thus institutionalised.

Institutionalisation on the grand scale occurs in the state and other large-scale organisations. Because states purport to, and to a considerable extent do successfully, monopolise coercive force in the territories over which they claim jurisdiction, the institutional normative order of the state can have a unique influence in contemporary human life and thought. But, as Twining underlines, this is not by any means the only, or an all-purpose all-important theatre of law, not even from the point of view of legal professionals involved, for example in human rights law or in international commercial law. It is, however, an important theatre and deserves to be taken seriously as such.

In this context, Julie Dickson's summary of my position about the character of state-law is clear and accurate. There are institution-agencies of the state that in various ways are responsible under a constitution for issuing new rules and repealing old ones. There are others responsible for seeing to the execution of rules validly made. There are yet others that adjudicate upon alleged breaches of or failures to implement properly the rules that have been made. This they normally do in the light of a body of interpretative precedents themselves established in prior judgements of the adjudicative institutions. The constitution under which they act, however formally established, has itself ultimately to be underpinned by a customary or conventional norm accepted by the personnel of most of the institutions and most citizens as well. This custom is to the effect that the constitution must be implemented and respected, for if this is not a prevailing attitude the state cannot function coherently.

This is neither boring nor obvious to my view, and without some such a grasp one cannot, as Fred Schauer argues, begin to comprehend the body of state-law which the courts (the adjudicative institutions) apply using interpretative arguments of various kinds. Certainly, such arguments are ideally guided by some attractive overarching conception of legal justice such as Tadros (and Dworkin) seek to place at the heart of jurisprudence. But neither Tadros nor Dworkin successfully shows that the explanatory (or, in a weak sense,[1] 'sociological') elements in the explanation are redundant or subordinate to the ideal element.

The claim to explain the essential character of a certain kind of law widely pervasive in human society and societies through unpacking the explanatory definition that says 'Law is institutional normative order' is vulnerable to attack for the very use of a definition of this kind at all. Yet there is in fact no justification for shying away from definition as one tool of explanation. Certainly, Twining and I now both agree on this notwithstanding the contrary view of our early mentor Herbert Hart, and Andrew Halpin's continuing disinclination to grant definition any exalted place in a well-constructed juristic methodology.[2] Definition or not is hardly the real issue, however. We need to face the more substantial risk that what is offered fails as an explanation, hence is pointless as a definition.

One test-bed for checking the adequacy of the explanation is to see how much it helps explain, and this proposition leads us at once into scrutinising the analytical part of *Institutions of Law*. Discourses of lawyers and many non-lawyerly discourses about law use a network of interrelated concepts and technical terms like 'persons', 'duties', 'rights' obligations', powers', 'immunities'. Many of these terms and the concepts they name are also in use in broader normative discourse beyond the range of institutional law – in ideal moral discourse, for example.

An analytical approach to elucidating the meaning of such terms is one that seeks to see how they all interconnect in linkages of mutual implication or opposition, or by way of enabling change at one level so as to confer a dynamic character on the whole conceptual network or framework. This is a kind of exercise in conceptual grammar or even (as is sometimes said) 'logical grammar'. It requires a reflexive inquiry into the norms of the discourse we engage in when we are discussing the legal rights and duties of persons, or their acquisition of property or their immunity from arbitrary arrest, or … . This can be a relatively abstract discourse, or, in a lawyer's chambers trying to solve a client's legal problem, an intensely practical one. The complexity of life under highly developed systems of law guarantees also that the network one analyses is a dense and thickly concatenated one. Jaap Hage's remarkable contribution to the present book about 'transactions' and the linkage of this with a discourse of 'legal power' (itself a form of 'normative power')

1 From a sociologist's point of view, bare observations about institutions would seem very pre-theoretical, and requiring theoretical construction to come within the domain of the sociological properly understood. So the Dworkinian-sociological is indeed sociological only in the weak sense of amounting to some kind of pre-theoretical 'raw data'. The approach embraced by legal-institutional theorists is to theorise institutions within jurisprudence in the hope of creating a serious bridge across two cognate disciplines, and constructively linking legal and social theory.

2 Halpin (this volume) quite reasonably says: 'We may enrich our understanding of something through arriving at a clearer idea or concept of it, without necessarily providing a definition of it.' He is correct, but equally it follows that it is not necessary to abstain from providing a definition where a definition does promote clarity.

shows some of this complexity and exemplifies an elegant approach to analysis that makes the complex appear in simple light. I hope that something of the same quality is to be found in Part II of *Institutions of Law*.

If the explanatory part did its work well, it will have made possible a clear and illuminating account of law's conceptual framework showing networks of mutual implication and the like – which at this level are indeed far more important than any essay into definitions of terms. This will not involve a slavish reproduction of everyday speech about law. Rather, it will to some extent have a reforming or at least a tidying-up purpose, showing how lawyers might use their special common terminology with a higher degree of accuracy than under the terminological compromises that daily life sometimes calls for. Nevertheless, analysis must respect ordinary legal speech as the basic data from which to start, and it must be faithful to its implicit grammar. The critical element will, however, be stronger in relation to earlier attempts at similar analyses (Hohfeld's or Hart's, for example) where these seem to have missed their mark, or badly distorted the 'basic data' with no compensating gain in achieved new clarity.

Analysis, as its name implies, breaks things down. It takes a complex conceptual framework and examines each component in relation to every other. It therefore needs to be complemented with synthesis. How do atomic concepts build up into complex molecular wholes, and how does this map on to ways of seeing law and divisions of legal practice? One way to look at this is to take well known branches of law, such as Public Law, Human Rights Law, Criminal Law and Private Law (and use the latter as a grab-bag for all those branches of law that bear on the 'private sector' of a market economy, hence not separating out such sub-sets as consumer law, commercial law, labour law or family law). This enables one to take a large view of the relations of Law, State and Civil Society.

Public law plainly has to do with the structure of the state and with its raising and spending of revenues necessary or desirable for the performance of state functions. Under the prevalence of social-liberal or social-democratic ideals and ideologies it is at least desirable and perhaps obligatory for the state to attend to matters of distributive justice among citizens and to provide the basics, or more than the basics, of a general system of social welfare. Thus public law can be associated both with principles of effective and efficient organisation of governance and with distributive justice. In analytical terms, a great deal of public law concerns empowerment of institution-agencies charged with the various tasks of modern government. Typically, but not exclusively, as Victor Tadros points out, powers of this kind are unilaterally exercisable. But they must be exercised for general public goods, not for the private good of those who, on behalf of the institutions, take the initiative in activating the powers vested in them. Typically, but not exclusively, the powers exercisable in private law differ in both respects.

Human Rights law, in the primary present understanding of Human Rights, affects 'vertical' relations between citizen and state rather than 'horizontal' relations among citizens. They confer wide immunities upon citizens protecting them from potentially oppressive exercises of state power and in general they confer complex rights in relation to states of being (like remaining alive) or states of affairs (e.g., no criminal penalties without prior fair trials). Hence it forms a bridge between general public law and criminal law, for criminal law is also an area in which citizens may face oppressive interventions by the state, not all of which are backed up by true claims of retributive justice. Ideally, one seeks a system of criminal law that does adhere rigorously to the requirements of retributive justice, with fair and objective prosecution services working through independent courts that fully respect the presumption of innocence in favour of all accused persons, but that punish appropriately those who are in the end convicted of crimes. Such a system is one essential background condition of the establishment and maintenance of peace and civility among persons and thus enables the society comprising a state's citizens to develop into genuinely civil society.

Magnus Ulväng and Victor Tadros, backed by Nils Jareborg, warn against any tendency to over-value the peace-securing function of criminal law, even in tandem with the claims of retributive justice and the maintenance among citizens of a sense that the state protects them adequately from criminal violence, robbery, theft and burglary, rather than leaving them to self-help and the risk of a spiral of mutual violence. There is much else that falls within the province of criminal law, as the thesis of the 'moral substratum' of criminal law developed in *Institutions of Law* tries also to show. Nevertheless, it is important when taking a broad view of law and society to acknowledge the essential part criminal law does play in securing and maintaining the civility among citizens that makes possible the existence of civil society. Thereby it also helps establish conditions in which, given an appropriate body of private law, a commercial market economy can also flourish.

In private law, justice in exchange ('synallagmatic justice') prevails so far as concerns dynamic interchanges in markets. When things go wrong, the corrective justice of civil remedies comes to the fore. But the overall distribution of property and resources that results from the workings of markets in goods, labour, services, and moveable and immovable forms of capital is quite undesigned and hence the issue of distributive justice lies largely outside the scope of private law. Large scale class-actions based on strict liability for harmful conduct, sometimes involving heavy punitive damages, may in some jurisdictions (chiefly in the USA) introduce substantial redistributive elements into the domain of private litigation. Yet this can often seem to exacerbate a sense of distributive injustice as between those who succeed in coming within the ambit of such a many-party claim and those who, similarly harmed in other contexts, do not.

However that may be, Victor Tadros is correct to say that one cannot too simply assign the task of distributive justice to public law, retributive justice to criminal law and corrective justice to private law by way of a simple and unquestioned division of legal labour. For each has elements of all aspects of justice in it. Comparably, Nils Jareborg's elegantly expressed doubts about the political wisdom and justice of imposing criminal liability on corporations as such, rather than on directors of such companies, show how a single topic may raise issues of justice on all fronts. Elements of both criminal and private law come into play together in this. A simple division of legal labour in the cause of justice does not exist.

What is more seriously arguable, and what I argue for both in *Institutions of Law* and here, is this. Taking a broad view, the main engagement of state law with distributive justice comes through the taxation system and the welfare and public service elements dealt with by public law. The main engagement with retributive justice is through criminal law, and with corrective, through private (or 'civil') law. The sustenance of the state is achieved through public law primarily; the most essential foundation of the civility of civil society lies in a satisfactory and reasonably well-working system of criminal law implemented through uncorrupted and efficient police, prosecution services and criminal courts. The market economy in turn depends on a similarly satisfactory system of private law that makes available machinery for enforcement of contracts, for securing of property and for compensating for harm achieved. This is done through the civil courts as instruments principally of corrective justice. There is perhaps some danger of over-simplification in trying to establish a large view of this kind, yet on the other hand in some contexts under-simplification can be as great a barrier to clear understanding as over-simplification. I hope to have achieved a mean between extremes here.

I turn now to the evaluative part and to final issues of method and methodology. The facts that criminal law has a moral substratum in popular or conventional morality and that different aspects of justice are engaged in different branches of law by no means determines the content of a state's law in any very confining way. For the issue of what justice requires in any of the domains we have considered and the issue of what is a satisfactory form of economy are the perennial issues of legislative politics and are continuously in controversy in democratic (or even partly democratic) political systems. There is no single justice that is *the* justice of law; there are rival conceptions of justice that contend for temporary mastery through legislative politics and ultimately through judicial interpretation and application of law. These processes are of course central to the achieved institutionalisation of state law as one particular manifestation of institutional normative order.

By contrast, moral argument, though it may address institutions, especially legislatures but often also courts, depends at base on the autonomous commitments of individual moral persons. In moral argument, people are autonomous; they are their own source of law-like imperatives or norms. These they can deploy in purely personal and social contexts or also in political ones. But not all views can prevail politically. Some become institutionalised as part of law in force for the time being, others do not. Moral discourse is essentially autonomous, discursive among equal discussants, and non-institutionalised. It therefore follows that law as institutional normative order and morality understood in terms of autonomy are quite distinct conceptually though mutually influential practically. Whether such an understanding in terms of autonomy is correct is a serious question. I attempt to re-state the case for this view in the fourth volume of the quartet on 'Law State and Practical Reason', *Practical Reason in Law and Morality*. If it is correct, it follows that one tenet of the legal theoretical stance known as legal positivism is true, namely that law and morality are conceptually distinct from each other. Vittorio Villa's view of constructivist epistemology perhaps applies here. We construct our concepts of law and of morality as outputs of philosophy; we do not start with them as raw inputs. But how we construct them, and with whatever reasonable claims to correctness in what we do, the issue of identity or difference is settled at the level of the output. By this epistemological approach, one identifies two domains of human activity that are conceptually and even ontologically distinct from each other.

As Villa notes, however, my trajectory in legal theory has been away from another main tenet of positivism, to the point that I would now describe my position as 'post-positivist'. What is at issue is whether there are any moral constraints on what can possibly be classified as genuine law. I think there are, and have come close to sharing the view of Robert Alexy and Gustav Radbruch – there are extremes of injustice that negate the existence of 'law' even where some of the normally necessary and presumptively sufficient conditions for existence of law are present. To adopt terms very appropriately used by Julie Dickson, normally rules made by legal institutions with legislative power are laws, all the more so when they are implemented as such by adjudicative institutions. This is precisely what the institutional theory of law asserts, with the rider that underpinning a constitution there always has to be some customary norm or convention that is not itself issued by any norm-creating institution.

Why or how, then, can there be an outer limit set in moral terms? Why hold that the normal conditions for law-ness are defeasible in extreme cases? Why say that institutionalisation is only presumptively sufficient for legal existence and validity?

There are both theoretical and (connectedly) practical reasons for holding this.

Theoretically, we start from the observation that understanding law synthetically, under such a heading as 'Law, State, and Civil Society', requires us to see how aspects of justice are implicit in the rules and principles and practices of the various branches of state law taken as a whole. Law exists, as Twining puts it, to serve justice and peace – also, Dickson adds, the common good and the cause of civility. But this is open to a detached understanding as well as to a committed one. Dickson's own work on methodology advocates that the theorist or student of law needs criteria of importance in identifying what matters about law, and these will refer to the practices of those engaged in law-work and legal practice in all its forms. But the theorist need not endorse the practical commitments of the practitioners at all, and must be guided by theory-determined criteria of importance. Hence, although law cannot be understood without understanding the values its participants think it should serve, the theorist has no commitment as a theorist to these values. So whatever they happen to be determines the content of law, whether the theorist thinks the content of the law very just and otherwise morally decent, or takes a radically opposed view. Law it is, either way. Villa and Twining both, I think, endorse this position of Dickson's, albeit with some differences of nuance among them.

What this overlooks, however, is the problem of the 'law' that no one is willing publicly to avow. The Nazi's anti-Jew Nuremberg Laws were open and published and vilely discriminatory, but there was a kind of public accounting given of them by the regime – expressed also in Hitler's *Mein Kampf*. When it came to the great crime of shipping Europe's Jews to death camps and there killing and incinerating about 6 million of them, the public record was silent. All was achieved by largely secret, at any rate unpublished, administrative decrees. The administrative institutions were empowered by some means to do as they did, and they acted with hideously consequential efficiency. Was this law in action?

When in spring and summer of 2008, a presidential and parliamentary election took place in Zimbabwe, the evidence appeared to be clear that the ruling President, Robert Mugabe and his ZANU-PF party had been defeated in both elections. But long recounts of votes took place and it was declared that Morgan Tsvangirai, the MDC candidate, though ahead of Mugabe in the first ballot, had not won an overall majority of votes, hence there had to be a run-off in the presidential election. Forces closely associated with ZANU-PF then went on a rampage of intimidation, beating and even murder to terrorise the opposition from participating effectively in the run-off election. They succeeded, and to forestall the risk of civil war, Tsvangirai withdrew from the election. This nevertheless went ahead, with terrified voters turning out to support the sole remaining candidate, who was in due course sworn in as lawfully elected President of Zimbabwe.

For Zimbabweans at home in summer 2008, the prospects for effectively challenging the lawfulness of Mugabe's presidency through any of the country's institutions are dim. It would also be an extremely dangerous course for anyone to take, given the coercive forces at the government's disposal and its track record of ruthlessness in using these. Outside, governments of other countries and Zimbabweans in exile can denounce the election as a sham and the result as illegal. But this changes nothing internally and does not make it impossible for President Mugabe to proclaim the legality of his government, with the support of such courts and other public institutions as remain in function. But of course the proclamation of this legality entirely suppresses and denies any suggestion of improper and violent means used to defeat opposition and deny it the democratic hearing it had won.[3] The history of dictatorship is littered with similar examples from elsewhere – Chile under Augusto Pinochet, Uganda under Idi Amin, to name but two.

One can even come nearer home and contemplate things that go wrong under conditions of relatively strong democracy and an effective implementation of the rule of law through independent courts. The case of *R. (Bancoult) v Foreign*

3 By the autumn of 2008, under external pressure, President Mugabe was prevailed upon to agree to establish a power-sharing government along with Mr Tsvangirai as Prime Minister, but the talks aimed to bring this about were for long deadlocked.

Secretary[4] concerned the rights of the Chagos Islanders, or 'Chagossians', to reside in their native isles in the Indian Ocean, these islands being part of what has been designated the 'British Indian Ocean Territory', sometimes abbreviated to 'BIOT'. The islands are very remote and were formerly a part of Mauritius, from which they were detached by a somewhat contested process in the 1960s. At that time there were around 1000 Chagossians resident in the island of Diego Garcia and certain of its neighbours, working mainly in copra plantations and well-fed from the plentiful fish stocks around the islands, but dependent on long and infrequent voyages to Mauritius or other neighbouring places for medical treatment and stores of various kinds.

The USA, in the circumstances of the Cold War then prevailing, sought an airbase in the Indian Ocean, with one essential feature – it must be on a vacant island with no indigenous population, and Diego Garcia was of convenient size and location. The UK was the colonial power and was approached by the US Government for its help. The upshot was that by various ruses – shipping out for medical treatment, with no return voyage, for example, many of the islanders were cleared off to Mauritius. Eventually those that remained were simply forced off the island with a single suitcase each for all belongings, their much-loved dogs being gassed with carbon monoxide and then incinerated. The UK supplied the USA with this now vacant, or, rather, vacated, territory for an airbase that remains in place and in very active use into the twenty-first century.

Some compensation was subsequently paid by the UK Government to displaced islanders, under the constraint of their giving up any right to complain of their treatment in being forced into exile. In 1971, an 'Immigration Ordinance' was enacted using powers under the Colonial Laws Validity Act of 1865, and this banned islanders (and others) from returning to the islands by 'immigrating' there save with permission. With great pertinacity, however, one of the leaders of the Chagossians took up and sustained a series of legal challenges to this Ordinance and eventually in 2000 succeeded in obtaining an order annulling it.[5] The next move by the UK Government was to mount an inquiry into the possibility of resettling some at least of the Chagos Islands. In the end, a negative conclusion was reached about this on the grounds that it could not be made economically viable and that the old economy of copra-production could no longer be revived. In 2004, by exercise of the royal prerogative power (effectively done by ministers of the Crown) a new 'British Indian Ocean Territory Constitution Order' was enacted by way of an Order in Council. This was made in the name of the Queen in Council, the highest authority under the Colonial Laws Validity Act 1865, with unqualified powers of lawmaking for the peace order and good government of colonial territories. The Constitution Order included a provision expressly banning islanders from returning to reside on the islands. An associated immigration ordinance provided for permission to be given for occasional visits,

4 *R. (Bancoult) v Foreign Secretary (No. 2)* [2007] 3 WLR 768.

5 See *R. (Bancoult) v Foreign Secretary (No. 1)* [2001] QB 1067.

all other visiting of the islands being prohibited. The Court of Appeal in London, however, ruled that, notwithstanding the near-absolute power held by the Queen in Council, the Order was void for irrationality. A power to make laws for 'peace, order and good government' implies that there is somebody to be governed, whose interest in peace and order and the common good justifies the law-making power. This is reduced to nonsense by an instrument that on its face excludes from the governed territory those persons whose good government is at stake. The Order bears its total irrationality on its face, and cannot be saved simply by appealing to the apparently absolute character of the law-making power conferred by the 1865 Act.[6] This seems a pretty convincing conclusion, but unfortunately it was not upheld on final appeal to the House of Lords, in which a majority of three to two overturned the Court of Appeal's reasoning. The Lords did so on the ground that the power to make laws for the 'peace, order and good government' of a territory is one in relation to which the judiciary cannot substitute its judgement for that of the executive branch, which is entitled to take into account the overall interest of the United Kingdom and the colonial territory considered as a whole. They considered that in the circumstances of the case, with a long lapse of time since the original clearance of the islands and the current attempt to re-open the islands to their previous inhabitants, the issue of a right of resettlement had become merely symbolic, except to the extent that it might be a lever to put pressure on the UK government to invest heavily in some form of economically unviable resettlement programme.

This case provides a clear example of a grave injustice visited by a colonial power upon indigenous colonial people. In respect of the original governmental actions of the late 1960s and early 1970s, the injustice was deplored by all the judges, including the final majority in the House of Lords. Most of what was done to the islanders was done secretively, and attempts were made to disguise the true character of their removal from the United Nations and other interested parties. Little public or Parliamentary comment was made on any aspects of the affair other than reference to the Treaty with the USA making the land available for the airbase. Yet when the litigation culminating in 2000 forced the UK Government into relatively more public action through enactment of the British Indian Ocean Territory Constitution Order, the irrational character, effectively the publicly unavowable character of the Order, became clear. It purported to be both a constitution and a ban on residence in the constituted territory of those whose citizenship was of that territory. In this case, there were independent Courts able to take a stand on the issue and insist on the minimal requirements of legal rationality in any purported law-making act no matter the source of the power to make laws of this kind.

---

6 *R. (Bancoult) v Foreign Secretary (No. 2)* [2007] 3 WLR 768. The report of the House of Lords decision to overrule the Court of Appeal (by a majority of three to two) is at [2008] UKHL 61.

But there might not have been such courts, and indeed the final instance of appeal backed off from holding the Constitution Order to be invalid. We cannot always depend on courts. In cases of incipient breakdown of the rule of law an early point of attack is the independence of the judiciary, and the substitution of place-persons for independent judges (not an issue in the *Bancoult* case, of course). That achieved, a slide away from legality in matters of direct interest to the executive head of government in a country readily follows. The individual in question frequently acquires also extensive powers to rule by decree, such powers being conferred under legislation that seemingly delegates power in a neutral if not innocent way.

Nothing constrains a legal theorist to continue counting as 'law' whatever institutionalised enactments there may be, however secret and lacking in public avowal by their authors, however on their face irrational, however lacking in any discursively statable principle of justice. Such defects of governance can properly be treated as defeating conditions for law. Where they are found, the presumptive sufficiency of institutional rule-making for law does not hold good and neither need nor should be sustained. In such circumstances, there may be a kind of institutional order, but any true normative as distinct from brute coercive character is lacking from what is done, certainly in extreme cases like those cited above.

In 'real time' in the 'real world' this theoretical absence of lawfulness may not make a practical difference. Brutal dictators will continue brutally to dictate; colonial civil servants will continue to pursue the dictates of *Realpolitik* (as happened in the Chagos Islands in the 1960s and 1970s) unless restrained by courts. Nobody will be safe from arbitrary treatment, or worse. But bad regimes eventually come to an end, and what is to be said then? Do we have to say that bad things were done but were legally done at the time? Or can we conclude that the worst of the bad things (at least) were never done under anything better than a pretence at legality which cannot protect the perpetrators from some due legal responsibility after the restoration of conditions of (better) legality? This seems the better answer – not all pretended legality is the genuine article, and simple institutional say-so is not alone enough to erect into legality whatever the institutions say at a given time under any circumstances, no matter how cruel and oppressive.

In this quite restricted sense, the extremely unjust 'law' is no law at all. It is never better than pretended law. It may purport to be law, but those who lie outside the malign sphere of the then governing powers should not countenance it as any kind of 'law'. Those who take this stand are not after the event cancelling the legality of something that was once really a law; they are denying the correctness of ever counting it as having at any time been truly law.

This extended reflection perhaps enables me to respond effectively both to Julie Dickson and to Vittorio Villa on the issue of my retreat from legal positivism. Dickson very perceptively observes that I make a use of the 'focal meaning' approach of John Finnis that differs from his use of it. We share the view – rather, I learned from Finnis the view, which I gratefully adopted – that in all matters of practical human concern there is a point to what we do and thus in domains of human activity some instances are more focally instances of the domain in view than others are. Law is an example. Where institutional normative order exists in a way that broadly serves ends of justice and the common good according to some reasonable conception of these, and where law helps to secure the conditions of civility and a viable economy, there one has 'law' in its focal meaning. Many are the examples of legal systems that fall short of this ideal condition, and some at least are thoroughly corrupt even if not yet across the extreme limiting line into non-law.

That line lies, for me, at the point at which instruments of government do not even purport to, or cannot do more than pretend to, serve any conceivable and discursively statable far less arguable conception of justice and common good. For Finnis, it appears that the issue is not one of what purports to be the case, but of what is the case. Deviation from focal meaning (but how far deviating?) tends to un-law, in Finnis's schema; in mine it is the total failure even to address the concerns of 'focal meaning' or a fortiori active opposition to them in some partisan cause that defeats the pretence at 'law'. I gratefully adopt Dickson's proposed clarification of my position on this, which does grasp the essence of what I was trying to say.

In the vein of Villa's preference for a constructivist approach to issues of ontology and epistemology, it seems to me that I am on safe ground in this argument. We are not indeed confronting in this discussion an absolute 'given', a 'raw datum' of 'law' before which we must simply bow down in mute obedience. We are to some extent at least the masters of our own conceptual apparatus. The ordinary discourses of lawyers, and of laypeople about law, do not contain or amount to a univocal or clear concept of 'law' and the 'legal' such as a legal theorist might try to construct in the light of these discourses. So far as we have 'raw data' of speech and discourse here, they are data that contain gaps and contradictions and internal conflicts of usage. They identify the broad domain of what it is worthwhile to discuss and attempt to theorise as 'law'. In no sense do they dictate that we have to construct a concept of law such that anything goes provided there is some semblance of institutional order to be found somewhere, however oppressive, irrational and incapable of public and articulate self justification it may be. It is not sensible to do so, but the objection to doing so does not depend on some kind of moral absolutism that claims to find a pre-ordained body of 'natural law' in the form of an ideal code that human law simply has to match. No such ideal code exists, and there is indeed scope for the qualified kind of relativism Villa advocates if we seek to establish what are the limits of a discursively statable conception of justice such as my account of the matter requires. Of course the world of legislative politics is a world of rival views on justice and the common good. Those who think divorce should be permitted or abortion allowed in certain circumstances differ from those who think both should be prohibited and arguments rage around such issues, with different outcomes in different countries. But those who disagree, disagree about what is just, and each has a well-argued case for the position advocated. The same can be said about most big issues concerning consumer law, the welfare state, the liability of corporations for crimes and so on. A theorist who insists that nothing is law in the way of institutional order unless it expresses some statable conception of justice does not propose a single template for all law, but acknowledges a great range of arguable possibilities. That, for me at any rate, is quite enough in the way of relativism, and as far as it is either necessary or desirable to go in the way of positivism.

Yet on one understanding of the term 'natural law', it is not a 'natural law' position either. For the 'ideal code' version of natural law is as firmly rejected as the out and out 'anything can count as law' version of positivism. In such a universe of false oppositions, a post-positivist stance such as that suggested here in repetition of the point in *Institutions of Law* seems much preferable.

A final word on methodology: save for one or two caveats expressed in the foregoing, I gratefully accept what Andrew Halpin's chapter has to say about the role of methodology in legal theory. I also thank him for the relatively clean bill of health he awards to *Institutions of Law* on this account. So far as I can detect any difference between us, it concerns at most the degree to which one should lean towards Villa's constructivism. That in turn depends on a point noted above about the character of the 'raw data' that one tries to deal with in advancing an institutionalist (or, perhaps any other kind of) theory of law. A theory of law that dealt with topics and things other than those that ordinary lawyers and ordinary citizens concern themselves about and talk about as law would be a very absurd sort of enterprise. We are tied to the discourses that we try to clarify and understand better. But they do demand better understanding. They do not speak to us clearly and unequivocally as though already incorporating some ideal theory. Inevitably, therefore, there is a 'constructive' element in any effort to produce an explanatory, analytical, synthetic and value-relevant overall account of law. What is produced is (or anyway ought to be) clearer and more informative than the 'raw data' that are available to begin with. It builds upon prior attempts at theorising much the same data, but tries to construct a clearer picture. To be an attractive account of its subject matter, it must convey some sense of the point and value of the whole enterprise when it is working well, and that is inevitably a point of possible controversy. We cannot escape such controversy, nor can we escape the task of constructing (as distinct from merely finding) an account of law in the light of what we propose as its point and value.

References

MacCormick, N. (2009), *Practical Reason in Law and Morality* (Oxford: Oxford University Press).

Index